THE
GLOBAL
RIVALS

ALSO BY SEWERYN BIALER

*Stalin's Successors: Leadership Stability and Change
in the Soviet Union* (1980)
*Stalin and His Generals: Soviet Military Memoirs
of World War II* (1984)
*The Soviet Paradox: External Expansion,
Internal Decline* (1986)

ALSO BY MICHAEL MANDELBAUM

*The Nuclear Question: The United States
and Nuclear Weapons, 1946–1976* (1979)
*The Nuclear Revolution: International Politics
Before and After Hiroshima* (1981)
The Nuclear Future (1983)
(With Strobe Talbott) *Reagan and Gorbachev* (1987)
*The Fate of Nations: The Search for National Security
in the 19th and 20th Centuries* (1988)

EDITED BY SEWERYN BIALER AND
MICHAEL MANDELBAUM

Gorbachev's Russia and American Foreign Policy (1988)

THE
GLOBAL
RIVALS

SEWERYN BIALER
and
MICHAEL MANDELBAUM

VINTAGE BOOKS

A DIVISION OF RANDOM HOUSE, INC.

NEW YORK

First Vintage Books Edition, september 1989

Copyright © 1988 by Seweryn Bialer and
Michael Mandelbaum

All rights reserved under International and Pan-American
Copyright Conventions. Published in the United States by
Vintage Books, a division of Random House, Inc., New York,
and simultaneously in Canada by Random House of Canada
Limited, Toronto. Originally published, in hardcover, by Alfred
A. Knopf, Inc., New York in 1988.

Library of Congress Cataloging-in-Publication Data
Bialer, Seweryn.
    The Global rivals / Seweryn Bialer and Michael
Mandelbaum.—1st Vintage Books ed.
        p.   cm.
    Companion volume to the television series
The global rivals.
    Includes index.
    ISBN 0-679-72649-7 : $9.95
    1. United States—Foreign relations—Soviet Union.
2. Soviet Union—Foreign relations—United States.   3. World
politics—1985-1995.   4. Arms race.   5. United States—
Foreign relations—1981-1989.   6. Soviet Union—Foreign
relations—1985-   I. Mandelbaum, Michael.   II. Global rivals
(Television program)   III. Title.
[E183.8.S65B53   1989]
327.73047—dc20   89-40161
                                                                    CIP

Manufactured in the United States of America
10 9 8 7 6 5 4 3 2 1

To my sister, Pauline Ganc

S.B.

To the memory of my brother,
Jonathan Edward Mandelbaum, M.D.
1949–1976

M.M.

CONTENTS

Preface   ix

Introduction   3

1 The Roots of the Conflict   10

2 The "Lost" Opportunities   41

3 The Gorbachev Difference   71

4 The Arms Race and the Human Race—
   The Past   92

5 The Arms Race and the Human Race—
   The Future   109

6 The Arenas of Conflict: The Third World and
   the Strategic Quadrangle   130

7 The Arenas of Conflict: Europe   148

8 The Future of the Rivalry   172

Index   201

PREFACE

This book is a companion volume to the television series "The Global Rivals," a co-production of WNET New York and Antelope Films of London. The book and the series are similar in overall design, many of the same themes can be found in both, and the authors took part in the production of the television programs.

The authors are grateful to their home institutions for support of various kinds during the writing of this book: Seweryn Bialer to the Research Institute on International Change at Columbia University, and especially to Lorraine Berger, Gertrude Garrettson, and Thomas Sherlock; Michael Mandelbaum to the Council on Foreign Relations, and especially to Cynthia Paddock.

THE
GLOBAL
RIVALS

INTRODUCTION

Relations between the United States and the Soviet Union have reached a turning point. The two great nuclear powers, whose rivalry has dominated international politics since the end of World War II, stand on the verge of a better relationship than at any time since 1945. Historians of the twenty-first century may well look back on the end of the 1980s as the moment when this global rivalry changed in fundamental ways.

What is different now? In the past, the two sides could deal only with the consequences of their conflict—the military rivalry. They could and did keep their political differences from exploding into a war that would devastate both, and they managed to place some limits on the huge nuclear arsenals with which such a war would be fought. Now, however, it may be possible to address the basic causes of the global rivalry. One of these is the series of political disputes that divide the United States and the Soviet Union the world over, especially in Europe. For the first time these may be amenable to resolution. The second fundamental cause of the global rivalry is the sharp differences in the two countries' political and economic systems. These, too, may become less pronounced through domestic changes on the Soviet side. The Soviet Union will not evolve into a Eurasian version of the United States, but it may well become less like the country that Stalin forged and thus less distasteful and menacing to the rest of the world.

The improvement in Soviet-American relations is already underway. As it proceeds it is likely to be more clearly visible in retrospect than as it happens. The changes that are possible will be less sudden and dramatic than the sweeping shifts in international politics and in the status of the great powers that have created previous historical watersheds.

Wars and revolutions marked the great turning points of the past. Often they occurred together. Regimes collapsed, new social forces and political ideas emerged, armies clashed, conquering and reconquering territory, and finally one side—often a coalition of great powers—defeated the other, divided up the captured territory among its members, and installed governments to its liking. The world looked very different in the wake of these great international upheavals than it had before them.

So it was with the war of 1939 to 1945. That conflict, with whose legacy the world still lives, followed a similar pattern. It left Europe divided between two great military blocs and so greatly weakened the French and British empires, which had survived World War I, that they could no longer resist the rising tide of nationalism in Africa and Asia and were dismantled over the next two decades.

This recurrent historical pattern is now obsolete. Nuclear weapons have put an end to the volcanic methods of international change. In the nuclear age a great war such as the wars of the French Revolution or World Wars I and II would be a horrible absurdity. It would destroy the countries that waged it and the stakes for which they were fighting. Both the United States and the Soviet Union have made it clear that they will go to great lengths to avoid such a conflict.

Nor is the collapse, without war, of either the American or the Soviet regime at all likely. In the last part of the twentieth century, it is true, sovereign, functioning governments have disintegrated. The Shah of Iran was forced from his throne, Ferdinand Marcos was exiled from the Philippines, the rule of the dictator Jean-Claude Duvalier collapsed in Haiti. But neither the American nor the Soviet government is vulnerable to their fate.

The United States is a democracy in which gradual peaceful change is possible, lessening the need for sudden, violent upheavals. In the Soviet Union, change comes with far greater difficulty. But the Soviet system does change, and the regime's reserves of stability and support, its capacity for self-preservation, and, not least, the determination of the ruling elite to retain power, are far greater than those on which the Shah, or Marcos, or Duvalier could draw.

Conflict between the two great nuclear powers will not end in the next decade. The two will not establish the kind of relationship that the United States enjoys with Canada, or the Federal Republic of Germany, or even a distant, nonaligned country like India. The Soviet Union will continue to be a rival of the United States; indeed, it will continue to be the preeminent rival, and vice versa, far into the twenty-first century. But the rivalry may become less bitter and more predictable. It is even possible that the two will find themselves cooperating on issues of common concern such as nuclear proliferation, terrorism, and Islamic fundamentalism.

Nor will the two do away with the weapons with which they confront each other, including—especially—nuclear weapons. But the military dimension of the global rivalry may become less costly, less volatile, and less dangerous than it has been—or has seemed to be—since the arms race began in the 1940s.

The conflict between the United States and the Soviet Union has deep roots, which cannot simply be pulled up and discarded. But the conflict can be moderated, precisely because its root causes can be addressed. If and as they are, the rivalry is likely to have less effect on international politics overall than has been the case since World War II.

Why has the global rivalry reached this turning point as it enters its fifth decade? Changes both within the two countries and in the international arena in which their rivalry is played out are responsible. The historical watershed that they have reached is the product both of changes of heart and circumstance.

For one thing, the circumstances of their military competition have altered. The arms race has reached a plateau. The two sides have accumulated enough weapons, and have enough experience in competing with each other to acquire them, to be ready to conclude that neither can achieve a decisive military advantage over the other and that the time has therefore come to settle for a draw. This conclusion has come harder, and later, to Moscow than to Washington. By the end of the 1980s, however, it was the Soviet Union that seemed eager to ratify the nuclear equilibrium with a series of formal arms control agreements, and the United States that aspired to break out of the deadlock by developing a system of space-based defenses against nuclear attack. But since the technical obstacles to any such defense appear insurmountable, it is still possible, though far from certain, that in the 1990s the two sides will embrace the idea of negotiating an end not to nuclear armaments but to the nuclear arms race.

The world, too, has changed in ways that promise a moderation of the Soviet-American conflict. That struggle has taken the form of a rivalry for influence all over the globe. Governments and political movements in Asia, Africa, and Latin America became surrogates for the United States and the Soviet Union in the decades after World War II. But over time the local forces have become more assertive of their own interests and more independent of—indeed resistant to—the aspirations and programs of the great powers. The global influence that the U.S. and the USSR have sought has become progressively more difficult to acquire and less rewarding to exercise. The two have therefore begun to reassess their stakes and their policies in the arenas where they have clashed. This, too, promises to moderate their rivalry.

Although the sharpest clashes between the United States and the Soviet Union during the last twenty-five years have come from—and their mutual suspicion and mistrust have been aggravated by—the arms race and their rivalry in the Third World, the core of the conflict has remained Europe. There the Cold War began. There the two sides confront each other directly, heavily armed. The division of the continent remains both the chief symbol and the principal cause of the Soviet-American rivalry. The conflict in Europe had become, in the 1980s, at once the most stable and least tractable part of that rivalry. Neither side is at all disposed to risk war there, but neither is likely to retreat from its European position, either. Even in Europe change is possible in the 1990s; but

Europe is also the place where developments that could break the pattern of improvement and worsen the conflict are most likely to occur.

Like the world, the two rivals themselves have changed in ways that make an improvement in their relationship possible. The greater shifts have taken place in the Soviet Union, coincident with the rise of the man who became general secretary of the Communist Party of the Soviet Union in March 1985, Mikhail Sergeyevich Gorbachev.

The hierarchical character of the Soviet system places enormous importance on the man at the top. Gorbachev plainly wants sweeping change in his country. The impulse goes beyond a single, powerful individual, however. Gorbachev stands at the forefront of a new political generation, which assumed power in the Soviet Union in the latter half of the 1980s. Its members' political experience, and therefore their views of their country and the world and their plans for both, differ from those of the older men whom they replaced.

The political slogans that Gorbachev and his associates have introduced—*perestroika* (reconstruction), *glasnost* (publicity, openness), democratization, and "new thinking" in foreign policy—bespeak the different perspectives they have brought to the governance of the Soviet Union. The new thoughts and ideas they have sought to introduce are familiar enough to the rest of the world, but novel for the Soviet Union. Some of them —particularly the idea that the Soviet people ought to take a greater part in the public affairs of their country, and that in the nuclear age military competition is futile and dangerous— promise, if translated into actual policies, to make relations between the global rivals considerably less hostile. The advent of Mikhail Gorbachev to power is the most important single reason that Soviet-American relations have arrived at a turning point.

Gorbachev has set as his supreme tasks modernizing the economy and invigorating the society and the political system. These are formidable, perhaps impossible undertakings, with which the leadership will be preoccupied for the rest of the century. They are tasks that will leave little time and few resources for the kinds of foreign policies that have aggravated the global conflict with the United States.

Gorbachev has recognized that to carry through his program of domestic reform he needs a respite from international competition. He began to pursue better relations with the United States almost from the moment he assumed power. Détente abroad, he has as much as said, is the necessary condition of restructuring at home.

The domestic changes, moreover, have the potential for moving Soviet policies at home and abroad in the direction the West has long favored: toward a more liberal political order at home, a freer Eastern Europe, and less emphasis on the accumulation of military might and the use of force.

The changes within the United States have been less dramatic. Nonetheless, the events of the 1980s have also disposed the other superpower to a moderating of the conflict between them. Historians of the twenty-first century may well consider the Reagan years a turning point in the American conduct of the global rivalry.

Ronald Reagan entered office as the most emphatically anti-Soviet American chief executive since Harry Truman, who presided over the beginning of the Cold War. The Reagan administration was committed to stepping up the competition with the Soviet Union·in the areas where the rivalry was sharpest. It orchestrated the most expensive peacetime military buildup in American history and began the Strategic Defense Initiative, which was designed to free the world from the nuclear stalemate in which each side's society was hostage to the weapons of the other. But the Reagan years have demonstrated the limits to both policies. They have made it clear that the United States, like the Soviet Union, will have to settle for military equilibrium in the great power rivalry.

The Reagan administration also provided support for insurgents against Third World regimes tied to the Soviet Union, a policy that came to be known as the Reagan Doctrine. The policy enjoyed some success. It raised the Soviet Union's costs of overseas influence, which dampened Moscow's enthusiasm for acquiring foreign clients. But the Reagan experience also demonstrated the limits to the American public's enthusiasm for contesting Soviet gains in the Third World.

Having entered office denouncing the détente of the 1970s as a fraud, the arms control agreements of that decade as fatally flawed, and the Soviet Union itself as an empire that was the focus of evil in the world, Reagan prepared to leave office having met with his Soviet counterpart more often than any other president, having signed far-reaching arms control treaties, and, like Mikhail Gorbachev, having proclaimed a new era in U.S.-Soviet relations.

....

1

THE ROOTS OF THE CONFLICT

....

THE BASIS OF THE RIVALRY

Why are the United States and the Soviet Union rivals? There is, in the first place, something in the very nature of international politics that promotes rivalry among great powers. Historically, the strongest states have consistently distrusted each other and have often become adversaries. This tendency can be traced to the earliest recorded chapter in international history, the relations among the Greek city-states in the fifth century B.C., which were dominated by the conflict between Athens and Sparta.

Thucydides' account of that conflict, *The Peloponnesian War*, includes many of the familiar features of the Soviet-American rivalry: differences in the ways the two states governed themselves, opposing alliances, an arms race, and rising mutual suspicion. (There is also an important difference: Most of Thucydides' narrative is taken up with what the United States and the Soviet Union have thus far managed to avoid—a war.)

Athens, Sparta, and all powerful states since their time have had to cope with a common condition: They have been part of an international order that lacks a central supreme authority. In the absence of any such authority capable of enforcing good behavior, each of them is ultimately responsible for its own safety; and so for each great power a measure of suspicion toward the others becomes a logical, rational, necessary policy. When there are only two great rivals, as has been the case since 1945, each is naturally disposed to be suspicious of the other.

The conflict has a second ingredient. It partakes of the most powerful force in international politics in the twentieth century—nationalism. It is nationalism that provoked the two great world wars of the century, and was responsible for the dissolution of the multinational empires that dominated the international system for much of the modern era. Both Americans and the Russians who dominate the Soviet Union have seen themselves as marked out by history and destiny to play a special role in international politics, especially since 1945. Their conflict has been especially potent because nationalist feeling has merged with a third dimension.

The global rivalry is not just a series of disputes between two powers mistrustful of each other. It is more than a clash between two strong states ambitious for influence in the world. It is a conflict between two countries and two coalitions with wholly different systems of social, political, and economic organization.

In 1944, as Soviet and Western armies converged on Germany from opposite ends of Europe, Stalin told a group of Yugoslav communists: "This war is not as in the past; whoever occupies a territory also imposes on it his own social system. Everyone imposes his own system as far as his army can reach. It cannot be otherwise." Historically, he was not entirely accurate. Victors in wars had imposed their own systems in the past, but seldom if ever had the members of a winning coalition and the systems they put in place been so dissimilar.

The American system was based on the supremacy of the individual. It was descended from the philosophical tradition that stresses individual rights and the economic school that emphasizes individual initiative, which together constitute the tradition of liberalism. The Soviet system gave priority to the claims of the collective, that is, of society. The instrument of the collective interest was the Communist Party, which drew its policies from the teachings of Marx and Lenin and the practices of Stalin.

At the heart of the liberal political order is the freedom of the individual to say what he likes, to practice the religion of his choice, and to take part in politics including the selection of his leaders in open elections with secret ballots. These rights are embedded in a series of practices and institutions: a free press and a host of social, cultural, and political organizations including political parties that contest regular elections.

In the communist political system the party enjoys a monopoly of power. Acting in the name of society as a whole, it selects the rulers from among a small, self-appointed elite group. Elections are ritual affirmations of the party's choices. Only the political ideas that the party favors can be publicly expressed; only political activity that it sanctions can take place. No organization of any kind independent of the state, which the party dominates, is permitted. Citizens of liberal societies have control over the policies of those that govern them in the sense that if they do not like those policies they can change the governors. Citizens of communist societies cannot do so.

In the liberal economic order, like the liberal political system, wealth and productive resources are owned by individuals, who can dispose of them as they like. Property and capital are privately held. Ultimately individuals decide how much is invested and where, what is produced, and the price at which it is sold, through the mechanism of the market. The market's unit of account is price, and price is set by supply of and the demand for products, services, labor, and capital. These are, in turn, the result of millions of individual decisions.

In communist economic systems property is owned by the collective, the state. Economic initiative comes from the top. The basic mechanism for economic decisions is not the market but the plan. Political leaders decide what will be invested and where. Planners set output targets for farms and factories and stipulate the prices at which their products will be offered to the public. All these decisions are based ultimately on political considerations, not the more narrowly economic standards—price determined by supply and demand—by which liberal economies operate.

In liberal societies, the role of the state is relatively limited. Its principal tasks are to keep order and to do the things that individuals cannot do for themselves and that the market, left to its own devices, will not do—building roads and schools, cleaning up pollution, recruiting and training the armed forces. The restriction of organized social power, the conviction that the work of private individuals is superior to the activities of the government, is the essence of the liberal tradition.

In communist society, by contrast, government is all-pervasive. It is spontaneous, unofficial, private conduct that is suspect, that is, indeed, for the most part illegal, although in practice there is a great deal of such activity, so much so that in the Soviet Union it is called the "second economy."

The differences between the two systems profoundly affect the daily lives of the people who live in them. In the West, to summarize those differences, everything that is not forbidden is permitted. In the East, anything that is not permitted is forbidden.

These differences have made the global rivalry between the United States and the Soviet Union an unusually bitter one, and the stakes in the contest unusually high. Whether a given country is in one camp or the other affects what choices its people can make in their lives, what social activities are permitted, where they can go and work, and what they can read, buy, and own.

The bitterness and intractability of the conflict stem not just from the sharp differences between the two forms of social organization involved but also from the relationship of the two systems to the two great powers that embody them.

Each system has deep historical roots in the country that is its most prominent example. Liberalism and communism are bred into the historical genes of the United States and the Soviet Union; they cannot be abandoned or ignored.

Nor has either country been content simply to serve as a showcase for its political and economic arrangements, without regard for the way that others govern themselves. Each has considered its own system to be suitable for export. Each country has put its political principles and economic practices at the center of its foreign policy. The Soviet-American rivalry has therefore taken the form of a contest to spread different, opposed, and incompatible systems around the world.

THE EVOLUTION OF THE TWO SYSTEMS

How did the United States and the Soviet Union come to have such radically dissimilar systems of political and economic organization? The lineage of the American system is the Western tradition, which begins with the ancient Greeks and Romans, and comes down through the Renaissance, the Enlightenment, and the French Revolution to the present. The Western tradition is the liberal tradition, and it was borne around the globe in the modern period by the expansion of Europe, notably of Great Britain, which brought the liberal approach to politics and economics to North America.

The Soviet system is of more recent origins, and is a sharp departure from the course of historical development that the United States represents. It was in fact intended to depart from that course, which partly accounts for the divergences between the two systems. The communist system is, as well, the product of a series of historical trends, social movements, and great political events, each of which moved Russia away from the path that the West has followed. It is the product of the socialist tradition, its Marxist variant, the form Marxism took in Russia, the weight of the long political history of that country, and the circumstances that the Russian Marxists faced when they took power there.

Since the time of the ancient Greeks, one of the central political debates in the West has pitted the claims of the individual against the needs of the collective. Socialism is the modern version of the collective side of the argument.

The industrial revolution gave the claims of society special urgency. It produced glaring, ugly inequalities. In the nineteenth century, manufacturing created great wealth but also great squalor in the urban areas where industrial workers were concentrated. Socialism became the creed of those who wished to temper the excesses produced by the individualist economic activity of industrial capitalism, and to do so through the great instrument of public purpose—government.

Socialists wished to employ government for two purposes.

One was to make available to everyone a level of social welfare —of food, housing, and social services—that private activity by itself was not providing. The other was to correct the irrationalities of the private system of production through government planning of the economy.

Socialism did have an impact on Western societies. In fact, the liberal political systems of the second half of the twentieth century have adopted both of socialism's themes. In every Western country the state has assumed some responsibility for the public welfare, and every Western government engages in economic coordination in some fashion. Such measures have been central to the programs of the social democratic political parties of the West. The German Social Democratic Party, the French and Italian socialists, the British Labour Party, and even the Democratic Party of the United States are in this sense the bearers of socialism. But for all of them, the provision of welfare and the coordination of economic activity by the government are designed to modify, and to soften, what have remained essentially liberal political and economic systems.

In the Soviet Union the collective principle has been carried much further. It has come to dominate politics and economics. In the West, the socialist tradition has tempered liberalism. In the East, socialism of a particular sort has excluded liberalism altogether.

Nineteenth-century socialism was not a united, uniform movement; indeed, it was not a single movement at all. It was rather an umbrella covering a wide variety of ideas, social experiments, and political movements, all of which were critical in one way or another of industrial capitalism. An important school of socialism, the one that took root in Russia and had an ultimately decisive influence there, was founded by Karl Marx.

Marx left a large body of books, articles, polemical essays, and scholarly studies that together make up the corpus of what has come to be known as Marxism, which is the distant ancestor of the communist order of the Soviet Union.

It was he who, drawing upon the utopian socialists who envisioned ideal, harmonious socialist communities, insisted that

socialism would be entirely different from, and morally superior to, the capitalist economic and political systems that he so
fiercely criticized.

From German philosophers, especially Hegel, he adopted the
idea that history proceeds in distinct stages. Each historical
stage, Marx believed, is dominated by a particular social class.
The motor of history is the conflict between the dominant class
and its principal challenger. In the feudal era the aristocracy
had held sway. Its place was usurped by the middle class, the
bourgeoisie, when feudalism gave way to the capitalist economic order that reigned in Europe in Marx's lifetime. But
capitalism was itself destined to be replaced by socialism,
through a process in which power would pass to the industrial
working class, the proletariat.

Drawing on his reading of the great British economists of the
nineteenth century, Marx contended that the capitalist
method of economic organization contained within itself the
seeds of its own destruction. Capitalism could only function,
Marx argued, and capitalists themselves could only prosper, at
the expense of the workers, who would become progressively
poorer and more viciously exploited until they finally joined
together, rose up, overthrew the capitalist system, and established the more humane, productive socialist one. Marx did not
anticipate what actually happened, namely that workers could
organize themselves politically and improve their conditions
within the capitalist order without overthrowing it.

If Marx took his philosophy from Germany and his economics from Britain, his understanding of politics was shaped by
the history of France. Just as the great French Revolution of
1789 had destroyed feudalism and opened the way for the bourgeois era, so the workers' revolution of the future would smash
capitalism, and erect the new Jerusalem of socialism on its
ruins. When Marx died, his collaborator, Friedrich Engels,
eulogized him as "above all, a revolutionary."

Marx assumed that the revolution he forecast would come in
the most economically advanced parts of Europe, where the
industrial revolution had gone furthest and the working class
was most numerous, sophisticated, and militant. The countries

that he had in mind were France, Britain, Germany, and the United States. He assumed as well that the proletarian revolution would occur simultaneously in all of these countries. He did not foresee revolution in just one country, and least of all just in Russia.

For Russia was the most backward of the major states; the process of industrialization had barely begun there. There was little class consciousness, and to the extent that it existed at all it was the property of the wrong class. Russia was a society of peasants, religious and superstitious people who venerated the tsar as the father of them all. Few had ever heard of socialism, let alone Marx. Most could not read. The idea of Russian Marxism was therefore something of a contradiction in terms.

Nonetheless, a small group of Russians did become disciples of Marx and devotees of his writings at the end of the nineteenth century. They considered themselves Marxists. Since Russia did not fit Marxism, they changed Marxism to fit Russia, which had momentous consequences for the development of the communist system once they took power.

Russia lacked the conditions that Marx had deemed necessary for overthrowing capitalism and constructing socialism. In place of bourgeois rule, a broad industrial base, and an aroused working class, the Russian Marxists, in particular the Bolshevik faction led by Lenin, put the revolutionary party. The party was to act on behalf of the workers, to do for them, if necessary, what they would not or could not do for themselves. Its ranks were to be filled with people whose grasp of Marx's teachings enabled them to act as the "vanguard" of the historically privileged proletariat.

The Bolsheviks arrogated to themselves the right to speak, plan, act, and ultimately govern in the name of the working class. At the time of the revolution, and especially during the bloody civil war that followed, the party did have considerable support from the ranks of the small Russian working class. It could not have succeeded without this support, and that of much of the much larger peasantry as well. But the Russian workers and peasants who rallied to the Bolshevik banner were not fighting for the sweeping changes that Stalin forced upon them a decade later, nor did he consult them before imposing these changes. The Bolsheviks' adaptation of Marxism made them, in their own eyes, the agents of history, the bearers of universal values, and the architects of the socialist society of the future. The Party, which Stalin controlled and embodied, assumed the right to carry out its program on the basis of the acute understanding it claimed to possess of the forces of history.

The authoritarian character of Soviet rule in Russia had its roots in the prerevolutionary period. The Tsarist government declared the Bolshevik Party and its activities illegal. In its early years many leaders were in exile, either in the eastern part of the Russian empire or in Western Europe. Lenin spent several years in Zurich, and Trotsky lived for a time in New York. The Party was therefore compelled to operate in secrecy, using many of the procedures common to clandestine activities in wartime.

Once in power, the Party permitted a degree of participation to its own members; but all others were prohibited from taking part in public affairs. Subsequently, Stalin abolished even the limited openness of the Leninist period, and the political system became a harsh, cruel, one-man dictatorship.

The communist political order was a Russian as well as a Bolshevik one. Although they considered their revolution the dawn of a new era in world history, the Bolsheviks were not writing on a blank page in Russia. The country had a long and distinctive political history. There is an ongoing debate among scholars about whether the communist system that Lenin and Stalin established owed more to their theories of governance or to the character of the country that they came to govern. Is the Soviet system chiefly a communist or a Russian one? Is it an example of historical continuity, with the general secretary of the Communist Party as the latter-day tsar, Marxism-Leninism as the successor to the dogmas of the Russian Orthodox Church, and the KGB as the descendant of the imperial secret police? Or is it, as Solzhenitsyn has written, "not a continuation of the spinal column, but a disastrous fracture that very nearly caused the nation's total destruction"?

In fact the system embodies both continuity and change. No doubt the history of communism would be different if the revolution had occurred in Germany; and the history of Russia would be different if some group other than the Bolsheviks had taken power in 1917 and held it thereafter. Although they were Marxists, the Bolsheviks were also partly the products of their country's political culture, for all their determination to eradicate it.

The Russian political tradition is not a democratic one; the country has no real history of liberty. The decisive events of Western history—the Renaissance, the Reformation, the Enlightenment, and the French Revolution—had only faint effects, or none at all, on Russia. Unlike Western Europe, Russia was conquered and occupied from the East. The period of Mongol rule left an authoritarian imprint on its political culture that has never entirely disappeared. While the prerogatives of the monarch were modified, limited, and ultimately abolished in most of Western Europe, in Russia the tsar retained absolute authority almost until the moment when the Romanov dynasty collapsed. The nobility never asserted prerogatives independent of the crown, the development that set Western Europe on the path to political liberalism.

None of the institutions of the Western liberal political order was firmly established in Russia. The country did not develop a free press, or parties that competed in genuinely democratic elections. No educated middle class emerged to serve as the mainstay of parliamentary government. Some democratic institutions were introduced at the very end of the tsarist period, dating from the defeat by Japan in 1905 to the outbreak of World War I in 1914. And the provisional government that succeeded the tsar in 1917 was a genuinely parliamentary regime. But it was feeble, with shallow roots in Russian society and the added burden of having to operate in the chaos of wartime; and it was swept away, almost unmourned, by the Bolsheviks.

Russia also lacked the basis for a Western economic system in 1917. Most of its people lived in villages and worked the land. They were peasants only a generation removed from serfdom, most of them cultivating land of absentee landlords, not the independent, land-owning farmers and ranchers of England or North America. Industrial and commercial practices similarly were not firmly entrenched in Russia as in the West. Much of the capital invested in the country came from abroad, or from Germans and Jews, whom most Russians regarded as alien even if they could trace their ancestry in Russia back for centuries.

Not least important, Russia lacked something that is essential for political liberalism and commercial civilization—the tradition of the rule of law, which protects the integrity of democratic politics and underpins the private transactions of capitalism.

Lenin and his colleagues disdained parliamentary procedures and civil freedom. In the 1930s Stalin set out to eradicate all vestiges of private economic activity. There was never a role for independently enacted and impartially enforced laws. None of these, moreover, had deep roots or a powerful constituency in Russia, which minimized the resistance the Party met when it swept them away in the aftermath of the revolution. Western values, Western customs, and Western institutions had not penetrated very far into Russian society in 1917. The bearers of Western civilization comprised a tiny fraction of the population. Between 1917 and 1937 these people were sent into exile, killed, or cowed into silent submission. Ironically, one of these Westernized groups was the original membership of the Bolshevik Party. As Marxist intellectuals they were steeped in what was, after all, a doctrine made by, in, and for the West. Many, like Lenin (but unlike Stalin) had lived for long periods in Western Europe. Most of the members of that original core who survived to the 1930s were killed by Stalin, cutting off one of Russia's few ties to the rest of the world.

The communist system was also shaped by the circumstances in which the Bolsheviks gained power; and the Party's responses to the conditions it encountered drew Russia further still from the course of Western development. Lenin and his followers gained power against great odds. The collapse of the old order under the weight of the war and the confusion that followed made their October coup possible. To win support in the Civil War the Bolsheviks promised not communism but peace, bread, and land. Because their initial political base was a very small one, the two principal tasks that Lenin and Stalin set for themselves—first to consolidate their rule, then to industrialize the country—turned out to require extreme and bloody methods to accomplish.

Communist rule was challenged immediately. Lenin announced shortly after the seizure of power: "We will punish with an iron hand the enemies of the revolution and the saboteurs." Almost everyone was a potential enemy or saboteur. Thus the Party introduced what would come to be a familiar strategy and a favored tactic. The strategy was the elimination of all opposition and the prohibition of any independent political activity. Since anyone could pose a threat to the Party, only the Party was permitted to operate legally. The tactic was terror.

Lenin sanctioned terror as an extraordinary measure on a modest scale during wartime. Stalin made it a normal instrument of governance, on a huge scale, during peacetime. For Lenin, terror was a tactic to be used against competitors for power during the consolidation of Bolshevik rule. For Stalin, it was a method to be turned on large groups within Russia—the peasantry, the army, the intelligentsia, and ultimately the Party itself—in order to eliminate all possible challenges to his personal rule and to reshape society in radical fashion. In Stalin's day people were arbitrarily arrested, sent to camps, and executed by the millions for trivial offenses, or on suspicion of trivial offenses, or for no reason at all. A popular Russian joke has two people meeting in a Stalinist camp in the 1930s. "How long is your sentence?" the first one asks. "Twenty years," the second replies. "And what did you do?" "I did nothing." "But that's impossible," the first man says indignantly. "For doing nothing the sentence is only ten years."

When Stalin died, his successors abandoned the use of terror. Doing nothing ceased to be a crime in the Soviet Union. But any form of political opposition continued to be swiftly and severely punished. No independent political activity, even unorganized, even if it did not challenge the regime or its policies, was permitted under Khrushchev and Brezhnev.

The crushing of all opposition, the proscription of independent political activity, and the practice of terror all stemmed from the weakness of the Bolsheviks at the time that they took power and for the two decades thereafter.

So, too, did the curious system of dual authority that came to typify communist rule. It began with the Red Army. Trotsky, the first commissar for war, recruited hundreds of tsarist officials to the Bolshevik cause. Their military skills were desperately needed, and proved decisive in winning the Civil War. But the Party leadership did not trust these officers and so assigned reliable Party functionaries to keep watch on them. Every unit was assigned a political commissar. The practice spread to civil government and the economy as well. Provincial and city governments, factories, collective farms, research institutes, and universities all came to have political watchdogs.

From the early days of communist rule in Russia, as a result of the Party's precarious grip on power, came one more feature of the communist system: the pervasive role of the secret police. The institution has operated under a variety of names since 1917. First it was the Cheka (an acronym for the "Extraordinary Commission for the Struggle against Counterrevolution and Sabotage"), then the OGPU, then the NKVD, the MGB, and most recently the KGB (Committee on State Security). Its power has waxed and waned. Under Stalin, it acted virtually as a shadow government and a law unto itself. Khrushchev reduced its role; Brezhnev rehabilitated it. Since 1917, however, the secret police has always had a much larger role than the internal security forces in Western countries. From 1917 on, the Soviet Union has been, in this sense, a police state.

By the end of the 1930s, communist power was secure in Russia. Contrary to everything that Marx had written and Lenin had believed, however, the revolution had not occurred in any of the advanced industrial countries. Russia stood alone as a revolutionary state. In response to this unexpected development, Stalin adopted a policy of building "socialism in one country." That task, he believed, involved converting the largely agrarian country that he ruled into an industrial giant. He had, as well, a more practical reason for hastening the process of industrialization. Industrial products form the sinews of military strength in the twentieth century. If they were more or less secure in Russia and in the non-Russian territories that the tsars had accumulated and they had reconquered, the communists nevertheless found themselves surrounded by hostile Western powers. Without the kind of military might only industrial production could bring, Soviet Russia was vulnerable to the counterrevolutionary designs of world capitalism.

Just as the consolidation of power was difficult because the Party was weak, so the task of building an industrial base in Russia was a formidable one because the country was backward compared to its neighbors and ideological adversaries. Here, too, therefore, the Party adopted extreme methods. Stalin shunned the capital and expertise that tsarist Russia had imported from the West and that Lenin had welcomed during the party's first five-year economic plan after consolidating power. To obtain resources for building steel mills, power plants, railroads, and factories, the regime proceeded to extract them forcibly from the population, conscripting workers, depressing wages, herding farmers into agricultural collectives and compelling them to turn over to the state everything they grew beyond the requirements for their own subsistence. Investment priorities were dictated from the top. Production quotas were set—often at unrealistically high levels—by the leadership.

The communist system was not, however, purely the product of circumstances and the way the Party responded to them. It was not only the result of a cynical effort to retain power at any cost, although that attitude was certainly present among the Bolsheviks. Nor was it simply the outcome of improvisation in the face of unexpected events, although there was a good deal of that, too, in the first two decades of communist rule. Nor, finally, was the communist system entirely the consequence of the sadistic whims of Joseph Stalin, although his personality undoubtedly helps to explain its most barbarous features. That system is also the result of deliberate design. It was based in no small part on the ideological convictions of its architects. Beneath the cynical opportunism, tactical flexibility, and cruelty of the men who made it there was a hard core of principle. Many features of the system that they created followed from what the communists believed.

They forced peasants to give up their land and work on collective farms controlled and managed by the state, killing millions in the process, because they considered private property historically retrograde and ethically unsavory. They attempted to control all economic activity with quotas, targets, and administered prices because they genuinely believed central planning to be a more efficient method of economic organization than what they saw as the wasteful disorder of the capitalist market.

They felt justified in resorting to violence and terror because they were, after all, the agents of history and the creators of a new, shining civilization. Trotsky said in 1924: "In the last analysis, the party is always right, because the party is the sole historical instrument the working class possesses for the solution of fundamental tasks." Since the Party was always right, it had the right—indeed, the duty—to do whatever was necessary to enact its program.

That program went beyond merely holding power in Russia and it involved more than mining coal, forging steel, and building tanks, planes, and rifles. It encompassed the construction of an entire civilization that was distinct from, and superior to, the liberal democratic capitalism of the West. Stalin imposed communist standards on art and literature, which, he insisted, had to serve the interests of the state. He decreed that there was a distinctive Marxist-Leninist method of conducting scientific research. He insisted that history be written—in many cases rewritten—to conform to the dictates of the official ideology. Maxim Gorky, who became an acolyte of Stalin, wrote that "We must know everything that happened in the past, not in the way it has been written about heretofore; but rather, in the way it appears in the light of the doctrine of Marx-Engels-Lenin-Stalin."

Stalin did not create an entirely new civilization, much less one superior to what existed in the West. The communist style of art and literature, which was called socialist realism, turned out to be a particularly banal form of propaganda. Stalinist science, such as the biological studies undertaken in the Stalin and Khrushchev eras by Trofim Lysenko, was simply bogus. Officially sanctioned history combined the worst features of both. It was written to demonstrate the virtues of the Party, and so resorted extensively to falsification. But if these ideologically inspired efforts did not yield a glittering new society, they did produce a series of social, political, and cultural institutions and practices that differed dramatically from what had developed in the West. Stalin did not create the new Jerusalem, but he did produce Russian communism.

SOVIET INTERNATIONAL AMBITIONS

Russian communism was not, in itself, necessarily threatening to the West. Russia had always been different from the rest of Europe, a hybrid, part Eastern and part Western. The two parts of Europe had generally managed to coexist, although sometimes uneasily.

The revolution of 1917 made coexistence between Russia and the rest of the world much more difficult. The authors of the revolution were convinced that coexistence was, over the long term, impossible. The revolution, they believed, would not and could not be confined within the borders of the tsarist empire.

Marxism was from its origins an internationalist creed. Marx believed that the social systems whose evolution he traced transcended the political units into which the world happened, for the moment, to be divided. Capitalism was more powerful than national sovereignty; so, too, was the might of the proletariat. French, Belgian, and German communists were all part of a great global movement. To Marx the workers of all nations had more in common with each other than with capitalists who happened to live in the same cities and speak the same language as they. National borders were artificial, bourgeois contrivances. The revolutionary tide would overflow them and wash them away.

Marxist doctrine drew much of its power from its international scope; and the Bolshevik claim to rule in Russia rested on the power of this doctrine.

The revolutionary aspirations of Lenin and his followers extended far beyond the tsarist kingdom that they conquered. They assumed, in 1917 and for a few years thereafter, that it was only a matter of time—a short time—before those aspirations would be fulfilled. After seizing power some of the Bolsheviks wanted to continue the war against Germany, but as a revolutionary conflict, on behalf of the workers of the world. Lenin overruled them, withdrawing Russia from the war by accepting humiliating terms from Germany at Brest-Litovsk in 1918. He calculated, no doubt correctly, that peace was necessary for the consolidation of Bolshevik rule. But he certainly expected the workers in the West, taking their cue from what had happened in Russia, to rise up and overthrow capitalism in the near future.

In 1920, having gained the upper hand in the Civil War and having repulsed a Polish attack that had reached Kiev, Lenin and his associates decided to continue their counterattack into Poland, which, once under communist control, was to serve as a bridge to Germany and the rest of Europe. The Bolsheviks organized a communist government in Moscow that was to take power in Warsaw once Soviet troops had conquered the country with the help of the Polish workers, who were expected to rally to its banner.

Instead, Poles of all classes opposed the Russian invaders. The Red Army reached Warsaw, but was stopped and thrown back. The Bolsheviks signed a peace treaty with an anti-Soviet Polish regime. Twenty-five years later the the Red Army arrived in Poland to stay; a communist government formed in Moscow was installed in Warsaw. While Lenin and his colleagues were surprised that their troops were not welcomed by the Poles, Stalin was more experienced, and cynical, about Polish attitudes toward a Russian-imposed political system. In 1919, even before the ill-fated campaign in Poland, the new Soviet regime established an international socialist organization, the third since Marx had helped to launch the first one.

It was called the Communist International, or Comintern. All communist parties belonged. Its mission was to coordinate and provide support for their revolutionary activities.

The Comintern became an instrument of Soviet foreign policy, the means by which Moscow controlled the activities of foreign communists. There were twelve conditions that a foreign party had to meet in order to gain admission. Their net effect was to subordinate these parties to the direction of the Soviet Union. Nor was the Comintern responsible for any successful foreign revolutions. Communism came to other countries either through the occupation of the Red Army or the independent efforts of foreign communists. Mao won power in China by ignoring Stalin's instructions. Nonetheless, the Comintern symbolized a basic, powerful tenet of Russian communism, the impulse to spread the revolution abroad.

Although he gave first priority to protecting the revolution in Russia, Stalin never abandoned the pursuit of worldwide revolution; he simply postponed it. He argued that a powerful Soviet Union was the key to the success of communism elsewhere. Socialism was to be built in one country for the sake of the global revolution that Marx had foreseen. Stalin's slogan, like the Comintern itself, embodied the intention to lead the proletariat to victory in Europe and beyond, if not necessarily a specific series of policies for doing so.

Moreover, Stalin presided over an important innovation in Soviet foreign policy: the fusion of communism with Russian nationalism. Soviet expansion drew its power not just from ideological but also from nationalist impulses.

Marx and Lenin had abhorred nationalism, considering it historically obsolete and counterrevolutionary. For Lenin, revolution in Russia was important only as the first stage in a worldwide upheaval. During World War I he endorsed the defeat of Russia because this was likely to topple the tsarist regime. He authorized the assault on Poland in 1920 to spread the revolution to that country. If a proletarian revolution had taken place in Poland first, he would have supported a revolutionary attack on tsarist Russia.

Stalin had a different view. Although he was a Marxist-

Leninist, he was also a fervent Russian nationalist. This was so despite—or perhaps ultimately because of—the fact that he was not an ethnic Russian but a Georgian.

It was he who fused the two political currents. The crucible in which they were fused was World War II. This was not, for the people of the Soviet Union, a war for the principles of Marxism-Leninism but rather a "Great Patriotic War," one fought initially to defend the motherland and then to expand its holdings.

The Soviet Union's attachment to the Eastern European empire it won in that war and its drive for influence beyond Europe stem ultimately more from the powerful urge for Russian international greatness than from the wish to spread communism abroad. Poland in the 1980s, for example, was not ruled by a communist party but by the army. This was acceptable to Moscow because the Polish generals were loyal to Russia.

In assessing the future of nationalism, Marx and Lenin were wrong and Stalin was right. It has been the most powerful political force in the twentieth century, far more powerful than the principles in which the founding theorist of scientific socialism and the architect of the October Revolution believed. Communism has triumphed when it has allied itself with the forces of nationalism, as in China, Vietnam, Cuba—and in Russia. This is a source of strength for Soviet foreign policy, but also of weakness. For when communism opposes nationalism, when Russian nationalism is pitted against the nationalist sentiment of other peoples, it provokes resistance. It is nationalist resistance that lies behind the Soviet Union's difficulties with Afghanistan, Poland, and China. Nationalism has fueled the extension of Soviet power; it also threatens what the Soviet Union has gained.

AMERICAN INTERNATIONALISM

The Bolsheviks' commitment to spreading the system that they established in Russia naturally evoked opposition from the non-communist world. The Western powers even intervened, halfheartedly and to no effect, in the Civil War that followed the Revolution. Still, the rest of Europe had had some experience with Russian international ambitions. In 1815 Alexander I's armies reached Paris. The other members of the coalition that had defeated Napoleon used their powers of persuasion to ensure that these armies returned home. In the last decades of the nineteenth century Britain engaged in an ongoing contest with the tsarist government for influence in Southwest Asia, a contest that centered on Afghanistan and was portrayed in Kipling's novel *Kim* as "the great game."

The October Revolution was bound to lead to a conflict between East and West. Given the Bolsheviks' attitudes toward Western political and economic institutions and the way they set about reshaping Russia, it was bound to be a conflict of systems. The fact that the chief Western opponent of the Soviet Union after 1945 turned out to be the United States, however, gave the conflict a special character.

The United States shared an adherence to liberal norms with the other Western democracies, but was more self-conscious about them. In addition, America was more committed than its European partners to introducing these principles throughout the world. The global rivalry became a particularly intense one because the principal Western adversary of the Soviet Union was an ideological as well as a nationalist power.

Americans do not think of themselves as an ideological people. The term evokes abstract systems of thought and queer foreign doctrines. The American self-image is of a straightforward, plain-spoken, and supremely practical nation. Americans favor what works. They are guided by what common sense dictates, not what some long-dead philosopher once wrote.

If an ideological nation, however, is one that is devoted to a particular set of political beliefs, beliefs that deeply influence its institutions and behavior and that are regarded with respect bordering on reverence, and if these are beliefs that the nation considers itself duty-bound to make available to others, then Americans are indeed ideological. For they are devoted to a particular set of ideas, the ideas of liberalism: the political freedoms incorporated in the Bill of Rights of the American

Constitution—speech, assembly, and religion—and the economic liberties that are integral to capitalism.

Americans believe that these ideas are fundamental and universal, that they are essential for the decent ordering of any society, and that they ought therefore to be honored, and practiced, everywhere. The founding document of the American republic, the Declaration of Independence of 1776, deemed it a self-evident truth that "all men are endowed by their creator with certain inalienable rights; that among these are the rights to life, liberty, and the pursuit of happiness." A broad, indeed a virtually unanimous devotion to that creed has been a consistent feature of American political life for more than two centuries.

American history has nourished this faith in liberal principles. As with the Soviet Union, the founding event of the United States was a revolution—a revolution grounded in political principles, more specifically in liberal political principles. These principles have been prominent in the great events of American history. Blessed with an extraordinarily favorable location, the United States waged wars because it chose to do so, not because it was forced to fight. Its foreign wars have all been conducted at least nominally, and to a considerable extent actually, on behalf of liberty. The great civil war of 1861 to 1865 was not a war of choice in this sense, but at its center, too, stood the issue of individual liberty.

The nature of American society has reinforced the popular appeal of liberalism. The United States has been peopled by immigrants. Many arrived in North America in flight from political and religious persecution. It was precisely the civil freedom of the country that attracted them; so it is not surprising that they came to hold these freedoms in high regard.

Even those who immigrated for other reasons had powerful incentives to absorb the tenets of American liberalism. For these form the basis of American nationalism, and are what unites the people of the United States. In a nation of immigrants it could hardly be otherwise. Citizens of France are French, after all, because they and their ancestors have been part of the culture, have lived on the land, and have spoken the language of the country for generations. Americans do not, for the most part, have such deep roots in North America. The social cement of the United States is not simply shared experience; it is a shared set of principles—liberal principles. Thus liberalism and nationalism have been fused more tightly in the United States than in the other Western nations almost from the founding of the republic.

The personal experiences of most Americans have validated these principles for them. The United States is a populist, decentralized democracy, in which opportunities for political participation are widely available. American politics are much more open, and far easier to enter, than the political systems of the other Western democracies, let alone the communist ones. Moreover, private property is widely held in the United States. The average American is not just a wage-earner; he tends to own his own home and hold shares in publicly traded companies—individually or through funds of various kinds in which he participates—at higher rates than others in the West. So an American tends to have a personal stake in the economic system.

Americans also tend to believe that that system rewards industry and initiative. Historically there has been greater social mobility in the United States than elsewhere. The sons and daughters of European, and more recently Asian, immigrants have entered the American middle class in large numbers. Liberalism means liberty, prosperity, and opportunity. American society has furnished people with firsthand experience of each on a large scale, and so generated a sizable reservoir of popular loyalty to liberal politics and economics.

American history is not, to be sure, an uninterrupted record of devotion to liberal principles. Chattel slavery was legally practiced in the United States until the middle of the nineteenth century, and the descendants of slaves were subject to legal discrimination for a century thereafter. Others have often had a less glowing view of American society. Where Americans have celebrated the liberty that permeates their society, others, particularly Russians, have seen license, disorder, excess, and lawlessness. Where Americans have glorified the dynamic power of uninhibited private economic activity, others—and not just Russians—have deplored the extremes of wealth and poverty to which unfettered capitalism can give rise. The American impulse to spread the blessings of free enterprise beyond North America has been seen by some as contributing to the economic exploitation of others, especially in Latin America.

Still, their devotion to the liberal principles on which the country was founded, and their conviction that the United States has embodied these principles more faithfully than any other political community, have created a feeling among Americans that theirs is an exceptional country. Since the founding of the republic, in the eyes of its citizens the United States has stood in marked contrast to the older European states, in which liberty was compromised and opportunity limited. That popular sense of "exceptionalism" has affected America's relations with the rest of the world, although in different ways during different historical periods.

During the nation's first century, American exceptionalism contributed to a foreign policy of isolation from the great power rivalries of Europe, a policy that aimed at preserving the purity of the American experiment by keeping the country aloof from the sordid quarrels of the Continent. George Washington's Farewell Address provided the rationale for American isolation.

This isolationism, however, was not meant to imply that the American experience had no relevance for other countries, or that the United States was uninterested in exercising influence abroad. On the contrary, from the outset Americans considered it their vocation to spread the blessings of liberty to others— though by the power of their example rather than by more active measures. The American republic would be, in the words of the Puritan leader John Winthrop, "a shining city upon a hill," to which others would look for inspiration and guidance.

In the eighteenth century and for most of the nineteenth, the United States was too weak to exert direct influence outside the western hemisphere. By the twentieth century, however, it had become one of the world's great powers. The sense of exceptionalism was still potent, but it came to underwrite a policy of active involvement in the affairs of other countries. Liberal isolationism gave way to liberal internationalism, which had two major goals: the promotion of democratic order within other countries, and the reorganization of international politics along the lines of a democratic state, so that nations, as well as individuals, would come to abide by the rule of law. Neither has proved easy to implement; the evidence of the history of this century (and indeed of all of recorded history) suggests that the second is impossible. Nonetheless, the aspiration to achieve both has colored American foreign policy since 1898.

In that year the United States made its debut as a great power by defeating Spain in a brief naval war and acquiring two Spanish imperial possessions, the Caribbean island of Cuba and the Philippine archipelago in the Pacific. The Philippines were subdued only after a protracted campaign against indigenous guerrilla fighters. The decision to embark on the campaign was made with the sense of mission to spread liberal values that was to weigh heavily on all American foreign policies thereafter. President William McKinley later said that he had gone down on his knees to pray for guidance, and felt himself compelled to take the Philippines to bring Western civilization to the inhabitants of the archipelago.

With its entry into World War I in 1917, the United States became caught up in relations among the great powers. For Americans this was a war of liberal principle from the beginning. President Woodrow Wilson declared that it was being waged "to make the world safe for democracy." The war aims that he announced, the Fourteen Points, were a compendium of liberal goals. After the war Wilson was the main proponent of an international organization, the League of Nations, that he hoped—vainly, as it turned out—would become the core of the kind of liberal world order that he envisaged.

Contrary to Wilson's wishes, the United States did not join the League, retreating instead from active political engagement in Europe. But America returned to Europe in World War II. The man who led the country into that war, Franklin D. Roosevelt, shared many of Wilson's ideas about international politics. The war was for him, as the previous conflict had been for Wilson, and as both were for Americans in general, a conflict on behalf of democratic politics and free markets the world over. Like the Fourteen Points, the American-sponsored aims in World War II, the Four Freedoms and the Atlantic Charter, were lists of liberal precepts. As after World War I, so in the wake of World War II the United States led the way in establishing an international organization. The United Nations has enjoyed a longer life than the League of Nations but has come no closer to reordering the international system along liberal lines.

In the postwar period American foreign policy has been preoccupied with the conflict with the Soviet Union. The Soviet-American rivalry was understood as an ideological conflict from the beginning. President Harry Truman, requesting money from Congress for economic reconstruction in Western Europe, said in 1947 that it was to prosecute a conflict "between alternative ways of life."

"One way of life," he continued, "is based upon the will of the majority and is distinguished by free institutions, representative government, free elections, guarantees of individual liberty, freedom of speech and religion and freedom from political oppression.

"The second way of life is based upon the will of a minority forcibly imposed upon the majority. It relies upon terror and oppression, a controlled press and radio, fixed elections, and the suppression of personal freedoms." Most Americans saw the conflict in similar terms.

In the 1950s the competition with the Soviet Union spread beyond Europe to Asia, Africa, and Latin America. For the United States it was consistently a conflict of creeds, of systems, and one on which America's own security was seen to depend. The zenith of the American commitment to waging that conflict outside Europe came in the 1960s. In his inaugural address in January 1961, President John F. Kennedy vowed that the United States would "pay any price, bear any burden, support any friend, oppose any foe, to ensure the survival and success of liberty on this planet." This was perhaps the clearest, as well as the most expansive, statement of the terms of the global rivalry as Americans understood them, emphasizing as it did both the ideological stakes and the national mission of the United States.

Western Europeans were part of the anti-Soviet coalition led by the United States. They, too, opposed Moscow's international ambitions. They, however, tended to worry more about Soviet military might and less about communist ideas and political practices than the Americans. The United States took Soviet ambitions to spread the communist system more seriously than the Europeans did, which made the rivalry more intense than a conflict between the Soviet Union and the rest of Europe alone would have been. The United States was more eager than its European allies to foster liberal principles within the communist bloc. Britain, Germany, and the United States all established radio stations to broadcast to Eastern Europe and the Soviet Union. The British service was called the British Broadcasting Corporation, the German the Deutsche Welle (German Wave). These names suggest what was intended in each case—one nation communicating with others. The names of the American stations bespoke a more ideological purpose: Radio Free Europe and Radio Liberty.

One reason that the Western Europeans were less concerned about communist doctrine was that many had sizable communist parties in their own countries. The French and Italian parties were especially important political presences in the postwar decades. They had ties to Moscow, and their programs were rejected by most of their countrymen, but they were not seen as alien intrusions. They had authentic roots in France and Italy. Their strength was not considered cause for undue alarm, nor were extraordinary measures thought necessary to cope with them. Over time the Western European communists either became more moderate and less oriented toward Moscow, as in Italy, or less powerful, as in France.

The Europeans differed from the Americans as well in that they were the heirs of a tradition of foreign policy known as *realpolitik*, which emphasizes the external behavior of other states and downplays the way they organize their political and economic affairs. A foreign policy of *realpolitik* strives to produce a stable balance of military power with rival states, without regard to how these rivals govern themselves.

This tradition has never found favor in the United States. In the 1970s, President Richard Nixon and his chief foreign policy aide, Henry Kissinger, tried to introduce the principles of *realpolitik* into the conduct of American foreign policy. They established formal diplomatic relations with the communist government of China and entered into a series of military and economic agreements with the Soviet Union. The purpose of their opening to China and their policy of détente with the Soviet Union was to contrive a stable balance of power, in which American international interests would be secure.

For all their diplomatic skill, however, Nixon and Kissinger found themselves under attack from both the left and the right of the American political spectrum for having cynically disregarded the internal features of other countries in conducting American policy. Conservatives disliked dealing with the Soviet Union, whose political system continued to deny the rights basic to liberalism. Liberals disliked the policy of friendship with regimes that also denied their citizens basic liberties but joined with the United States in opposing the Soviet Union and communism, regimes like those of South Vietnam, Chile, and South Africa. Both wanted political values and domestic political practices, not simply considerations of military power, to stand at the center of America's relations with other countries. They desired an ideological foreign policy, which meant, among other things, a foreign policy that opposed not only the expansion of Russia but also the extension of communism.

THE POSTWAR PERIOD

The features of the United States and the Soviet Union that have made their rivalry so intense, in particular their common sense of national mission to spread their own social systems, dates from the end of the eighteenth century in the American case and the second decade of the twentieth for the Soviet Union. The basis for their rivalry was thus in place in 1917, yet it began in earnest only after 1945. The eclipse of the other great powers cleared the way for it.

The defeat of Germany and Japan in World War II and the reduction in the status of Great Britain and France after that conflict—and partly as a result of it—left the United States and the Soviet Union as the two preeminent countries in the world. It meant that their rivalry, with its emphatically ideological tone, would dominate international politics. Stalin's prophecy about each side implanting its own system proved true for Europe. The continent was divided along ideological lines, roughly where the Russian and Western armies stopped in 1945.

World War II also led, directly or indirectly, to the collapse of the great empires—the Japanese, the British, and the French—that had governed much of the world outside Europe before 1939. Their disappearance left political vacuums all over the globe, into which the two rivals were drawn. The end of empires made the Soviet-American conflict not just a European but a global rivalry.

After 1945 direct imperial control went out of fashion. Indeed, the United States and the Soviet Union were both vocal opponents of formal empire. Both agreed that Africa should be governed by Africans, Asia by Asians, but they disagreed about the form these governments should take. The two competed to foster their systems. The United States encouraged the forces of economic and political liberalism; the Soviet Union supported local communists, or at least groups it believed would be responsive to Moscow's wishes.

Ideological affinity became the source of influence for both great nuclear powers. The United States assumed that capitalist, democratic (or at least non-communist) countries would be well disposed toward Washington. The Soviets calculated that communist regimes would incline toward Moscow. Both were right. Indeed, the Soviet experience with Third World leaders of nationalist persuasions in the 1950s and 1960s was sufficiently disappointing that in the 1970s they tried to encourage the formation of full-fledged communist regimes, with ruling parties enjoying a monopoly of power. Most of all they strove for control of Third World governments, through communist parties if possible but at least through the presence of Soviet troops or their proxies.

Having emerged as the two most powerful states, the United States and the Soviet Union would have had difficulty maintaining cordial relations no matter what their domestic systems, because of the tendency of the international system to promote rivalry among its strongest members and because of the nationalist ambitions of these two huge powers. A capitalist Russia would not necessarily have been easy for the United States to live with; a communist United States would not likely have settled into a comfortable partnership with the Soviet Union: the communist regime in China, after all, did no such thing.

The differences between the two systems, however, made the conflict one in which compromise was particularly difficult to achieve. In the eighteenth century, the great powers of Europe could divide disputed parts of the continent among themselves. In the nineteenth century, they could partition large areas of Africa and Asia. Each power would get something. One might regard another's share as excessive, but none disputed the right of the others to have a share of some size.

The stakes in the Soviet-American rivalry are not so readily divided. Neither has regarded the other's system as fully legitimate. The right to have any share at all of international influence is precisely what has been in dispute.

Each country has seen not only the other's influence, but in some sense its very existence, as illegitimate. Each has had reason to assume that the two systems could not coexist over the long term, that one or the other would have to disappear. For Americans at the beginning of the Cold War, the Soviet Union and communism were like Fascism—an aggressive, evil force with which conflict could hardly be avoided. The liberal world had fought, defeated, and eliminated Fascism. For their part, the Soviet leaders, as Marxists, could only regard the liberal system as transitory, destined to be supplanted by their own form of government and economic organization. The end of European overseas rule fortified their assumption that the entire liberal enterprise was historically doomed.

Each side objected, ultimately, not only to what the other did but also to what it was. Or rather, because the rivalry took the form of competition to spread the two systems, what each country did beyond its own borders seemed to the other to be an extension of, and therefore indistinguishable from, what it was at home. Neither side had any intention of modifying what it was, of changing its own system, to accommodate the other. Thus the rivalry between the United States and the Soviet Union after 1945 took on the features of a global civil war, in which each side contested the basic legitimacy of the other. Civil wars, because their stakes are supremely high and not readily subject to compromise, are the bitterest kinds of conflicts.

Contrary to the expectations on both sides in the 1940s, the two countries have learned to live with each other. The coexistence that seemed impossible at the outset of the rivalry has become a permanent, accepted, even celebrated feature of international politics. Nuclear weapons made the avoidance of war necessary, and therefore possible. The United States changed its attitude and the Communist Party of the Soviet Union adjusted its official doctrine accordingly.

Still, if the two rivals have managed to prevent their conflict from exploding into a cataclysmic war, the conflict has nonetheless persisted. The two have controlled its military consequences but have not removed its causes. Forty years after it began, the core of the rivalry remained intact. It remained not only a clash of great powers and a national rivalry but also a conflict of systems. The two countries have continued to adhere to the doctrines on which their different systems were based.

The faith in Marxism-Leninism that was so powerful among the Bolsheviks in 1917 has long since faded in Russia. In the elaborate, confident detail of its early-twentieth-century form it has few serious believers. But it remains the basis for the rule of the Communist Party. The presumed truth of the doctrine, and their fidelity to it, are what entitle the Party elite to direct the vast bureaucracies that govern the Soviet Union and to control its armed forces. They cannot abandon this doctrine without putting at risk the system that they have inherited and their own positions in it. Indeed, they cannot afford not in some general fashion to believe in it. Because they must believe in it, they do believe in it. None of the current Soviet leaders is as wholeheartedly committed to the tenets of Marxism-Leninism as was, for example, Nikita Khrushchev. Neither, however, are they utterly cynical, concerned only with preserving their own power. For them there is something called socialism, which is distinct from capitalism and which they are striving to create.

In the United States, by contrast, the principles of liberalism still evoke broad and enthusiastic acceptance. The historical forces and individual experiences that gave life to these principles continue to operate. The truths that the signers of the Declaration of Independence embraced in 1776 are just as self-evident to most of their 240 million political descendants in 1988.

The Russian elite, therefore, remains faithful, in a fashion, to communism because they need it; the American people retain their allegiance to liberalism because they believe in it.

2

....

THE "LOST" OPPORTUNITIES

....

The end of the 1980s is not the first period in which Soviet-American relations have appeared to be on the verge of significant improvement. This is not the only occasion when a more cordial alternative to the animosity that has marked the relationship has seemed at hand. High hopes for accommodation between the two powers have in fact been a regular feature of their rivalry. Such hopes have appeared once in every postwar decade: at the end of World War II in 1945, upon the death of Stalin in 1953, in the wake of the Cuban missile crisis and the signing of the Limited Test Ban Treaty in 1963, and with the flowering of the first period of détente in 1972. In 1988, after four summit meetings in as many years between President Ronald Reagan and General Secretary Mikhail Gorbachev, they returned.

On none of the previous occasions were these hopes fulfilled. Each proved a false dawn. Why, therefore, should this moment be different from the others? Why, that is, were the hopes of 1945, 1953, 1963, and 1972 disappointed?

There is, however, a prior question: Given the deep divisions between the United States and the Soviet Union, given the differences of ideology and the powerful conflict of national ambition between them, how could it ever have been supposed that the rivalry *could* be tempered? What was the basis for the optimism of the past, unfounded though it proved to be?

The American ideology, the same liberal precepts that have brought the United States into conflict with the Soviet Union, has also nurtured the hope that that conflict could be resolved.

Liberalism provides a series of ideas not only about how states should be organized internally but also about how they should, and can, deal with one another in the international arena.

In the liberal view of the world, harmony is the natural order of things; conflict is both unnatural and avoidable. International conflict is, for liberalism, a problem to be solved rather than a condition to be managed where possible and endured when necessary. The optimism that is a natural characteristic of Americans reinforced this approach.

The idea that a particular conflict can be solved is an expression of the characteristically practical American approach to public and private problems. The idea that any and all conflicts are susceptible to settlement with the application of hard work and goodwill is, however, a profoundly ideological one, and it is an idea that has affected the American approach to the global rivalry with the Soviet Union.

There is another reason for the persistent American hope that the Cold War would end: The effort that the conflict required was not one that the Americans were especially anxious to make. The liberal creed emphasizes private values—life, liberty, and property. Great public undertakings such as the role the United States has played in the world since 1945 do not fit comfortably into the liberal outlook. Americans have accepted that role but have not, on the whole, been enthusiastic about it. They have generally preferred that their values, practices, and institutions be promoted and protected throughout the world by the force of the American example, as in the nineteenth century, rather than by the use of American armed forces, as has been the pattern of the second half of the twentieth century. The American public balked at the price it was asked to pay—in money and in lives—to promote these values in Korea and in Vietnam.

Not surprisingly, there has been an historical connection between the price Americans have been asked to pay to promote the cause of liberalism abroad and the hopes that changes in the Soviet Union would eliminate the need for such payments. When the cost of the American role in the world has risen, so have the hopes for accommodation with the Soviet

Union. Those aspirations were highest immediately after World War II and in the wake of the war in Vietnam.

The American disinclination to become involved in international affairs, and the short attention span for matters of public policy in general, have led political leaders to overstate the consequences of the foreign policies they have devised. Advertisers in the United States routinely exaggerate the virtues of their products. Presidents have done the same thing for their foreign policies. Threats tend to be portrayed as apocalyptic, and agreements as the harbingers of a new age of harmony and tranquillity.

The impulse to end the rivalry received additional impetus in both countries from a new force in international politics, which appeared shortly before the Cold War began and that has shaped the global rivalry from the very beginning: nuclear weapons.

The existence of nuclear weapons has made the avoidance of war between the United States and the Soviet Union a matter of necessity. Although it cannot be proven that nuclear weapons and nuclear weapons alone have been responsible for the sometimes uneasy peace since 1945, it is plausible to assume that they have made a contribution to it. Leaders on both sides have acknowledged the dangers of nuclear weapons. They have declared that these dangers shape their policies. There is no reason to doubt them. In the postwar period, the prudence that nuclear weapons impose on both sides has overridden the impulses for conflict that arise from the differences between their political and economic systems and their ambitions to spread them.

The nuclear peace has rested on mutual deterrence. Each side deters the other from attacking its vital interests by threatening to respond with a nuclear salvo. Deterrence has proved a sturdy foundation for peace, but a foundation with which Americans, and others, have felt uneasy. Deterrence is a unilateral policy, based on the presumption of opposed interests. It is designed to keep the rivalry within bounds.

In the nuclear age there has been a powerful and broadly felt desire, chiefly in the United States but also in the Soviet Union and elsewhere, to go beyond deterrence, to find a basis for peace between the United States and the Soviet Union that involves cooperation and that addresses the basic causes of the conflict. Out of the recurrent attempts to address these causes, or perhaps more accurately out of the recurrent belief that they are being addressed, have emerged a series of occasions when the opportunity for ending the Cold War seemed to have arrived.

Paradoxically, however, nuclear weapons have also had the opposite effect. Even as they have triggered the impulse to solve the fundamental political conflicts between the United States and the Soviet Union, they have made it less than urgent to do so as the two countries have come to recognize that neither was prepared to risk war in pursuing those conflicts.

There has been no war between the United States and the Soviet Union and over the course of four decades such a war has seemed progressively less likely. The two sides have accepted the idea that, unlike similar conflicts of the past, theirs cannot be settled by force of arms. They have negotiated modest limits on their stockpiles of nuclear weapons.

Still, if they have agreed, tacitly, that a third world war would be too destructive to fight, and if they have understood that that agreement has made the resolution of their political disagreements less urgent than would have been the case if war were likelier, they have not managed to ignore or accept their differences. They have continued to hope periodically for their resolution.

THE ORIGINS OF THE COLD WAR

At the end of World War II, the United States looked forward to the creation of a new world, a world of free governments engaged in free trade and belonging to a strong international organization, the newly founded United Nations, which would play a vigorous role in keeping the peace. Americans hoped—indeed, they expected—that the Soviet Union would be a partner in this new world order. Instead, during the half-decade between the end of World War II and the outbreak of the

Korean War, the United States and the Soviet Union, allies at its beginning, became bitter adversaries.

The rivalry began with the division of Europe. When Roosevelt, Churchill, and Stalin met at Yalta in 1945, the American side thought the Soviets had made a commitment to conduct free elections in Poland, which the Red Army had occupied on its march westward to Berlin. Whether the Western powers pressed their view of Eastern Europe on Stalin as vigorously as they might have at Yalta, and at the summit conferences that preceded and followed it, at Tehran and Potsdam, and indeed whether Stalin had reason to believe that the United States and Great Britain had conceded him a free hand there, are questions that are debatable and have been extensively debated. Whatever impression he received from his Western counterparts, Stalin proceeded to install a communist government in Warsaw that was run for the most part by men who had spent the war in Moscow and were agents of the Soviet Union.

The Soviet policy in Poland set the pattern for the rest of Eastern Europe. Soviet-style rule was imposed most dramatically on Czechoslovakia, where communists staged a coup against a democratic government in 1948. By the next year Hungary, Bulgaria, Romania, and the Soviet occupation zone in Germany were firmly under communist control. An iron curtain, in Churchill's famous phrase of 1946, had descended across Europe.

The issue of nuclear weapons also divided the two wartime allies. The American government recognized that the question of what to do with the new explosive would be crucial for the postwar world. President Truman commissioned a study of the issue, whose conclusions, in modified form, were presented as an American proposal to the United Nations in 1946. The Baruch Plan, as it was called, provided for the establishment of an independent international organization that would control all phases of the atomic energy process from the mining of uranium to the fabrication of bombs. The Soviets rejected it. Three years later they exploded a nuclear device of their own.

The nuclear arms race had in fact begun well before then, when the Soviet Union learned of the American atomic energy program. By 1949 the arms race had come out of the laboratories into the testing grounds, and had produced not just experiments but real weapons.

In 1947 the American government created the European Recovery Program, better known as the Marshall Plan. It provided loans and grants to the war-torn countries of Western Europe. The United States offered to include Eastern Europe and by implication the Soviet Union in the Marshall Plan. Again the Soviets refused. Americans considered economic ties among sovereign states—trade, investment, and the transfer of technology—to be the foundation for peaceful political relations. That, too, was a basic precept of the liberal view of international politics, which was one reason that free trade was basic to the American program for the postwar world. The Soviets' refusal of Marshall aid, both for themselves and for the countries of Eastern Europe, ensured that the two parts of Europe, and the United States and the Soviet Union, would not be part of a common economic network.

By the time the Soviets declined to take part in the Marshall Plan, relations with the United States had already deteriorated. Several months before, upon deciding to send assistance to government forces fighting communist insurgents in Greece (who were, to be sure, receiving relatively little Soviet assistance), the American President had proclaimed the Truman Doctrine, according to which the United States stood ready to assist nations, like Greece, threatened by communist subversion. The next year the rivalry took on a military coloration. Having consolidated his rule in Eastern Europe, Stalin probed to see if further gains were possible by imposing a blockade on the western sector of Berlin, the former German capital. Each of the four victorious powers—the United States, the Soviet Union, Britain, and France—had occupation rights there but the city itself was located 80 miles inside the Soviet occupation zone of the country. The United States supplied the sector by air in what was, in effect, a military confrontation between East and West.

In 1949, several Western European countries and the United States formed the North Atlantic Treaty Organization (NATO), by whose terms each member pledged to come to the aid of the others in the event of attack. In 1950, with the outbreak of the Korean War, NATO was transformed from a simple guarantee pact to an integrated military alliance, with a complement of American troops permanently stationed on the European continent.

Hopes for postwar cooperation with the Soviet Union had been high in the United States in 1945. Americans' sense of disappointment with what happened thereafter was therefore acute, and led to a sense of betrayal that reinforced the dislike and distrust of the Soviet Union that Stalin's policies had already aroused. Their hopes stemmed from a belief in the precepts of liberal internationalism that seems, in retrospect, naive, and from a weariness with conflict that four brutal years of war with Germany and Japan had created. Roosevelt had believed that, in the end, he would be able to coax Stalin into going along with his version of a postwar order. Americans in general mistook the wartime alliance with the Soviet Union for permanent friendship.

To justify his alliance with the Soviet Union, Churchill once declared that if Hitler invaded hell he would at least make a favorable reference to the devil in the House of Commons. His was a jaded (although not inaccurate) view of the dynamics of international politics. The rift between East and West after the defeat of Hitler did not surprise him, and indeed, even while the war against Germany was being fought he had tried— without notable success—to turn Roosevelt's attention to the problem of dealing with the Soviet Union in the postwar period. Churchill's view was one that most Americans did not share. An alliance with the devil was a distasteful proposition. The United States was undeniably allied with the Soviet Union. Therefore Stalin was not a diabolical dictator. He was, rather, friendly Uncle Joe, with whom Americans could stay on good terms after the war ended. When this proved not to be possible, the American reaction was first one of surprise and then anger.

Could the great global rivalry have been avoided or at least

modified through wiser policies in the years immediately following the war's end? The question cannot be answered defini-
tively. What can be said with certainty, however, is that the
conflict arose from policies that were basic to the two countries.
The division of Europe, the nuclear arms race, and the failure
of economic cooperation were all due not to misunderstandings
or misjudgments but to values deeply embedded in the two
political systems and interests of supreme importance to the
leaders on each side.

Had the division of Europe been avoided, the history of the
postwar period would have been dramatically different. That
division, however, could have been avoided only if non-communist regimes had been established in Eastern Europe. It was the
character of the Soviet-imposed regimes there to which the
United States objected, and that led to the fear that the Soviet
Union would, if unchecked, impose similar regimes in Western
Europe. Not surprisingly, moreover, the imposed regimes
proved unpopular with, indeed unacceptable to, the people
whom they governed. The constant tension between rulers and
ruled in Eastern Europe erupted into open protest and organized opposition in 1953 in East Germany, in 1956 in Hungary
and Poland, in 1968 in Czechoslovakia, and in 1980–81 in Poland.

The power to determine how Eastern Europe was to be governed rested, in 1945 and thereafter, with the Soviet Union.
The Soviet campaign against Hitler's forces brought the Red
Army into the countries of the region, where it remained at the
end of the war—and to this day. As long as Soviet troops were
in place, the Soviet Union could decide the political fate of
these countries. The West could have dislodged them only by
force. Despite the rhetoric in the early 1950s about "rolling
back" Soviet control there, neither the United States nor Western Europe ever seriously contemplated going to war to liberate Eastern Europe.

Part of the mission of the men who had seized power in
Russia in 1917 had been to spread the revolution abroad. Their
early efforts to do so had failed. For three decades the Soviet
Union had been too weak to implant communism elsewhere;

but the Soviet leadership had never repudiated the idea of doing so. The course of World War II had made it feasible. In taking advantage of the opportunity that history had presented, Stalin was simply being true to one of the founding principles of the Soviet state.

Quite apart from considerations of ideology, the Soviets felt they had compelling reasons for seeking to dominate Eastern Europe. In the wake of the terrible war, one nearly fatal to the regime, the Soviet leadership was bound to give high priority to creating postwar conditions in which it could feel secure. It required a friendly regime in Poland, through which a Western invader would have to pass to reach Russia. But the Poles were hardly well disposed toward the Soviet Union. The battles of 1920, the brutal division of Poland between Germany and Russia that the Nazi-Soviet Pact and the German conquest of 1939 had produced, and Soviet treatment of Poland during the war had all aggravated the deep resentment Poles had long felt for the Russian role as one of their executioners and occupiers, along with Prussia and Austria, in the partition of their country at the end of the eighteenth century. An independent Poland had been reconstituted only after World War I. No popular Polish government was likely to be friendly to the Soviet Union. A friendly government would only be one controlled by Moscow, which meant a communist government.

The same logic applied to Germany. The Russians were determined to prevent the Germans from rising to threaten them for a third time in the twentieth century. The surest way to do so was to control at least part of Germany, which in turn required ultimately installing a communist regime in the Soviet zone of occupation.

Besides ideology and security, Moscow had a third reason for incorporating the countries to the west into a Soviet sphere of domination: Eastern Europe was a spoil of war. The Soviet Union had paid for it in blood. Hundreds of thousands of Soviet soldiers had died to liberate Poland, Czechoslovakia, Romania, Hungary, and Germany. Having freed Eastern Europe from one occupation, the Soviet Union proceeded to impose another. For Russians the Soviet position in Eastern Europe, no matter how it appeared to the Eastern Europeans themselves, was a matter of justice. It was accompanied by a sense of entitlement that was vividly expressed twenty years later by Leonid Brezhnev, when the Czech Party leader Alexander Dubček complained in 1968 about Soviet interference in his country's internal affairs. Brezhnev replied, evidently with some surprise, "But you belong to us."

Public opinion does not play the same role in the Soviet Union that it does in the West, but so far as it is possible to judge the sentiments of the average Soviet citizen, the continuing occupation of Eastern Europe is not unpopular. Certainly the periodic protests against, and open resistance to, Soviet hegemony there have not evoked much sympathy in Russia. Stalin would scarcely have faced a rebellion at home had he permitted free elections in Poland, but his policies there probably found favor with the Soviet public.

The competition in developing and building nuclear weapons has been the most visible, troubling, and perhaps the most dangerous feature of the global rivalry. Had it been avoided the conflict itself, although still a fact of international life, would have taken a different form. Given the deep political differences between the two sides, they might actually have gone to war against each other if they had been armed only with the kinds of weapons with which the war in Europe had been fought from 1939 to 1945. The stakes in such a war would have been high, but not as high as those a nuclear war would involve. At issue would have been political primacy in Europe, not the survival of the nations of the Continent as functioning societies. Nuclear weapons have made the Soviet-American rivalry a global conflict in the sense that it threatens the lives and property of everyone everywhere, as pre-nuclear and nonnuclear war do not. Like the forcible imposition of communist rule in Eastern Europe, however, the arms race was the product of basic features both of the two great powers themselves and of international politics. Like the division of Europe, it is difficult, in retrospect, to see how it could have been avoided.

The American-sponsored Baruch Plan was not a promising way to avoid it. The Plan implied the creation of a world government: an international body that monopolized the most powerful weapon known to man, after all, could easily impose its will on any sovereign state. It was therefore unlikely to be adopted under any circumstances. States do not surrender their independence, that is their sovereignty, voluntarily. It was the Soviet Union that rejected the Baruch Plan, but it is far from clear that, had the Soviets for some reason been willing to accept it, the United States would actually have turned over its nuclear weapons—the only ones in existence—to a new and untried international organization.

The Baruch Plan was misconceived in another way. It addressed the symptoms rather than the cause of the Soviet-American rivalry. The cause of the rivalry was the conflict of political aims. Weapons, nuclear and nonnuclear, were instruments of the conflict. Nations are armed, it is often said, because they are adversaries; they are not adversaries because they are armed. So it has been with the United States and the Soviet Union. In this sense the arms control agreements the two have managed to conclude over the last quarter-century are descendants of the Baruch Plan. They deal with the consequences rather than the root causes of the global rivalry.

There is a final reason why the Baruch Plan never had a realistic chance of being implemented. It would have frozen the Soviet Union into a position of nuclear inferiority. In 1946 the United States had already designed, built, and exploded several atomic bombs and would have retained the knowledge of how to do these things even if it had put all of its nuclear facilities into the hands of the international authority that the Baruch Plan envisioned. The Soviets lacked this experience, and the Baruch Plan would have prevented them from acquiring it.

As important a part of Soviet international aspirations as spreading Marxism-Leninism was achieving equality with the United States. Indeed, this national ambition has probably been more powerful than ideological motives in shaping Soviet foreign policy. To be equal, the Soviet Union had to be equally powerful, which required a Soviet nuclear stockpile. Indeed, to be inferior to the Americans, especially to permit them to have a monopoly of the new explosive, would place the Soviet Union at the mercy of the United States. At stake for Moscow in the early stages of the arms race was not simply pride or ideology, but, as the leadership saw it, the very independence of the Soviet Union. Shortly after the United States dropped the first two atomic bombs on Japan, Stalin summoned a group of scientists and told them, "A single demand of you, comrades. Provide us with atomic weapons in the shortest possible time. You know that Hiroshima has shaken the whole world. The balance has been destroyed. Provide the bomb—it will remove a great danger from us."

The Soviet rejection of the Marshall Plan was not a cause of the conflict with the United States, as were the imposition of Soviet-style governments in Eastern Europe and the decision to acquire nuclear weapons; but the rejection did contribute to American suspicions of the Soviet Union. It seemed perverse. The Soviet Union and the nations of Eastern Europe certainly needed assistance, having been badly damaged in the war. Moscow had eagerly accepted American Lend-Lease assistance during the war, and had bridled when President Truman abruptly terminated it shortly after the war's end. In the eyes of Americans, moreover, commercial ties formed the basis of friendly political relations, and so the Soviet refusal to establish an ongoing economic relationship with the West connoted a disinterest in peace.

For the Soviet Union to have accepted Marshall aid, however, would have violated its powerful allergy to any form of international inequality with the United States. The Soviets would have been in the position, if not quite of supplicants, then at least of receiving rather than conferring benefits. More important, Marshall aid appeared to Stalin to be a kind of Trojan horse for unwanted Western influence in the communist world. It would have required the Soviet Union to furnish considerable information to the United States. It would have generated pressure to adopt Western—that is, capitalist—economic practices. It would ultimately have tied the socialist countries to the market economies of the West, which, given the West's greater strength, would have made them dependent on international capital. Stalin was in the process of making

Soviet satellites of the countries of Eastern Europe. Marshall aid would have loosened his grip on them. It would have lifted the iron curtain.

Much later, Leonid Brezhnev sought economic relations with the West, but within strict limits and at a time when the Soviet leadership felt less vulnerable to the rest of the world. Accepting Marshall aid in 1947 would have undercut fundamental goals of communism in power: the construction of an economic order separate from that of the West, the maintenance of tight control over the economy and the society by the party, the establishment of a series of economic rules and practices different from the capitalist norms that Marx had so passionately criticized, and most of all the establishment of a Soviet sphere of domination in Eastern Europe.

The United States and the Soviet Union have been rivals because issues basic to both sides have divided them. Neither has been willing to give up the commitments and values that brought them into conflict. Only by sacrificing the things that liberalism deemed basic for the United States and that Marxism-Leninism, not to mention the Russian national interest, made supremely important for the Soviet Union, could the rivalry have been avoided. The beginnings of the Cold War represent not a lost opportunity for accommodation but the emergence of fundamentally divisive issues that the war against Hitler had temporarily submerged.

THE DEATH OF STALIN

In 1953 Stalin died, giving rise to hopes in the West for an end to the East-West conflict. Ordinarily the disappearance of a single person cannot make such a sweeping difference in international politics. Stalin, however, was no ordinary man. For two decades he had dominated the Soviet Union. He was the chief architect of its centrally planned economic system. He had exercised supreme political power; the other members of what was in theory a collective leadership were merely the executors of his will. In fact, they were terrified of him. To the rest of the world Stalin *was* the Soviet Union.

He embodied the regime, and even the country itself, for many people inside the Soviet Union as well. Within Russia his death inspired fearful uncertainty. The rest of the leadership appealed to the country not to panic, but something like panic was one widespread response to the end of the Stalin era.

What was cause for alarm in some circles, however, provided grounds for optimism in others. In the West, Stalin's departure heralded a new era, one in which the terrible practices and oppressive institutions he had introduced might be modified or abolished, and in which the conflict with the West that he had begun might be tempered. President Eisenhower responded to Stalin's death with a major address urging the new Soviet leaders to capitalize on the "chance for peace."

Important changes did occur in the Soviet Union after Stalin's death. The terror that he had used as a routine instrument of political control was, by the common consent of his successors, abolished. They put an end to the terrible era of wanton, arbitrary political murder. In 1956, in a secret speech to the Twentieth Congress of the Soviet Communist Party in Moscow, Nikita Khrushchev, who had emerged as the most powerful member of the post-Stalin leadership, denounced Stalin, his crimes, and the practice of heaping excessive, nauseating, and wholly undeserved praise on him known as the cult of personality. Hundreds of thousands of people who had been sent to detention camps for political reasons—or for no reason at all— were allowed to return home.

Soviet foreign policy changed as well. Despite his instructions to Soviet physicists on the morrow of Hiroshima to develop a Soviet atomic bomb as quickly as possible, Stalin never fully grasped the strategic implications of the atomic age. He had decreed that war between the capitalist and communist worlds remained unavoidable. His successors repudiated his thesis. They made more concrete changes as well. They gave up bases Stalin had seized at the end of the war in Manchuria in then-friendly China, and in neutral Finland. In 1955 they signed the Austrian State Treaty, under whose terms Eastern and Western troops withdrew from their zones of occupation in Austria and the country became formally neutral.

The essential character of the Soviet system and the main elements of Soviet foreign policy did not change, however, after Stalin's death. The basic causes of the global rivalry therefore remained. Even without the systematic use of terror the Soviet Union remained very much a police state, with a single party monopolizing power, planning and controlling the economy, and denying the rights and liberties basic to the liberal political orders of the West.

The arms race continued. Stalin's successors were as determined as he to draw even with the United States. They took a startling, and to the West unnerving, step in that direction in 1958 with the launching of the first earth-orbiting satellite, *Sputnik*.

The division of Europe persisted. In the wake of Stalin's death it became clear how deep and durable that division was. The year 1956 was an important one in the history of the Cold War. Partly encouraged by the changes Khrushchev had set in motion in the Soviet Union, a popular uprising against communist rule occurred in Poland and a full-scale revolution erupted in Hungary. In Poland the disturbances were ended with the return to power of Wladyslaw Gomulka, a Polish communist whom Stalin had purged in the late 1940s. In Hungary, however, the revolution was put down by Soviet troops with considerable bloodshed. The United States condemned Soviet repression, but did nothing to stop it.

The fate of the Hungarian revolution demonstrated that, contrary to the hopes of many Eastern Europeans, the West was not prepared to use force to liberate them. But the uprising also showed that communist rule in the region had virtually no popular support and was thus prone to outbursts of resistance. Since the people of Eastern Europe did not accept as legitimate the regimes the Soviet Union had imposed on them, the West could hardly do so. Thus the division of Europe was bound to be a continuing source of conflict between East and West.

In some ways the Soviet-American conflict became more rather than less intractable after Stalin's death. For all his cruelty to the people under his direct control, Stalin had pursued a generally cautious foreign policy, particularly toward the West after 1945. The regime he created within the Soviet Union was comparable to Hitler's in Germany, but his approach to the rest of the world was quite different. He gave only meager assistance to the communist forces in the Greek Civil War. He withdrew from northern Iran in 1946 after the United States objected to the Soviet presence there. Although he imposed a blockade on West Berlin in 1948 he did not attack the Western zone or prevent food from reaching it.

Khrushchev, his successor, conducted a bolder, riskier foreign policy. Several times during his term as Soviet leader Western officials were persuaded that he was preparing to go to war over Berlin; and it was he who installed missiles in Cuba in 1962, setting in motion the crisis that brought the two great powers, by general reckoning, closer to nuclear war than at any time before or since.

Stalin, moreover, had disdained the Third World. Khrushchev was intrigued by it. He believed that the disappearance of the European colonial empires in Africa and Asia and the emergence of independent states in their places offered fertile opportunities for the expansion of Soviet political influence and military presence. He tried to cultivate nationalist leaders like Nehru of India, Sukarno of Indonesia, Nkrumah of Ghana, and Nasser of Egypt.

The first major Soviet venture into Third World politics in the postcolonial era came in 1955, when, with Soviet approval, Czechoslovakia agreed to sell arms to Egypt. The next year the Soviet Union stepped in to replace the United States as the principal sponsor of the Egyptian Aswan Dam. The rivalry that had begun in Europe had spread to the Middle East. It would not stop there. Conflict in the Third World would come to be an important feature of Soviet-American relations.

THE CUBAN MISSILE CRISIS AND AFTER

It was the Cuban missile crisis of October 1962 that led to the next period of hope for a transformation of the conflict. The Soviet Union began to install missiles in Cuba capable of carrying nuclear warheads to targets in the United States. American intelligence discovered them through aerial photography. The Kennedy administration demanded their removal and imposed a naval blockade of the island to affirm its intention to remove them if necessary. After a nerve-wracking week the Soviets agreed to take them out.

The event rattled both sides. In its aftermath the leaders of the two countries felt a common need for a more stable relationship. They searched for ways to reduce tension. The result was a brief period when, unlike 1945 and 1953, relations between them did improve modestly, owing to the efforts of both governments. Kennedy and Khrushchev publicly expressed hopes for a less contentious relationship, Kennedy most pointedly in a speech at American University in Washington in June 1963. The Limited Test Ban Treaty, the first arms control agreement of the nuclear age, was signed in Moscow in July of that year. The United States agreed to sell grain to the Soviet Union for the first time in the postwar period.

The limits to the accommodation were apparent, however, even at the time. The Test Ban Treaty demonstrated that the two could conclude an agreement, but it had no effect on either side's weapons stockpiles, let alone on the political issues that divided them. In prohibiting nuclear testing in outer space, in the earth's atmosphere, and underwater while permitting it underground, the treaty's principal effect was to protect the environment. It was not a step toward restraining the arms race.

In its wake, in fact, the nuclear competition accelerated. In the mid-1960s the Soviet Union stepped up its production of offensive nuclear weapons. By the 1970s, like the United States, it had thousands of explosives. The missile crisis may have given a push to the Soviet program. In October 1962, thanks to a spurt in acquiring weapons launched by the Kennedy administration, the United States enjoyed a substantial advantage in nuclear weaponry over the Soviet Union. Finding themselves outgunned at the time of the crisis, the Soviet leadership, it has been speculated, was determined never to be in a position of nuclear inferiority again.

The missile crisis marked the end of the period when war in

Europe seemed likely. Berlin had been the flashpoint of the Soviet-American rivalry for fifteen years. When they imposed a naval blockade on Cuba to compel removal of the Soviet missiles there, Kennedy and his advisors thought Moscow might respond by putting pressure on the Western position in Berlin.

This did not happen, nor were the periodic threats to West Berlin renewed. A chapter in the Cold War had ended. It was formally sealed in the late 1960s and early 1970s by a series of accords involving the Soviet Union and the Western governments, principally that of the Federal Republic of Germany, which put the status of Berlin on a firmer political basis.

If one chapter of the global rivalry ended in the Caribbean in the autumn of 1962, however, another began there. If the conflict assumed a more regular, settled form in Europe thereafter, it became sharper in other parts of the world. The Cuban missile crisis was a milestone in the rivalry in the Third World. Its conclusion left Fidel Castro firmly in control of the island and solidly in the Soviet camp. This was a victory for Soviet foreign policy. A Soviet client state had been established in the western hemisphere, only 90 miles from the continental United States. Communist Cuba was the first installment of a Soviet empire outside Europe, whose growth in the 1970s would alarm Americans.

Finally, the goodwill that emerged in the wake of the missile crisis proved transitory. It was very much the creation of the two leaders who had guided their countries through it, and little more than a year after the Test Ban Treaty was ratified by the United States Senate both had left the scene—Kennedy assassinated, Khrushchev deposed. Relations between the two powers soon came to be dominated by another Third World conflict, in Vietnam.

THE DÉTENTE OF THE 1970S

The Berlin agreements and the West German policy of conciliation toward its eastern neighbors known as *Ostpolitik* proved to be the precursors of the broadest, most deliberate, and most ambitious effort to improve relations between the United States and the Soviet Union in the postwar period. The détente of the early 1970s partly re-created if not the events then at least the expectations of the immediate postwar period. It aroused hopes for an end to the global rivalry. The failure to fulfill them, and the collapse of détente, created disappointment and bitterness—and not just in the United States, as at the beginning of the Cold War, but on the Soviet side as well. The final demise of détente at the end of the 1970s ushered in the harshest relations between the two rivals since the early days of the Cold War; and that period, in turn, was the prelude to the present moment.

The centerpiece of détente was a series of summit meetings between American presidents—there were three during the decade—and Leonid Brezhnev. Six such meetings took place: in 1972 in Moscow, in 1973 in the United States, in May 1974 in Moscow and later that year, in November, in Vladivostok—the first involving Richard Nixon before his resignation, the second with his successor, Gerald Ford—in 1975, when Ford and Brezhnev traveled to Helsinki to sign, along with the leaders of the European countries, the Treaty on Cooperation and Security in Europe, and finally in 1979, in Vienna, where Jimmy Carter met Brezhnev to sign the SALT II treaty.

The summits were powerful symbols of change in the relationship between the two countries. The sight of two leaders greeting each other warmly, conferring intently, signing treaties and protocols calling for cooperation in various spheres, and proclaiming a new era of friendship between them made a powerful impression on Americans, Russians, and others. In politics, as in art, style is meaning; and the style of the summits left the world with the message of reconciliation and cooperation. It was a message that the American people, then still bearing the political, psychological, and economic burden of the war in Indochina, were happy to receive.

The most important business the leaders transacted at these summit meetings was arms control. They signed a series of agreements imposing restrictions—most of them modest, to be sure—on their nuclear arsenals. The Strategic Arms Limitation Treaty of 1972 (SALT I) froze the long-range offensive forces on both sides. A successor agreement, SALT II, which was signed in 1979 but never ratified by the United States Senate, put further limits on these weapons. There were other accords, of which the most important was the Antiballistic Missile (ABM) Treaty of 1972, which effectively prohibited the construction of systems of defense against missile attack.

In 1972 and 1973 the two sides attempted to work out a code of international conduct to regulate their relations. These were efforts to institutionalize the restraint with which they had come over the years to deal with each other. They also committed themselves to expanding trade considerably and to broadening scientific, scholarly, and cultural exchanges.

The new relationship that Nixon and Brezhnev said they were constructing soon began to unravel. The trouble did not, however, come in Europe, where the stakes were highest and the two sides were most heavily armed. Détente in Europe preceded and outlived the efforts by the United States and the Soviet Union to reach accommodation on the whole range of issues that divided them. The German accords were in place by the time the American president and the Soviet general secretary met for the first time in 1972; and the Europeans, in particular the Germans, were reluctant to follow the American lead in adopting a more hostile stance toward the Soviet Union after the invasion of Afghanistan, indeed even after the crushing of the free trade union Solidarity in Poland two years later.

Détente did not bring the arms race to an end. The Soviet Union continued to add to its arsenal (as did the United States) even after the two treaties of 1972 had been concluded, leaving many Americans with the feeling that in the arms negotiations the Soviets were acting in bad faith.

No sooner had the ink dried on the first military, economic, and cultural agreements of the détente era, moreover, than the Soviet Union began to behave aggressively—in American eyes, at least—in the Third World. The Soviets were already providing substantial military assistance to the Vietnamese communists. In October 1973, with Soviet connivance as Americans saw it, Egypt and Syria launched their attack on Israel. (The

Soviets in turn found grounds for complaint about American policy in the Middle East in the skillful diplomacy of Secretary of State Henry Kissinger that excluded them from the postwar peace process between Israel and Egypt.) They later extended their influence to Africa. With Cuban assistance, pro-Soviet regimes took power in Angola, Mozambique, and Ethiopia. The invasion of Afghanistan in December 1979, to ensure that the government in Kabul remained under the control of friendly Afghan communists, was the final and, to the United States, most flagrantly provocative Soviet initiative in the Third World of the decade.

The political support for détente in the United States eroded steadily. The initial agreements of 1972 and 1973 encountered a wary reception from American conservatives, who grew increasingly disenchanted with the policy of cooperation, conciliation, and formal agreements as the Soviet presence in the Third World expanded and as it became clear that the arms competition would continue.

In 1976, in recognition of the change in mood on the right, the Republican president Gerald Ford discarded the term "détente" from his political vocabulary. He adopted a markedly more skeptical attitude toward the Soviet Union than he had displayed when he had first succeeded Richard Nixon in the summer of 1974. He was moved to do so in part by a challenge for the Republican presidential nomination in that year by the vehemently anti-Soviet former governor of California, Ronald Reagan.

Ford was nominated but not elected. The Democratic Party, which was still by and large committed to détente, took control of the presidency. The administration of Jimmy Carter negotiated another series of limits on offensive nuclear weapons with the Soviet Union, which were codified in the SALT II treaty. But the invasion of Afghanistan prompted Carter to withdraw the treaty from consideration by the Senate and destroyed the last vestiges of détente. The most elaborate effort to abolish the Cold War, and the high hopes that that effort had inspired, had come to an end.

What went wrong with détente? At the heart of its failure

was each side's misunderstanding of the other's intentions. Each side presumed a friendlier, more cooperative, more conciliatory approach on the part of the other than was warranted. Each placed too benign an interpretation on the other's definition of their new relationship.

The United States thought that the Soviet Union was agreeing to abide by American standards of international conduct, and was shocked when this did not occur. The American government oversold the benefits of détente to the American public. Although he and his colleagues privately held a much more sober view, President Nixon proclaimed that he and Brezhnev had laid the basis for a "full generation of peace." The American public received the impression that the Cold War was at an end, that the Soviet Union was prepared to abandon the policies that had created the conflict. This was not so. The Soviets, for their part, assumed that the Americans were acknowledging their right to an international status equal to that of the United States. The policies they pursued were well within the bounds of their own definition of international equality. Unlike Stalin in 1945, the Soviet leaders of the 1970s seem to have been genuinely surprised when the United States professed shock at those policies.

The United States hoped, and believed, that the Soviet Union had accepted the American concept of nuclear equilibrium. The idea was expressed by the term "mutual assured destruction," which was often abbreviated by the acronym MAD. It refers to a condition in which each side can deliver a devastating blow in response to an attack by the other no matter how fierce that attack and no matter what measures the attacker adopts to defend itself against retaliation. Since each is vulnerable to retaliation, neither will dare attack. Because each can deliver a crushing second strike, neither will launch a first strike.

When each side has enough firepower to mount a devastating second strike—and both had more than enough nuclear weapons for this purpose by the early 1970s—then neither needs to add weapons to its arsenal. The doctrine of mutual assured destruction implies the end of the arms race. Many Americans thought that the Soviet Union had accepted the doctrine, and its implications, by signing the 1972 ABM Treaty. By the terms of the treaty, both sides renounced defenses against nuclear attack. Each accepted permanent vulnerability, as the doctrine prescribes. At the same time, the two agreed to freeze their offensive launchers—although not the warheads attached to them.

For the Soviet side, adherence to the ABM Treaty was evidently not so much a way of embracing the American definition of nuclear equilibrium as a tactic to forestall a competition in the deployment of systems of ballistic missile defense, a competition in which the United States had considerable advantages. The Soviet government agreed to some limits on their offensive forces as the price for a prohibition on defense. For Moscow the treaty did not, however, imply a wholehearted commitment to a general principle that would govern its entire nuclear arsenal. It did not agree to cancel ongoing programs—nor did the United States.

One of the Soviet programs involved putting multiple warheads (MIRVs) on existing missiles. The United States had been the first to perfect this technique. In 1972 MIRVs were already affixed to American missiles, but not to Soviet ones. Over the next several years the Soviet missiles received MIRVs, leading to an imbalance that the United States found troubling.

The Soviet Union had, for a variety of reasons, built bigger missiles than the United States. These missiles could thus carry more warheads. In the 1970s the guidance systems for the warheads on both sides became increasingly sophisticated. They could be aimed with ever-greater accuracy. This meant that each side was better able to launch a preemptive blow. Each could assign several warheads to each of the other's missiles. With the improvements in accuracy at least one of these warheads was certain to strike each missile before it could be launched in a retaliatory salvo. Since the Soviet Union had larger missiles and thus more warheads, its capacity for making such a preemptive strike was greater than that of the United States.

The Soviet Union could not hope to destroy all of the American nuclear arsenal with such a blow. Thousands of warheads, each capable of devastating a Soviet city, were carried on submarines and were thus invulnerable to preemptive attack. The United States could still crush the Soviet Union in response to a first strike. Mutual assured destruction remained a fact of international life. The Americans who worried about the Soviet advantage in striking land-based missiles did not expect Moscow to launch a surprise nuclear attack. But they did worry that the Soviet superiority in this one category of strategic proficiency might be translated into gains in the ongoing political competition between the two countries. The mere existence of this inequality, they feared, might make Soviet foreign policy more aggressive where the two sides confronted each other than it would otherwise have been.

This asymmetry in nuclear capabilities came to be known in the United States as the "window of vulnerability." It preoccupied American strategic planners. One of the chief American aims in the arms talks with the Soviet Union was to close it, but the Soviets would not oblige. In response to American complaints they argued that whatever advantage they enjoyed in land-based missiles was offset by the American superiority in nuclear weapons based at sea, on submarines, and on manned bombers with intercontinental range. They may also have believed that their larger missiles could provide them with political advantages, which they were determined to preserve and exploit after twenty-five years of trailing in the nuclear competition.

Like its determination to control Eastern Europe in the 1940s, the Soviet interest in the Third World in the 1970s stemmed partly from ideological considerations. Circumstances presented Moscow with the opportunity to spread its own system. Doing so was important for Brezhnev, as it had been for Lenin, Stalin, and Khrushchev before him. Although they had long since abandoned the idea that revolution was imminent in the advanced countries of the West, as Lenin had believed almost until his death, the Soviet leaders of the 1970s retained the conviction that Marxism-Leninism was, or per-

haps more accurately had to be, something more than a paro-
chial Russian creation. The belief in the relevance of its governing principles remained an important part of the political
outlook of the Soviet leaders. That belief continued to be part
of their claim to rule in Russia.

Their early encounters with the newly independent states of
the Third World were not particularly rewarding. Some of the
leaders they cultivated turned on them; others were overthrown. All were intent on pursuing their own interests, which
often turned out not to advance the interests of the Soviet
Union as Moscow saw them. The Soviet leadership therefore
adopted a new strategy for gaining influence in Africa and
Asia. In places like Angola, Mozambique, Ethiopia, and South
Yemen Moscow sought at least some form of direct or indirect
control.

The drive to achieve international equality with the United
States also drew the Soviet Union into the Third World in the
1970s. The United States had built a network of clients, friends,
and allies and a string of military bases around the world. The
Soviet Union aspired to a comparable international standing.
It had reached parity with the United States in nuclear weapons. Parity in the other indices of international status was the
next step.

The Soviets did not set out purposefully and systematically
to acquire their own network of clients. They took advantage
of opportunities that presented themselves, but they did not
create these opportunities. The war in Vietnam was at root an
internal affair; the Soviet Union assisted, but did not control,
the Vietnamese communists. Nor did they exercise controlling
influence in Egypt or Syria. The Arab-Israeli conflict had a
wholly indigenous basis. The collapse of the Portuguese empire, in which the Soviet Union played no part, created opportunities for the expansion of Soviet influence in southern
Africa. In each case the Soviet government was fishing in trou-
bled waters; but in none did Moscow play a significant role in
causing the instability from which it profited.

Americans were surprised and disturbed by the growth of
Soviet influence in the Third World. Détente, they believed,

involved a Soviet commitment to forgo the kind of international aggression that the spread of this influence involved. Like the window of vulnerability, the expansion of Soviet influence in Africa and Asia seemed to demonstrate that détente was a sham, another postwar occasion for Soviet duplicity.

From the Soviet point of view, however, the acquisition of Third World clients was an affirmation rather than a violation of the spirit of détente. It was a prerogative to which international equality with the United States entitled Moscow. It would have been perverse, in the view of the Soviet leaders, to deny themselves the kind of international network that the United States had long possessed.

It undoubtedly crossed the minds of some in Moscow that such policies might not sit well with the United States. But the Soviets believed that the Americans could not, or at least would not, do anything in response. For they interpreted the American decision in favor of détente as a concession, made out of weakness. In the early 1970s the United States was divided at home and beleaguered abroad. The riots in the urban ghettos of the late 1960s had barely subsided. The war in Vietnam was a source of ever-louder protest and rising disaffection. The war itself was costly, and the United States had little prospect of winning. The policy of détente in fact had its origins in the Nixon administration's early efforts to enlist Soviet help in ending the war through pressure on its Vietnamese allies.

The collapse of the authority of the executive branch in the United States contributed to the Soviet assessment. As Richard Nixon was progressively weakened by the Watergate scandal, his capacity to adopt policies that would offset Soviet initiatives in the Third World and elsewhere ebbed. Nor was his successor, Gerald Ford, able to carry out such policies. Although at first mystified by the Watergate affair, the Soviets ultimately came to see it as another sign of the decline of American power, which opened the way for the expansion of their own.

In the Soviet political vocabulary the term *correlation of forces* occupies an important place. It stands for the balance of strength broadly defined—including not only a country's military might but also the health of its economy and the cohesion of its society. By this broad measure the Soviet Union seemed to be rising in the 1970s while the United States was falling. The Soviet leaders saw détente as part of the process by which they were gaining power and status in the world. They understood Washington's willingness to agree to it as a way of coming to terms with American decline.

In addition to the arms competition and Soviet policy in the Third World, a third issue subverted the détente of the 1970s. That issue was human rights. The Soviet government denied to its citizens the rights and liberties basic to liberal political systems like that of the United States. Freedom of speech, of assembly, and of worship and the people's right to choose their own government were all unavailable in the Soviet Union.

This scarcely constituted, in the 1970s, a change from traditional Soviet practices. These rights and liberties had never been available to the Russian people, and it was the essence of the communist political order to deny them. The sharp differences between the two political systems were, after all, among the chief causes of the conflict. Still, in the flush of goodwill produced by the first phase of détente, these enduring differences disappeared from the center of public attention in the United States.

The disappearance proved to be temporary. The American distaste for internal Soviet political practices soon came to affect the course of Soviet-American relations. It crystallized around the desire of a large number of Soviet Jews to leave the Soviet Union.

The Soviet period had not been an especially happy one for Russia's large Jewish population. Many who inhabited the territory conquered by the Nazis in 1941 and 1942 were killed. The defeat of Hitler ended the severest threat to them, but shortly before he died Stalin began to prepare the ground for an anti-Semitic purge. The rumor was put about that Jewish doctors were plotting against him. A number of prominent Jews—physicians and others—were arrested. Before the purge could take on the dimensions of the mass killings of the 1930s, however, Stalin died. Still, even in the post-Stalin period, Jews were denied a religious life.

In theory, Jews are one of the constituent nationalities of the Soviet Union, endowed with all the rights nominally accorded to each of them. Many of the nations within the Soviet Union have in fact enjoyed a measure of cultural autonomy, even if nothing approaching genuine political independence, because they have been concentrated in their own homelands: Armenians, Georgians, Kazakhs, Azeris, and others have their own republics, in which they can speak their native languages and practice many of their traditional customs. Jews, however, have no geographic base, being dispersed throughout the Soviet Union. They have therefore suffered from double discrimination. They do not have the power to carve out a separate cultural sphere for themselves; but they also have difficulty assimilating. They cannot live as Jews, but they are often not accepted as Russians, either.

The 1967 Middle East war, with Israel's stunning victory, had a catalytic effect on Soviet Jews. It kindled an active sense of religious and ethnic identity among many of them, and they began to agitate for the right to move to their true national homeland—Israel. Emigration was generally forbidden to Soviet citizens. For its own reasons, however, the regime began to allow some Jews to leave, which increased the number of those wishing to do so.

Their cause was taken up abroad, especially by the Jewish community of the United States. In 1974, Senator Henry Jackson of Washington and Congressman Charles Vanik of Ohio introduced a measure in Congress calling for denying Most Favored Nation trade status (MFN)—which meant simply giving the preferences and exemptions that were normal for trade with the United States—to any country that did not permit free emigration. This measure, commonly called the Jackson-Vanik Amendment, was aimed at the Soviet Union. It passed by an overwhelming majority.

Its popularity had something to do with the political strength of the organized Jewish community, but more to do with the broad American commitment to the liberal precept of freedom of movement. To oppose the measure was to deny one of the most cherished of American principles.

The Soviet government was unhappy with the Jackson-Vanik Amendment. The Nixon administration tried to find a form in which it would be acceptable both to them and to its sponsors, but the effort was unsuccessful and the Soviet Union was denied MFN. With the final collapse of détente at the end of the 1970s, the flow of Jewish emigrants was closed off almost completely.

The human rights issue assumed a different form in the wake of the Helsinki Conference of 1975. The Soviet leadership had long sought such a conference in order to ratify the postwar boundaries of Europe and so, in their view, reinforce their control over Eastern Europe. To get the Western countries to sign a document to this effect the Soviets had, in turn, to agree to a series of articles on human rights.

Moscow presumably had no intention of permitting freedom of speech and movement as the terms of the document it signed committed it to do. But in the wake of the Conference a series of independent groups was formed in the Soviet Union and Eastern Europe to monitor their governments' compliance with the terms of the Helsinki accords. The communist regimes turned on these groups harshly. Their members were harassed and arrested. Their plight received wide attention in the West, and produced shock and outrage, especially in the United States.

The Soviet leaders objected to the Jackson-Vanik Amendment and to the Helsinki Watch Groups because these impinged on their right to govern their country as they chose. Moscow regarded these measures as attacks on the Soviet system, as indeed they were. To Americans, however, they were expressions of principles with universal validity. Soviet opposition dramatized their disregard for such principles. The right of Soviet Jews to emigrate and the provisions of the Helsinki accords were matters of fundamental principle for Americans. They were basic to the American ideology. Their violation reminded Americans of the basis of the global rivalry. It reemphasized that the conflict was one of social and political systems.

In this way the human rights issue was similar to the events that began the Cold War. Both brought to the surface the basic differences between the United States and the Soviet Union, differences that had been artificially, and temporarily, submerged.

CONCLUSION

Why, in summary, was it impossible to end the global rivalry for the first four decades of its existence? Why were what seemed at the time occasions for dramatic improvement in relations between the United States and the Soviet Union not genuine opportunities for change at all? There are three principal reasons.

First, the two powers were deeply divided over the political character of Europe and ultimately at odds politically elsewhere. Although they accepted that the division of the Continent could not be undone by force, the Western countries never regarded this division as legitimate and permanent. They could not have done so even if they had wished, because the Eastern Europeans refused to accept it.

Second, for the first twenty-five years of the rivalry the Soviet Union was inferior to the United States in military might and political influence. Initially for reasons of security, then for ideological and national reasons, Moscow was determined to catch up. When the Soviet Union did catch up there seemed no reason to stop. The prospect of superiority beckoned.

Third, the conflict of creeds, of systems, persisted. The principles of communist political, social, and economic organization were considered illegitimate in the West, especially in the United States. Even when leaders were prepared to set aside these internal differences, the American public was not. This was not a cause of war, but it was certainly a barrier to peace based on mutual respect and friendship.

3

THE GORBACHEV DIFFERENCE

In the first half of the 1980s relations between the Soviet Union and the United States were as bad as at any time in the post-Stalin era. The SALT II treaty negotiated between President Carter and Leonid Brezhnev was not ratified by the American Senate. The arms control negotiations between the two super-powers stalled. The Soviets continued deployment in Europe and Asia of new, mobile, intermediate-range ballistic missiles, the SS-20s. NATO responded to the SS-20s by beginning to place American-controlled Pershing II and cruise missiles, both armed with nuclear warheads, in Europe. The Soviets mounted a nasty political campaign to prevent the Europeans from ac-cepting the missiles but it failed, handing them a major diplo-matic setback.

A large contingent of Soviet combat troops fought a bloody war in Afghanistan in defense of a weak puppet communist regime, with the goal of transforming Afghanistan into a So-viet satellite. The nonviolent struggle of the entire Polish na-tion against its communist rulers, under the banner of "Solidarity," led to the creation of a military government and an "internal invasion" by Polish security forces, with the War-saw Pact armies in the background as a potential source of support. Solidarity was dissolved and martial law imposed on the Poles. Soviet domestic and foreign propaganda directed at the United States reached hysterical proportions, going so far as to compare President Reagan to Hitler and warning of an inexorable movement toward war. The paralysis of decision-making in the Kremlin in the last years of Brezhnev's rule and the ensuing interregnum made Soviet policies particularly rigid.

The United States, under President Reagan's leadership, responded to the Soviet arms buildup of the 1970s with a sharp increase in military spending. For the first time in its postwar history, the United States supplied arms to a force that was engaged in direct combat with Soviet troops—the Afghan resistance. In 1983, President Reagan launched his Strategic Defense Initiative (SDI), which aimed at creating a defensive umbrella in space to repel a Soviet nuclear attack. The Soviets saw SDI as an American scheme to develop the means to launch a nuclear strike against the Soviet Union free of the fear of retaliation.

By the mid-1980s, however, things had changed dramatically. Soviet-American relations had entered a new phase. The tensions that had arisen with the Soviet invasion of Afghanistan in 1979 began to ease. In late 1987 the two governments agreed to the destruction of all medium-range Soviet and American nuclear missiles and to extensive provisions for on-site inspection to ensure that both were observing the agreement. Soviet troops began to withdraw from Afghanistan. Four summit meetings were held between the fall of 1985 and the summer of 1988. An agreement on strategic armaments, the first to involve major cuts in the two arsenals, was imminent.

How did the two reach this point, which offers the greatest opportunity for improvement in Soviet-American relations since the advent of the Cold War over forty years ago? Developments in both the United States and the Soviet Union contributed to it.

President Reagan took seriously his promise to work for peace while strengthening the United States. By the end of his first term, he had made it clear that he was interested in mutually acceptable solutions to outstanding problems.

The balance of military power between Russia and America did not change meaningfully during Reagan's administration, but the United States did make clear its intention to compete militarily with the Soviet Union. The national mood also changed. The country proved eager to leave behind it the frustrating decade of the 1970s and regain its traditional confidence and optimism. Reagan's leadership served this purpose well. As his term of office drew to a close, he became receptive to new opportunities that would, without betraying his deeply held ideological convictions, permit agreements with the Soviet Union.

These opportunities appeared with the coming to power in the Soviet Union of Mikhail Gorbachev. He is both the architect and the product of powerful social and cultural currents in his country, which have the potential to produce sweeping internal changes and have a significant effect on foreign policy as well, including relations with the United States.

THE SOURCES OF CHANGE IN THE SOVIET UNION

By the spring of 1988, the Soviet Union had reached a stage of creative turmoil. What was happening could best be described as a gigantic experiment, touching virtually all fields of endeavor and calling into question the traditional ways of thinking and governing. This experiment was only at its beginning. To take hold and to change the Soviet system, the new course initiated by the general secretary will require at least a decade.

The changes that are taking place have many sources. They have arisen from the domestic performance of the Soviet system in the Brezhnev era and the necessary conditions for Soviet economic growth in contemporary circumstances. They are the product of the changed nature of Soviet society, the character and consequences of the technological revolution in capitalist societies, and the deterioration of the international position of the Soviet Union.

Major reforms grow out of major crises. The Soviet Union is no exception. The leaders who took power in the mid-1980s understood that they had inherited a country in a state of crisis, both material and spiritual. At the June 1987 Plenum of the Central Committee, Gorbachev said candidly that the Brezhnev era was characterized by the appearance of "pre-crisis phenomena." The implication was that, without urgent measures, the Soviet Union would have found itself in an actual crisis. The rector of Moscow State University, in a speech published in *Pravda* in November 1987, described the situation more dramatically: "We were sliding into the abyss and are only starting to stop the slide."

The speeches of the new leader and the discussions in the Soviet press are, by the standards of the past, extraordinarily frank. They are designed to shock people into action, to mobilize them for corrective action. The new leadership has also made it clear that the problems are national in scope, and affect all areas of social, cultural, and economic life. They have grown not from specific policies but from the very nature of the Soviet system. To overcome them, therefore, requires not simply new and better policies but a change in the system itself.

The Soviet Union has been steadily running down. Its performance has been poor in every sphere except the military. The official reports proclaiming how well it was doing have been simply lies. Without urgent and extensive reform the problem could still be transformed into a crisis of survival threatening the very existence of the Communist system.

By the end of the Brezhnev era, Soviet society was chronically ill. Politically, the most significant development was the alienation not only of the population at large, but also of the Party, from the rulers and from the regime. Aside from coercion, political stability was achieved through mass political apathy, the privatization of the people's concerns, and a complete absence of civic spirit. The government became highly bureaucratized, and thoroughly corrupted by Mafia-like cliques in the various ministries and provincial party organizations.

Even the enforced mask of "socialist realism," with its emphasis on optimism at all costs, could no longer hide the deep cultural pessimism prevailing among educated Russians. This was matched by feelings of hopelessness among the workers. The Soviet Union was probably the only major country in the world where the youth did not rebel but lacked any youthful enthusiasm that could be channeled into creative public activity. The heroes of the youth were their own private poets and balladeers. They placed great value on artifacts of Western mass culture like blue jeans and records that were often officially tolerated but not encouraged.

At a speech at a Plenum of the Central Committee in February 1988, Gorbachev made the extraordinary statement that in the twenty years before he took power, Soviet national income, with the exception of production of alcohol, did not increase at all in real terms. The Stalinist model of the economy that served the Soviets well in the first phases of their industrial revolution, that had built their heavy industry and military might, could no longer promote growth. It could not provide a better diet, the mass production of durable consumer goods, or the development of high technology. The Stalinist model stifled initiative and creativity. As it grew it became more and more cumbersome and unmanageable.

The Stalinist model of economic organization went hand in hand with an extensive strategy of economic growth. The Soviet leaders tried to achieve economic expansion by increasing the inputs of labor, capital, and land.

In the 1970s, however, the supply of new labor diminished. Cheap raw materials, so abundant in the past, were being exhausted. Costs increased sharply when production moved from the easily accessible European parts of the country to the vast wastelands of Siberia. Expanding the land under cultivation was no longer possible. Ever-increasing capital expenditures became difficult to sustain. The declining rate of capital formation reinforced the tendency toward stagnation. The monumental neglect of the Soviet economic infrastructure created extraordinary bottlenecks in the Soviet economy—the shortage of railroad capacity, for instance—and accounted for unbelievable waste of materials and labor. An estimated 20 percent of the agricultural harvest and perhaps half of all the vegetables and fruits were lost due to the lack of roads and storage facilities.

The Soviet political leadership, and of course the country's economic experts, were aware of the obsolescence of the extensive strategy of growth before Gorbachev came to power. They knew in a general sense that the Soviet economy had to switch to an intensive strategy of growth, one depending upon the increased productivity of labor and capital through technological progress and incentives, declining costs of production, and the conservation of raw materials and energy. Yet even when they tried to switch to an intensive growth strategy they were determined, because of inbred conservatism, to avoid serious changes. And an intensive growth strategy cannot be reconciled with the Stalinist economic model.

When Gorbachev and his colleagues came to power, they soon recognized that they confronted economic difficulties of major proportions. They concluded that what was required was both a change of growth strategy and a change of economic organization from the Stalinist command system to an as yet undefined model in which the market would play a much more important role.

The social sources of the Soviet crisis and of the Gorbachev response to it can be summarized simply: In the post-Stalin period, Soviet society has changed significantly, while the increasingly antiquated political order of a different era has remained largely in place.

The Soviet social system, which rewards those with political power and is indifferent to performance, has killed the population's work ethic. Official corruption and years of unfulfilled promises have led to the far-reaching alienation of the society from the Party and the regime. The Soviet middle class, and particularly its professional component, has had no power or autonomy. Finally, the growth of a huge welfare state has given the Soviet Union the worst of both worlds. Where it was necessary, the quality was poor—as with medical services; where it was unnecessary, it expanded dramatically—for instance, the enormous subsidies of food prices.

For the Soviet leadership and political elite (as well as its professional groups), the key measure of progress was and remains Soviet accomplishments in comparison with those of the advanced capitalist countries. This "relativism" is a Soviet tradition. Starting with Lenin, but especially under Stalin and continuing in the post-Stalin era, the slogan of "catching up and surpassing" the West, the United States in particular, has expressed a powerful impulse.

The comparative perspective on Soviet achievements serves as a reference point for the Soviet leadership. And while Sputniks, space stations, and intercontinental rockets may bolster morale, the competition between capitalism and socialism will be decided on earth. The important standard of comparison, moreover, is not extraordinary, heroic deeds but the quality of everyday life.

In the last fifteen years almost all capitalist countries have entered the era of the Third Industrial Revolution, the age of complex communication systems, the enormous and previously unimaginable expansion of information collection, retrieval, and exchange, and rapid change in durable consumer goods through electronics and miniaturization. Science has come to play a greater economic role. Markets have become truly global and international economic and technological interdependence has grown. A number of previously unindustrialized countries in Asia have managed to benefit from these changes.

The Soviet Union has not even begun to enter this Third Industrial Revolution. It has yet to create many of the prerequisites, from reliable telephone networks to the much more complicated production of such primary electronic components as miniaturized microchips. Part of the Soviet political and professional class was by the end of the 1970s well aware of the revolution that was sweeping the West and the East, but the Soviet leadership apparently did not understand the nature of the challenge and did not contemplate a realistic response to it.

The combination of Soviet economic and technological stagnation with the explosive growth in the capitalist world is calamitous for the Soviet Union and the aspirations of its ruling circles. Excluding the Second World War, the years from the 1970s to the mid-1980s were the first prolonged period in Soviet history in which the country fell behind the major capitalist nations in important economic indicators. The technological gap between the Soviet Union and advanced capitalist countries widened.

Yet even these comparisons do not tell the main story. The most important comparisons concern things that can seldom be quantified. The indices of Soviet production, once the visible signs of accomplishment and the source of great pride, suddenly seemed either irrelevant or the expression of backwardness. The Soviet Union produces, for example, twice as much steel as the United States with a GNP half the size, yet has chronic shortages of steel. The explanation is simple: the country is wasting steel. There is too much steel in capital and consumer goods. Lumber, electrical energy, and oil are also wasted on a large scale.

The present Soviet leaders are well aware of this state of affairs. They feel threatened. Their patriotic pride is wounded. The example of Japan and the newly industrial nations of East Asia such as Korea, whom the Russians have traditionally scorned, must be a particularly bitter pill for them to swallow. What they see as their destiny of international greatness is now in question. Their sense of urgency in meeting the economic and technological challenges coming from the rest of the world is reinforced by their fears of its potential military consequences. They recognize that their international aspirations cannot be reconciled in the long term with the narrow range of their foreign policy resources. In the last analysis, this is the deepest source of the present leaders' commitment to real change.

The final source of the changes that have begun is the deteriorating Soviet international position. Toward the end of the 1960s and during the early 1970s this position was improving. It appeared to the Soviets that a monumental change was taking place in the world, that the international correlation of forces, as they call the military and political balance, was moving sharply in their favor, perhaps irreversibly.

To the Soviets, détente looked like a guarantee against dangerous confrontations with the United States, for the stabilization of Europe including the recognition of the Soviet sphere of influence there, and the expansion of economic relations with the West including the large-scale technology transfer required by the Soviet economy, while at the same time offering an almost free hand for Soviet expansion outside Europe.

By the late 1970s and the early 1980s, however, the Soviet international position had worsened markedly. While détente with Western Europe was still alive, the Soviet invasion of Afghanistan in 1979 ended it with the United States.

Although still wary of military involvement abroad, the United States left behind its opposition to international activism, regained much of its past sense of confidence, and increased its military budget.

At the same time, the Soviet Union found itself overextended internationally, straining its resources without the promise of near-term victories. The national liberation movements that had been in the 1970s a symbol of increased Soviet influence had become by the early 1980s an anti-Soviet force. The Soviet Union found itself with almost no major friends and with trouble in its empire to boot. In Eastern Europe the Polish events that started in 1980 brought together the working classes and the intelligentsia in a massive national movement against the communist regime.

The Soviet Union's decline internationally, combined with its domestic difficulties, reinforced the feeling in the ranks of the Soviet leadership, political elite and experts, that Soviet foreign policy resources were inadequate to support Soviet global aspirations.

In the early 1980s, therefore, powerful pressure for change began to build. Yet change was not inevitable. It required a catalyst. That catalyst turned out to be Mikhail Gorbachev.

THE LEADER

Any leadership succession in the Soviet Union after Chernenko's death in March 1985 would have led to reforms. The pressure for change was enormous. The breadth and depth of these reforms, however, are the result of several exceptional features of the succession.

First, there were three changes in the position of the general secretary. Consequently, personal loyalties sometimes established by decades of association were weakened or broken. The possession of a political network ceased to be necessary to contend for the top position. This permitted a leader who did not have a political machine, who was a newcomer and a relative outsider in the top leadership, and whose support for reform was known before his victory, to win the top prize.

Moreover, the succession involved major turnover within the top leadership and the elite in all spheres of Soviet life, and coincided with a generational change. Gorbachev inherited a leadership group that, with the exception of China, was probably the oldest in the world. The succession has replaced the political generation that grew up in Stalinist Russia with a leadership that is more apt to support change and to recognize the need for reforms.

Finally, the historical accident that placed Mikhail Sergeyevich Gorbachev in the position of the general secretary at a particular moment in history is of major importance. Gorbachev's personal role looms large. He has promoted a much more elaborate and far-reaching vision of change in the Soviet Union than his comrades.

When Gorbachev took power he was an almost unknown quantity in the West. He soon demonstrated that he was a strong leader, who would inspire and motivate others. He has stamped his personality on the powerful position that he holds. Even people who do not believe in the ultimate success of his program are impressed by him. Among his close supporters and aides he has been able to create in a short time an aura of exceptionality, of charisma.

Gorbachev also showed himself to be an astute politician. He came into office without a personal political machine of his own. He arrived at a time of domestic and international crisis, accompanied by high and probably exaggerated expectations of what he could achieve and how quickly he could do so. And yet without producing any visible improvements at home, he managed to consolidate his power in the Politburo and prepare the conditions for a similar consolidation in the Party's Central Committee. As a politician he has proceeded cautiously, working with the Politburo and through the Politburo, yet at the same time dominating the body by his self-assurance, his tenacity, and his intellect. When decisive personnel and policy decisions have had to be made he has not procrastinated. In response to setbacks he tends to be fatalistic or complain about his bad luck, but he quickly sets them aside and moves on.

By Soviet standards Gorbachev is well educated, and he is known to be an avid reader. He is cerebral in approaching problems. He is inclined both to plan ahead and to improvise where necessary. He is a quick learner. More important, in his process of learning he is critical and skeptical. At heart he is an innovator who does not accept the conventional wisdom. He shows great determination to put his views through and by all accounts has a forceful personality. He is a man driven by both patriotism and personal ambition to reverse the decline of his country.

Gorbachev quickly established himself as an international statesman and seized the initiative in the crucial area of arms control. Lacking extensive experience in international affairs, he surrounded himself with experts and can now hold his own in meetings with other world leaders. His popularity abroad arose largely from the difference between his appearance and style and that of his predecessors. For the non-Communist world Gorbachev is exotic; he has the status of celebrity and a television personality. But this celebrity status is also partly a response to the inner power and conviction that he conveys.

Gorbachev believes deeply in the force of ideas in human affairs. He is emotional about them, even sentimental and romantic. He feels that he and his small band of associates will convince a growing number of supporters of the necessity for his program of *perestroika* and will revitalize Russia. He seems to see himself in Lenin's situation when he arrived in Russia in April 1917, with the tsarist regime already overthrown, and proclaimed that Russia was ripe for a socialist revolution. In the Russia of 1917, it should be noted, power was, figuratively, lying in the streets waiting to be picked up by a determined revolutionary, while in today's Russia it is tightly held by determined bureaucracies.

Gorbachev is the first modern leader of the Soviet Union—modern in his goals, in the means by which he pursues his policies, and above all in the style of his leadership, which is unprecedented in the Soviet Union. The visibility of his wife, Raisa, in his domestic and foreign trips and receptions for foreign heads of state is unconventional for the country.

Gorbachev is the first Soviet leader since Lenin who does not read his speeches but actually talks to the people. He is adept at informal exchanges, jokes, and working the crowd. He has learned to use television, where he comes across as a serious, powerful, and sincere personality. People have responded to him partly because he seems to show genuine curiosity about their work and their lives. He is modern also, and most importantly, in the sense that he has started to conceive of "modernity" in Russia primarily as a set of attitudes or approaches that are innovative and dynamic in all spheres of activity.

The mere existence of a man like Gorbachev, with his talents and independent thinking, at the upper levels of the Party apparatus—let alone his elevation to a position of top leadership—is extraordinary. And Gorbachev's political personality is important for the future of Soviet-American relations not only because he is the supreme Soviet leader, but also because it is on his personal efforts that the scope and pace of reform will depend; and the progress of reform will in turn influence relations with the United States.

THE GORBACHEV DIFFERENCE: PERESTROIKA

Under Gorbachev's leadership a new Russian word has entered the language of politics—*perestroika,* which is his programmatic domestic response to the crisis of the Soviet system.

Gorbachev's first two years in office constituted a process of education about the enormity of the mess that he had inherited. Parallel to this education and as its consequence, his program of change became increasingly radical. At first he defined the task at hand as the "quickening" of the developmental process. Then it was the "revival" of the society, next the "reconstruction of the system," and finally a "revolutionary transformation."

The hallmark of this program of change is its comprehensiveness. It involves not only a determination to replace the people who were responsible for the failures of the past but also a plan to change policies in almost all areas of endeavor. Gorbachev in fact aims to alter not only policies but the very structures of public life and economic activity in the Soviet Union.

The core of Gorbachev's *perestroika* is the determination to bring Russia up to the standards of the industrial capitalist world. In economics, modernization means stressing productivity and quality. In technology, it means self-sustaining progress. In politics, it means subordinating the distribution of power to the effectiveness of economic performance and technological creativity. In the social area, it means adjusting society to serve the needs of economic and technological progress.

Gorbachev does not yet really know how to achieve his goals and may still underestimate the difficulties of the process. But the basic orientation of *perestroika* is clear. The economic reforms are intended to move in the direction of a rather eclectic kind of market socialism. This reverses the trend of Soviet history, with the exception of the nine years of NEP in the 1920s. Gorbachev proposes to limit central planning, give greater rights and responsibilities to plant and firm managers, increase economic incentives, and redefine the indicators of success from plan fulfillment to productivity, cost-efficiency, and quality.

The decisions of the Central Committee Plenum in June 1987 and the state decrees that followed it are the most far-reaching steps Gorbachev has taken in the economic sphere. He defined his proposals as a plan for the "fundamental reconstruction of the management of the economy." They contemplate organic changes in the Soviet systems of planning and management.

Yet, in key respects they do not cross the line separating the Stalinist "command economy" from "market socialism." At the interfaces of economic activity, such as price formation, quality control, and competition, it is not market forces that will play the decisive role, but the old administrative structure. Still, the proposed reform is of great importance because it prepares the ground for later measures. These future reforms will introduce the market mechanism into price formation, new techniques of quality control, and competition.

Further movement toward market socialism will impose norms of behavior, standards of success, and rules for the distribution of economic rewards that will run counter to the entire Soviet tradition.

To advance his program of modernization Gorbachev will have to push and pull his lethargic country, as so many Russian and Soviet leaders have tried to do before him. He needs to establish his power over the Soviet political elite, the bureaucracies, and to mobilize support among its educated strata and working people. Whether and how he will be able to accomplish this is not yet clear.

Gorbachev is a stable and sophisticated leader who works closely with his colleagues. Of course, if in the next three years, positive results of his *perestroika* are lacking while its unintended consequences appear to be dangerous, his position as general secretary might be in jeopardy. Yet even then, it will probably be Gorbachev and his associates who will define what success means; and they might well alter their policies in order to remain in power.

As of 1988, Gorbachev had not yet achieved a significant breakthrough in domestic reforms. The resistance to *perestroika* has increased as Gorbachev has consolidated his power. This was not illogical. In 1986 Gorbachev was speaking about changes in a very general way, and everybody could agree with the need for change. But in 1987 he took major steps to expand *glasnost* and democratization and to reorganize the economy, thereby weakening those who wanted to preserve their own privileges and power. It was not surprising, therefore, that the resistance to his reforms grew. This was not an organized opposition, but rather bureaucratic resistance by those who simply paid lip service to *perestroika*.

This resistance will be broken only by a combination of personnel purges, incentives and disincentives, and persuasion.

Gorbachev wants to achieve what can be called a "revolutionary breakthrough," in which the principles of *perestroika* will take hold in the activities of the bureaucracies, managers, and workers. To this end, he will try to combine steady pressure from above, using the advantages of the highly centralized Soviet political system, with pressure from below created by *glasnost* and democratization.

Unlike all his predecessors, Gorbachev does not rely on any particular power base, such as the party apparatus. Instead, he is forging an unorthodox and heterogenous coalition that includes high and low Party, government, and economic officials and managers, liberals in the Western meaning of the term from among the intelligentsia, "pure" Leninists who believe that Lenin's vision of socialism was betrayed by his successors, military men who see Gorbachev's program of modernization as the only way to ensure Soviet international security, Russian nationalists who desire to make Russia great again, intelligence officials who know Soviet weaknesses intimately, anti-Stalinists who participated in Khrushchev's reform campaigns and now have the opportunity to resume what was interrupted twenty years ago, young professionals who want to hitch their wagon to a rising star, political and cultural leaders in the non-Russian republics who see in *perestroika* a chance to defend the cultural heritage of their nations and increase their autonomy vis-à-vis Moscow, those like Andrei Sakharov who are concerned about world peace and believe that Gorbachev is moving in the right direction, and many others.

The Yeltsin affair and the nationalist turmoil probably encouraged the centrists in this "rainbow coalition," who want to modernize Russia yet are wary of *glasnost* and democratization. It discouraged the leftists, for whom the instruments of modernization are as important as the goal of modernization itself. But neither the centrists nor the leftists have any real alternative to Gorbachev and his personal vision. Whether this coalition will be sufficient to implement reform remains, of course, an open question.

Gorbachev is a determined reformer, but politics, even in the Soviet Union, is the art of the possible. His course is likely to follow a zigzag pattern—a push for comprehensive reforms followed by periods of consolidation, to be succeeded by periods of all-out offensive.

Western observers often ask the question, "How can Gorbachev decentralize economic power, which is necessary for modernization, dilute the Party's political power by democratization, liberalize the media and culture, create an atmosphere of greater permissiveness and yet, at the same time, preserve the hegemony of the Communist Party and its leadership?" This is a question to which there is as yet no satisfactory answer. It is quite possible that these two aims, reform and the maintenance of Party control, are simply incompatible.

The task facing Gorbachev is, however, even more difficult than the question implies. The image of the Soviet Union as highly centralized is partly incorrect. During the last year of Brezhnev's rule and the interregnum, the flow of information from the provinces and republics to Moscow and the flow of effective authority from Moscow to the rest of the country broke down. The reporting from the peripheries to the center was to a large degree based on lies. The directives from the center were acknowledged and then routinely ignored. The enormous machinery of the Party and the government was drifting without a plan or direction. The elite in the provinces and republics, who frequently occupied their offices for fifteen to twenty years uninterruptedly, enjoyed considerable de facto autonomy.

Gorbachev's task is to restore or rather create a flow of accurate information and reporting from the bottom up and the effective flow of power from the center outward. Yet at the same time, he is trying to give greater autonomy to economic units, political groups, municipal governments, cultural organizations, and the like. To do both at once will be immensely difficult—yet without effective centralization, his reforms will not get off the ground, and without greater autonomy, they will not succeed. The solution to the dilemma is to give priority to centralization rather than to autonomy. This, however, is only possible if the process of devolution of power and greater autonomy is controlled. The nationalist turmoil in the south showed that this process will be largely spontaneous and difficult to control. The task that faces Gorbachev in his quest to modernize Russia is herculean. The extent to which he succeeds will influence Soviet-American relations; it will also depend on his, and others', foreign and security policies.

THE "NEW THINKING"

Domestic conditions in the Soviet Union and the change of leadership cannot but influence Soviet international behavior and security policies.

The new leadership has understood, as has no other from the time of Stalin in the 1930s, the decisive influence of domestic strength on foreign policy. In this sense Gorbachev's program of domestic reform is his most basic foreign policy statement.

The shifts in Soviet foreign policy that are taking shape are not only tactical, indeed not only strategic in nature, but also programmatic. Tactics concern primarily short-term changes of form. Strategy deals mostly with intermediate-range changes of direction. Programmatic changes concern long-range redefinition of goals and aspirations.

It is sometimes said that changes in Soviet foreign policy under Gorbachev have been limited to words. Words are important, however, particularly in a centralized and ideological state like the Soviet Union, especially if the words are those of authoritative leaders. Moreover, policy changes begin with words. The principal short-term objective of Soviet foreign policy was expressed in a speech by Soviet foreign minister Eduard Shevardnadze to the Soviet Diplomatic Academy in June 1987. "The main thing," he said, "is that the country not incur additional expenses in connection with the need to maintain its defense capacity and protect its legitimate foreign policy interests. This means that we must seek ways to limit and reduce military rivalries, eliminate confrontational features in relations with other states, and suppress conflict and crisis situations."

The linkage between domestic conditions and Gorbachev's foreign policy course is also strong. The general secretary made it quite clear by a rhetorical question addressed to the editors of *Time* magazine in the spring of 1987: "You know our domestic plan of *perestroika,* draw your own conclusions about what kind of a foreign policy these plans require." Foreign Minister Shevardnadze expressed the idea more explicitly: "If foreign policy is an extension of domestic policy . . . and the goal of diplomacy is to form an external environment that is favorable for internal development . . . then we are compelled to recognize that the backwardness of our power and its steady loss of status is partially our fault too."

The international environment has encouraged the rethinking of the major premises of traditional Soviet foreign policy. The resistance to Soviet influence in the Third World has increased, the stability of the East European empire is in question, the economic and technological superiority of the West is growing, and new dangers like Islamic fundamentalism are emerging. At the same time the perception of danger from the traditional adversaries—the U.S., NATO, China—has declined substantially. A theoretical journal of the Soviet Communist Party of January 1988 carried an authoritative article which for the first time since the advent of the Cold War (and for the first time in Soviet history) made the simple and, for the Soviet reader, astounding statement that "The Soviet Union is not in danger of war from the United States and NATO."

The new Soviet thinking about international relations in general, and relations with the United States in particular, has led to the revaluation of some old concepts, the birth of new perceptions, and the development of new principles. Every student of foreign relations knows that each country's international behavior is shaped by two factors: domestic and historical forces and the actions of other states. The Soviets, however, when explaining American actions or those of their other adversaries, used to put all the emphasis on the first while ignoring the second.

For instance, when the Soviets discussed Afghanistan among themselves they did not ask whether it was proper or sensible to have invaded, but rather why the Americans reacted as they did to the invasion. They put all the blame for the collapse of détente on the Americans and tended to consider all Soviet actions not only as justified but also largely irrelevant to détente's failure. There are indications that this blindness is giving way to a more realistic and truthful interpretation of events. Still, for most Soviets, American foreign and security policies seem to have a logic of their own that has nothing to do with Soviet behavior.

A key concept in Soviet relations with the United States and other capitalist countries has been revived and reassessed by the new thinking—the concept of the peaceful coexistence of countries with different social and political systems. According to the Soviets, this fundamental concept was originated by Lenin. This is true, but its meaning for Lenin was, it is to be hoped, quite different from that in the post-Stalinist era and today. For Lenin (and Stalin), peaceful coexistence meant simply that in the struggle with the capitalist countries, Soviet revolutionary pressure cannot continue at a constant level of intensity. When conditions do not favor revolutionary goals, the Soviet Union should retrench and wait for better times. Peaceful coexistence therefore signified simply an enforced pause in the attack on capitalism that would end when conditions become ripe for another round of revolutionary expansion, leading ultimately to a war between the Soviets and the West.

Peaceful coexistence acquired a different meaning under Khrushchev, the first Soviet leader to understand some of the realities of the nuclear age. He proclaimed that wars between capitalist and Soviet countries were no longer inevitable. For Khrushchev and Brezhnev, peaceful coexistence meant that Soviet expansion could occur without armed conflict with capitalist countries. It was for them a program of victory without war. For Gorbachev, peaceful coexistence seems to have acquired yet another meaning. The idea of a worldwide victory of socialism, even without a war, is being abandoned. An advisor to the Soviet leadership wrote in July 1987 in *Pravda* that: "Interstate relations . . . cannot be the sphere in which the outcome of the confrontation between world socialism and world capitalism is settled." Between Soviet foreign policy and communist ideology "fire breaks" should be established that separate the one from the other. "We have taken," said Gorbachev in his book *Perestroika,* "the steps necessary to rid our [foreign] policy of ideological prejudice." The Soviets are seeking doctrinal justifications for these unorthodox ways of thinking so as to make them legitimate to the believers.

Another element of the new thinking concerns interdependence. This is at the center of discussion of international relations in the West but is a new theme in the Soviet Union. One result of the Third Industrial Revolution is the growth of global interdependence, first in the economic sphere but also in science and culture. The new Soviet leaders are beginning to recognize this. They are aware of the inadequacy of Marxist and Leninist concepts to explain it. The idea of a global economy is especially troublesome for the Soviets because the Soviet Union, except for the initial phase of its industrialization, developed in a state of virtual economic autarky. While Stalin's successors rejected economic isolation, their economy, despite its immense size, has played an entirely marginal role in the global arena. The structure of Soviet exports is typical of an underdeveloped country, dominated by raw materials.

Several communist countries past and present have tried to form links with the global economy to support their plans for modernization. Hungary and China are current examples. The new Soviet leaders want to increase international economic contacts through credit, joint ventures, and trade. They do not envisage either capital imports or joint ventures, however, as substitutes for domestically generated technological progress. In this respect, at least, their understanding of the patterns of technological progress today is accurate.

Gorbachev's economic reforms envisage opening up more of the Soviet economy and Soviet science to outside influences. These steps, however, are still mostly on paper, and pitifully inadequate. Soviet participation in the global economy, and worldwide science and technology, combined with decisive domestic efforts to create favorable circumstances for managerial interest in technological progress are the *minimal* prerequisites for a modernization that will at least stabilize the widening gap with the capitalist states. The Soviets are only beginning to understand this.

The new Soviet thinking about economic, scientific, and cultural interdependence, if serious, will have significant consequences for its international relations. Economic and scientific needs will play a much larger role in Soviet foreign policy than in the past. The opening of the scientific and cultural sectors of society to global interchange will curb the pattern of secrecy. In order for global standards of modernity to influence Soviet development, enterprises will have to enter into international competition, not primarily for the sake of earning hard currency but to expand the islands of modernity within the Soviet economy. Whether in the long run the political requirements of the Party's monopoly of power will permit such transformations is an open question.

The Soviet understanding of interdependence goes beyond strictly economic, scientific, and cultural matters. It stresses shared interests and ceases to view international relations as a zero-sum game only. This type of thinking, alien to the traditional Soviet world view, will take a long time to influence the new leadership's basic approach to international relations. To win over the Soviet elite, it will have to evoke a response in the West.

The "new thinking" about international relations is of central importance to the rest of the world. It marks a shift from established Soviet approaches to a more Western way of thinking. But it is still confined to a relatively small group of Soviet officials and specialists, although some of its elements have found their way into Gorbachev's security and foreign policies.

To what extent Gorbachev and his colleagues are willing to sacrifice long-standing Soviet international ambitions, how far they are willing to go to demilitarize the global conflict and respect vital Western interests, is yet unclear. The unanswered and currently unanswerable question of the new thinking's staying power, future course, and practical consequences will shape American attitudes and the American course of action toward the Soviet Union.

4

....

THE ARMS RACE AND THE
HUMAN RACE—THE PAST

....

Of all the issues that divide the United States and the Soviet
Union, nuclear weapons and human rights have had the greatest public visibility and the strongest popular resonance in the
West. Each is represented in the public mind by several broadly
recognized and powerfully evocative symbols.

Newspapers, magazines, and television frequently carry pictures of sausage-shaped ballistic missiles with nuclear explosives at their tips, often igniting with a fiery tail and launching
into space—the world's largest, deadliest bullets. The Washington *Post*'s editorial cartoonist, Herblock, depicts the bomb as a
leering, stubble-bearded missile-shaped figure, surely the most
menacing cartoon character ever created. By far the most familiar symbol of nuclear weapons, however, is the mushroom-
shaped cloud, the characteristic formation of billowing smoke
created by a nuclear explosion, which the world first saw rising
above the ruins of Hiroshima on August 6, 1945. It is a symbol
that is universally recognized, a symbol of death, destruction,
and dread.

The familiar symbols of human rights, and the struggle to
secure them in the forbidding political terrain of the Soviet
Union, are not objects but particular people. Two Russians
emerged in the 1970s as the most famous protagonists in that
struggle. Natan (formerly Anatoly) Shcharansky, a young Jewish mathematician, came to embody the quest for the religious
liberty that was unavailable to Jews in the Soviet Union and

for freedom of movement, in his case the right to leave the country to settle in Israel.

Andrei D. Sakharov, one of the Soviet Union's most distinguished physicists and an honored member of the Soviet Academy of Science, who had made an important contribution to the Soviet nuclear weapons program, became the most visible member of a small group of Russians who sought political liberties, notably the right to dissent publicly from the government's policies.

Each was an articulate and sympathetic figure. Each made his views known to the rest of the world through Western reporters who were stationed in Moscow. In the 1980s Shcharansky and Sakharov were, along with whoever was the general secretary at the time, probably the three Russians best known to the rest of the world. Both were punished by the Brezhnev regime for their activities on behalf of human rights. As a consequence, each became the living symbol of terms that found their way into the vocabulary of the West. Shcharansky was the most famous "refusenik"; Sakharov the best-known "prisoner of conscience." Shcharansky went to prison in 1977 and was kept for long periods in solitary confinement. Sakharov was sent into internal exile, and put under virtual house arrest, in the provincial Russian city of Gorky in 1980. Their suffering made them heroes.

THE TWO ISSUES

In some striking ways these two most visible parts of the global rivalry, nuclear weapons and human rights, make an odd couple. As issues in international politics they differ markedly. For one thing, their scope is different. Rights are the property of individuals; a single nuclear weapon can kill hundreds of thousands, even millions of people.

For another, Soviet and American nuclear weapons policies have a strong family resemblance to one another, as their policies on human rights do not. The weapons' technical features impose a certain range of choices upon their possessors that are independent of any ideological convictions. The Soviet Union and the United States occasionally made separate choices, and these were consequential; but both fashioned the same kinds of armaments, deployed them in similar ways, and made their central purpose deterrence—the prevention of war.

The two countries' policies on human rights, by contrast, diverge dramatically. Those differences are at the heart of the huge gap between democratic and communist political systems. Political rights that are honored, protected, and freely practiced in the United States are systematically denied in the Soviet Union. If nuclear weaponry is the issue on which the two are most alike, human rights was and is perhaps the one over which the disparities are sharpest. Indeed, in response to the steady Western criticism of their practices of political repression, and in recognition of how deeply embedded the idea of human rights, as symbolized by Shcharansky and Sakharov, had become in the world's political discourse, the Soviet leaders began to insist on a different definition of the concept. Rights, they claimed, were to be understood in economic and social rather than political terms. All people were entitled not to political liberty but to housing, employment, and medical care. The performance of their own system in providing what they defined as rights, they always implied and often said, was superior to that of the United States and the West.

Much of what Moscow said was merely political propaganda. Behind the contrasts in the definition and observance of human rights between the United States and the Soviet Union, however, lay not just the determination of the Soviet oligarchs to exercise control over their country, but also genuine and deeply rooted differences in values.

In the West, and especially in the United States, individual liberty is highly prized. In the Soviet Union, as in Russia for centuries, social order is important and what threatens that order is resisted. The story of the Moscow grandmother who, seeing someone push ahead in the line for a bus, cries out "Anarchy," illustrates an attitude that is still widely held, which creates a far broader tolerance for authoritarian government than is found in the West. Partly as a consequence, neither the Soviet Union nor tsarist Russia before it has had any significant experience with democracy, with its civic participation, free elections, and independent parliamentary bodies.

In the West, and especially in the United States, efficiency is a virtue because it is the basis of individual prosperity. In the Soviet Union equality—that is equality of material conditions —is important. Someone who had lived in both countries once observed that when an American gets a flashy new car his neighbor's reaction is to try to figure out how to get the money to buy one for himself; whereas if a Russian manages to obtain a new car his neighbor's response is to complain to the local authorities that he is getting above his station. In fact, with the conspicuous exception of Party and government officials, Soviet society is marked by considerable economic equality. This is something that Gorbachev is trying to change. The most skilled and energetic people have little incentive to work harder at their jobs because there are strict limits to how much more they can hope to earn.

Competition is basic to Western economic and political life. Westerners are accustomed to many different products and many different ideas all clamoring for their favor. The Russian and Soviet tradition is different. Monopoly has always been the norm.

The Soviet predilections for order, for equality, for monopoly are not inevitable, and some of Gorbachev's reforms are aimed at introducing more spontaneity, merit-based distinctions, and diversity into the life of the country. But neither are these values wholly the artificial imposition of Stalin. They have deep roots in Russian society, and have helped to create a social and political climate hostile to the protection of the rights that Western Europeans and North Americans deem fundamental.

The United States and the Soviet Union engaged in extensive negotiations about nuclear weapons, beginning in the 1970s. Here, too, the nuclear issue differed from human rights. Each country tacitly conceded that the other had a legitimate interest in the composition of its own nuclear arsenal. But the Soviet leadership resisted the idea that the United States, or any other country, was entitled to pass judgment on, let alone promote a change in, the way it treated its own citizens.

Moscow welcomed the SALT talks but not the Jackson-Vanik Amendment.

For all the distinctions between these two uncommonly visible issues, however, they do have important common characteristics. They are the features of the global rivalry that distinguish it from the many great power conflicts of the past. The two issues are important elements of the conflict for the same reason that their symbols are so familiar: they arouse popular passions. People care about them, especially in the United States. The prospects for moderating the rivalry therefore depend heavily on finding common ground on nuclear weapons and human rights.

The importance of nuclear weapons and human rights in Soviet-American relations makes the rivalry different in degree from the long series of great power conflicts that preceded it. The two issues represent the furthest extension of social and political trends that began in Europe two centuries ago. They also make the global rivalry different in kind from those of the past because together they prevent it from ending as previous conflicts have.

For most of recorded history, international politics was a game played by kings and princes. Monarchs raised armies as large as their treasuries could purchase. They sent these armies against the forces of rival rulers in conflicts that often involved more maneuvering than fighting. At stake was the control of territory and of the people living in it. But the people themselves were little affected by the clash of those who ruled them. Some wars were bloody and destructive—the Thirty Years' War of the seventeenth century devastated the various German principalities where it was fought—but often, especially in the eighteenth century, they had little effect on the lives of ordinary people. The name of the ruler to whom they owed allegiance, and taxes, might change, but everyday life did not.

Then came the French Revolution, which expanded the scope and the stakes of international conflict. Those who made the revolution and carried it across Europe were not interested simply in exchanging one flag or one monarch for another.

Their aim was to overthrow an entire system of governance. This is the political meaning of the word *revolution,* whose modern usage dates from 1789 and its aftermath. At issue was not just who would rule in the different European jurisdictions but how the continent would be ruled. Napoleon's armies spread ideas and institutions across Europe that proved more durable than the assorted relatives whom the French emperor placed precariously on the thrones from which he had driven his opponents.

The wars of the French Revolution were wars of creeds, conflicts of differing social and political systems. The global rivalry between the United States and the Soviet Union is a direct descendant of those wars. It, too, is an ideological conflict, pitting against each other two distinct systems of political and economic organization, at whose core lies a sharp dispute over the theory and practice of human rights. These rights have gained increased political importance since 1945 and especially over the last twenty years. World War II was a central event in raising the international salience of human rights. It was a war fought in the name of these rights, a war that produced a number of official covenants and agreements that proclaimed their importance, such as the United Nations Charter.

The political prominence of human rights owes a great deal, as well, to postwar changes in the means of communication. Television has made a difference. The victims of human rights violations now have faces as well as names that are broadcast around the world.

The wars of the French Revolution also saw a sudden expansion in the military force that governments could muster. All of French society was mobilized to fight the Revolution's enemies. The new French army was larger and more powerful than the legions of mercenaries that the monarchs who opposed the Revolution and France were able to put into the field and it adopted much more aggressive tactics on the battlefield.

The practice of enlisting all able-bodied citizens in the war effort constituted a revolution in military art. It was followed by another military revolution in the nineteenth century, the harnessing of mechanical power for warfare, which came to full flower with the tanks, airplanes, and machine guns of World War I. Three decades later, at the end of the second world war of the twentieth century, came the third—nuclear—military revolution.

Human rights and nuclear weapons therefore represent the culmination of a two-centuries-long trend. The tendency for the stakes of international conflict to become progressively higher has reached its zenith with the global rivalry. Once very little depended on the outcome of such conflicts beyond the power and glory of the monarchs who happened to be waging them. In the Soviet-American rivalry, the fate of all the inhabitants of each country, and of most of the rest of the world, is involved. The stakes are as high as they could possibly be.

The deep differences over human rights and the existence of nuclear weapons also keep the Soviet-American conflict from following either of the two courses such conflicts have commonly taken in the past. Often they have been resolved by war. War between states that are heavily armed with nuclear weapons like the Soviet Union and the United States, however, would be too destructive to risk. The two rivals are condemned to a military stalemate.

Alternatively, great power conflicts have ended in political reconciliation. But the differences between the two systems, to which their contrasting approaches to human rights are central, are too deep to permit this. For either to abandon the conflict entirely, each would have to accept as legitimate the political and economic principles of the other—which would call into question its own system. If nuclear weapons prevent war, the issue of human rights, with all its implications, inhibits the construction of a peace based on anything more benign than the balance of terror and the prudence that it imposes on each country.

POPULAR PASSIONS

The United States and the Soviet Union will not go to war over the issues of human rights and nuclear weapons. It is geopolitical disputes like those that have been familiar throughout history which are the most explosive ones in today's global rivalry. The closest brushes the two powers have had with war have come over such geopolitical issues—Berlin in 1961 and Cuba in 1962. It is over Europe that the two make their most elaborate and expensive preparations to fight.

There was never any thought in the West of fighting to free Shcharansky or Sakharov. Nor are nuclear weapons themselves, or the state of the nuclear balance, a likely cause of war. Still, the two issues are important parts of the rivalry. They are matters over which the two powers are in direct contact, questions that stir popular feeling, especially in the West, and therefore issues on which the future course of the relationship will partly depend. They are also issues on which compromise is often difficult.

Soviet-American relations in different regions of the world involve third parties. Their rivalry in Europe is influenced to a growing extent by the Europeans themselves. So it is with the rivalry in Asia and other parts of the Third World, where it is increasingly a complicated multilateral affair in which the two great powers exercise considerably less than total control over their allies and clients. Nuclear weapons and human rights, by contrast, are the province of the United States and the Soviet Union and of the two of them alone. Unlike their geopolitical rivalry, these two issues are strictly bilateral affairs.

Each country threatens the other directly with its nuclear armaments. In the twentieth century, technology has eclipsed distance. Nuclear explosives, in combination with jet aircraft and intercontinental ballistic missiles, have made the two great powers neighbors in military terms despite the thousands of miles between European Russia and the east coast of North America. Moreover, although France, Britain, and China also have nuclear weapons, their arsenals are modest in comparison. Thus arms control negotiations have concerned the weapons of these two countries and no others. The negotiations are conducted directly between them.

So it is with human rights. The United States is not the only country with a political system based on liberal principles but it is the one most deeply committed to spreading these principles and the only one that puts them at the center of its relations with the Soviet Union. The West Europeans are not indifferent to political liberties and human rights, but they do not regard such issues as proper subjects for visible, high-level diplomacy.

Nuclear weapons and human rights take up much of the time that Soviet and American officials spend with each other. Since the 1970s high-level meetings between the two have almost always had a tripartite agenda. One part is what are called "regional issues," the term that refers to the various theaters of the geopolitical conflict between them. The other two are nuclear arms control and human rights.

Nuclear weapons and human rights, moreover, stir popular feelings in the West, especially the United States, in a way that geopolitical issues, although they carry a much greater risk of war, do not. Wars in southern Africa, in Southeast Asia, and in Afghanistan, when none of their countrymen are directly involved, are remote, obscure affairs for most Americans and evoke little response from them. Nuclear weapons and human rights, by contrast, have given rise to popular protests on a large scale.

Hundreds of thousands of people have demonstrated all across the United States on behalf of Soviet prisoners of conscience and refuseniks. Writers and artists have written letters and circulated petitions protesting the harsh treatment of their counterparts in the eastern bloc. Scientists have supported their Soviet counterparts in various ways, some even flying to Moscow to conduct unofficial seminars with colleagues dismissed from their scientific posts for political dissent or for seeking to emigrate.

The protests against nuclear weapons differ from the popular response to the denial of human rights in the Soviet Union in that they have a longer history, have taken place in Europe as well as in the United States, and have generally been directed against Western governments rather than the Soviet regime. The British Campaign for Nuclear Disarmament was founded in the late 1940s, at the beginning of the nuclear age. Large demonstrations were mounted in the Federal Republic of Germany in the early 1980s to protest plans for installing American-controlled intermediate-range nuclear missiles there.

In the United States, public expression of discontent on nuclear issues has been episodic. Protests were staged in the 1950s and early 1960s against the testing of nuclear weapons aboveground, which spewed poisonous radioactivity into the earth's atmosphere. In 1969 opponents of the plan to deploy a nationwide antiballistic missile (ABM) system organized a grass-roots campaign that had a considerable influence on the congressional debate about the project. In the early 1980s the rhetoric and the policies of the Reagan administration created public confusion and alarm in the United States, and inspired large demonstrations, some of them bringing out hundreds of thousands of people.

The movement to support the struggle for human rights in the Soviet Union and the various episodes of opposition to nuclear weapons programs in the West have a common basis. Each has expressed urgent, concrete concerns about issues that directly affected either the people taking part or others with whom they could readily identify.

Human rights are not, for Americans, an abstract matter. They involve real people being mistreated, people for whom Americans have enormous sympathy and with whom they have no difficulty in identifying. Americans care deeply about the rights being sought by dissident Russians, moreover, for the same reasons that liberal principles are so important in American public life: the emphasis that the country's history has placed on them and the way that the social experience of most Americans reinforces a commitment to them.

The reason that Americans, Europeans, and presumably citizens of the Soviet Union are concerned enough about nuclear weapons to bestir themselves to march to express their sentiments is even more straightforward. Their own lives are at risk. All of us can imagine everything we know, everything we value, being destroyed. Nuclear weapons conjure up visions of the apocalypse.

Human rights and nuclear weapons are the features of the global rivalry that strike closest to home. They are central to

Soviet-American relations because the people of the West and in particular the people of the United States deem them important. Popular interest has occasionally forced the two issues onto the official agenda of the two countries despite the efforts of political leaders to avoid them. The Nixon administration regarded the issue of human rights as at best a diversion from the principal business of East-West relations, at worst an obstacle to the kind of relationship with the other great nuclear power that it was trying to establish. Public pressure on the American government to make plain to the Soviet regime how strongly Americans felt about political liberty, however, proved irresistible to Nixon and each of his successors.

The United States is often accused of hypocrisy about human rights, since it has consistently supported governments that, although they may be hostile to the Soviet Union, themselves do not permit civil liberties and political participation. Even those who favor such support, however, concede that it is a regrettable if necessary departure from the preferred norm of supporting democracies. Moreover, anticommunist authoritarian regimes have been the objects of both public American protests and official pressure from Washington, particularly in the last decade. Nor have such regimes been able to count on consistent and forceful American support, as the Shah of Iran, Marcos of the Philippines, and Duvalier of Haiti all discovered.

Nuclear weapons policy has also been the subject of public pressure. The Reagan administration entered office determined to avoid arms control negotiations, which it regarded as a diversion from the urgent business of rearming the country at best and a way for the Soviet Union to trick the United States into unfavorable agreements at worst. Public protests against the Reagan nuclear weapons policies both in the United States and Europe forced the administration, after a year in office, to resume arms control negotiations with the Soviet Union.

Human rights and nuclear weapons are sources of tension because they are not only important issues, they are volatile ones. Over the last quarter-century the arms race has proceeded apace and the agitation for human rights in the Soviet Union has grown.

The two issues aggravate Soviet-American relations for another reason. They are difficult to compromise in ways satisfactory to the Western and especially the American public. The two countries have compromised on nuclear weaponry. They have signed several arms control agreements. These, however, have not abolished nuclear weapons and so have not removed the root cause of the anxiety that they generate; nor is there any prospect that the process of arms control will lead to a world entirely free of nuclear armaments.

The Soviet regime has released prisoners of conscience and allowed almost 250,000 Jews (as well as ethnic Germans and Armenians) to leave. It has not, however, conceded the political rights that dissidents have sought for all Soviet citizens, nor the general right to emigrate. Nor can the authorities concede these things, especially the kinds of rights and liberties that people in the West enjoy, without transforming their political system and undercutting their own power.

Nuclear weapons and human rights are not problems that can be solved once and for all. They are conditions of the global rivalry, and are therefore likely to persist.

CONNECTIONS BETWEEN THE TWO

These issues not only have a great deal in common, they are connected. The American effort to draw an explicit relationship between them, to make successful negotiations on security issues, most of which involved limitations on nuclear weapons, dependent on changes in the way the Soviet Union treats its own people, came to be known as the policy of "linkage." The Nixon administration attempted to link Soviet foreign policies in different areas. It tried to make accords on nuclear weapons contingent on Soviet cooperation in other parts of the world, like Indochina. But for the American public, the policy of linkage came to mean that cooperation on security issues and the Soviet approach to human rights were, or ought to be, connected.

The Soviet government rejected the concept of linkage. It insisted that a sovereign state's internal policies were entirely its own affair. Still, linkage of this sort did occur, at least indirectly. Treatment of dissidents and would-be emigrés affected public opinion in the West, particularly in the United States, which in turn influenced the political climate in which the arms negotiations took place. Moreover, the two issues were directly connected in at least three ways.

They were linked by international statute. The Final Act of the Helsinki Conference of 1975, which was signed by the United States, the Soviet Union, and all the countries of Europe, East and West, included provisions both for security and human rights.

The conference had its origins in the long-held Soviet desire to secure international ratification of Europe's postwar boundaries. The leadership calculated that this would lend legitimacy to its sphere of control in Eastern Europe. (The calculation turned out to be incorrect. The Helsinki accords did not prevent the rise of Solidarity in Poland, the greatest threat to the Soviet-imposed system in that country's postwar history. If anything, the Helsinki Final Act may have indirectly encouraged the formation of Solidarity and weakened the Soviets' standing in Eastern Europe by giving international attention to the rights denied the people of those countries.) The Western powers agreed to what the Soviets wanted on condition that the conference deal with other issues, including human rights, as well.

The result was a Final Act, signed on August 1, 1975, that had three parts, or "baskets." The first dealt, in accordance with Soviet wishes, with security. Although it did not mention nuclear weapons specifically, it did commit the signatories to refrain from the use of force and respect the frontiers and the territorial integrity of European states. It was, in effect, a promise not to go to war, which, given the forces arrayed on the continent, would likely be a nuclear war.

The second basket dealt with economic, scientific, technical, and environmental cooperation. The third committed the parties to the freer movement of ideas, greater access to broadcast and printed information, and the reunification of families—that is, emigration. It did not embrace the entire Western human rights agenda, but it did touch on important parts of it.

The Soviets accepted the provisions of the third basket of the Helsinki accord not because they had become convinced that the free flow of information and people across national borders was desirable in itself, but because they were anxious to get the West to agree to the first basket, and were willing to pay a price for this. The Western governments had insisted on the human rights provisions in no small part because of their publics' insistence. Such sentiment was particularly strong in the United States. In the minds of Americans, the internal order and the external behavior of the Soviet Union could not be separated.

The character of the Soviet system and nuclear weapons have been tied together as well through one of the central issues in the arms control negotiations—verification. Because the Soviet Union is a closed society, where movement is restricted and information closely guarded, Americans have always feared that its government would cheat on arms control accords. American violations of such agreements could not be concealed in the open society of the United States. Soviet violations, however, could go undetected, or so Americans feared, giving Moscow a military advantage.

Thus Washington has consistently refused to sign any arms control agreement unless compliance with its terms could be independently verified. Until 1987 the Soviet Union refused to allow foreign inspectors on its soil to monitor compliance with such treaties. The means for independent verification became available in the early 1960s. Cameras mounted on reconnaissance satellites circling the globe far above the earth's surface could take extraordinarily precise pictures of military deployments. Each side could therefore see exactly how many missiles the other had deployed. The cameras were reputed to have become so accurate by the 1980s that they could record the serial numbers of each missile. Whether or not that level of detail was available, the various agreements of the 1970s were verified by satellite photography. Technology solved a problem whose roots lay in the American conviction that a government that routinely denied human rights would not hesitate to cheat on a treaty that it had solemnly signed, and would be able to get away with the cheating because of the unchallenged power of the regime over the society.

Nuclear weapons and human rights are also related in a more abstract way. Together they define the requirements for the end of the Soviet-American conflict. Nuclear weapons are so powerful that they constitute a threat simply by their existence. Any state possessing them is potentially menacing to others. There is simply no chance that these armaments will be abolished entirely. They will continue to exist, the United States and the Soviet Union are certain to have them, and each will therefore continue to pose a threat to the other. This does not mean that war between them is unavoidable. The geopolitical issues over which wars are fought can be and have been compromised.

But the nuclear threat can be reduced to a minimum only insofar as the differences in the two political and economic systems can be narrowed. If the United States and the Soviet Union were as similar as the United States and Canada, their differences would be much easier to manage, although even then the differences would not disappear altogether. The heart of the disparity between the two systems is their sharply contrasting approaches to human rights.

SOVIET POLICIES BEFORE GORBACHEV

Soviet policies on nuclear weapons and human rights have moved perceptibly, if slowly and unevenly, toward Western standards. In Stalin's day the gulf was immense. To say that his regime violated human rights on a large scale is an understatement; indeed, "human rights violations" is a euphemism for Stalin's murderous rampages.

Stalin presided, as well, over the creation of the Soviet nuclear weapons program. His foreign policy at the end of his rule was relatively cautious. But he insisted that, whatever the state of East-West relations at the moment, and however great the destructive powers of nuclear weapons, war between the capitalist and communist worlds continued to be unavoidable in the long run, just as Lenin had said it was.

After Stalin's death his successors modified Soviet policy on both issues. Mass terror ended; hundreds of thousands of political prisoners were allowed to leave the camps and return home. At the same time, the Soviet leadership repudiated the thesis that war was inevitable. The new leaders decided, as one official statement put it, that the atomic bomb did not conform to the class principle.

The Soviet Union was not a model of civil liberties or nuclear restraint after 1953, but it did cease to be the large and, at least rhetorically, aggressive death camp that Stalin had seemed to make it.

In the Brezhnev era, nuclear weapons and human rights became the subject of official discussions with the United States for the first time. It was in the 1970s that the tripartite agenda for high-level meetings between the two governments was established. Brezhnev further modified Soviet policy on these two issues. He signed agreements limiting Soviet offensive and defensive nuclear forces in exchange for similar limits on American forces. And he permitted several hundred thousand people to leave the Soviet Union.

Both policies made the Soviet Union appear more humane, reasonable, and peaceful in the eyes of the West, and in no small measure had been adopted by Moscow for precisely that purpose. This was, however, an instrumental purpose—to create a favorable political climate for Soviet-American relations. The new policies did not represent a fundamental change either in the Soviet definition of the basis of security in the nuclear age or in Moscow's conception of human rights.

The Soviet regime was not willing to restructure its nuclear forces in conformity with the principles of equilibrium to which the United States subscribed. Nor was it prepared to allow every Soviet citizen who wished to do so to leave the country. Nor was it willing to permit independent political activity, especially if it involved opposition to policies like the war in Afghanistan. Those, like Sakharov, who engaged in political dissent, no matter how modest and peaceful, were punished.

Nonetheless, Brezhnev's more accommodating policies did have the effect of raising Western expectations concerning Soviet performance. When Moscow failed to meet these higher standards the response was disappointment, bitterness, and even a sense of betrayal, especially in the United States. The public pressure on the American government to press the Soviets on these issues increased. The Brezhnev policies thus had the effect, clearly unintended from the Soviet point of view, of making human rights and nuclear weapons more rather than less important features of the global rivalry.

5

THE ARMS RACE AND THE HUMAN RACE—THE FUTURE

Given the absence of any democratic tradition in Russian and Soviet history, and the social and cultural emphasis on order rather than liberty, on equality over efficiency and spontaneity, and on monopoly instead of competition, is there any reason at all to hope for the evolution of a more liberal Soviet society, one more hospitable to Western concepts of human rights? In fact, there is. The hope lies in the sweeping changes in Soviet society over the last thirty years, the emergence of new social groups that are discontented with the old authoritarian ways, and the leadership's recognition of the need to accommodate these new groups.

THE NEW MIDDLE CLASS

The society over which the new leadership presides is markedly different from the one that existed at the death of Stalin in 1953 or the ouster of Khrushchev in 1964. It is a younger society. It has made a quantum leap in its overall level of education, and in this respect is now comparable to other industrial nations. It is a society with a professional class that is in absolute numbers the largest in the world. It is also a society where the social structure of class, status, and power has become more settled and durable than before.

The new middle class of the Soviet Union has felt itself increasingly frustrated by the wide gap between its social status and its political and economic power. It has had no political influence. It has been fragmented and politically vulnerable, its members isolated from each other and from the political elite above them and the working people below whom they have treated with ill-concealed disdain.

The lower and middle segments of this new class were especially frustrated by their economic position. They were the victims of the policies of economic leveling and egalitarianism practiced by both Khrushchev and Brezhnev. They received salaries lower than those of highly skilled workers or cotton growers. Moreover, the wages of many were deliberately frozen starting in the early 1970s.

The cream of the new middle class are the professionals. Their frustration has been particularly intense because they are treated by the rulers in the same way as plumbers, carpenters, or tractor drivers. The autonomy that is the essence of professionalism is missing in the Soviet Union.

The basic features of the system are at odds with professionalism: secrecy pursued to the point of absurdity, a preemptive and all-powerful censorship, and the strict compartmentalization of information. Soviet professionals must contend with zealous administrative authorities that regulate contacts with the outside world, including other communist countries, with state control over the agenda of professional discussions, and with the lack of freedom to express one's views and have them published. Professionals must work in poor conditions, which are sometimes improved for a narrow group of outstanding individuals in particular professions.

The professional victims of the Soviet system are numerous: The medical doctor who has no syringes or needles available for necessary injections; the playwright whose work is transformed beyond recognition by censorship and constant "advice and suggestions" from cultural officials; the economist who has less—and less accurate—information about the economy than his Western counterparts; the filmmaker whose movie disappears into the vaults of the Ministry of Culture; the professor of Renaissance history who is never permitted to visit Italy;

the physicist who is cut off from contacts with his Western colleagues working on problems similar to his own; the journalist who is forced to deny in print an outrage that he has witnessed.

The Soviet professional class has reached a socially critical point. Its role in running the system is indispensable. Most of its members aspire to a truly professional status, an aspiration that is in conflict with the role assigned to them by official Russia. Gorbachev and his colleagues are much more attuned to their wishes than the Brezhnev generation and recognize that the enthusiastic participation of the professional class is indispensable to the success of reform. To the extent that doctors, economists, and scientists achieve wider professional independence, the Soviet Union will become a more tolerant, less restrictive society.

ECONOMIC REFORM AND LIBERTY

Gorbachev's economic reforms have as their overriding goal the modernization of the Soviet Union, the narrowing of the gap with the West, and the creation of a consumer society. This requires, in Gorbachev's view, the expansion of the private sector of the economy.

In modern history, liberty is at least partly associated with private economic activity and income. The development of the Stalinist economic system involved the eradication of legal free enterprise and the absence of private income independent of the state. In a measured and cautious way, and against the serious resistance of those within the Party who see it as a betrayal of socialism, Gorbachev has started to reverse this trend. The Soviet economy will remain overwhelmingly a nationalized one. But seventy years after they came to power, the communist authorities have hesitantly concluded that private restaurants and small marketing and service institutions do not present a serious threat to their rule.

The Supreme Soviet has legalized individual and family firm activities in two dozen areas, as well as the creation for the

same purposes of cooperatives that are in essence private part-
nerships. Farms have obtained the right to sell any grain and
other produce beyond what the state plan requires at free-
market prices. Special cooperatives that work for profit have
also been created to market the surplus produce of the farms
and of the farmers' private plots in cities at free-market prices,
even in cities that are located far from the farms.

The profits from those private enterprises, it should be noted,
are taxed, and on a sharply progressive scale. Private prices are
higher than those of state enterprises.

By permitting private economic activities, the government is
pursuing three parallel goals: to legalize parts of the vast underground economy so as to be able to tax it; to bring to the
consumer goods and services that would otherwise be unavailable; and to counteract inflationary pressure by draining surplus
money from those who can afford to pay the higher prices in the
private sector.

It is clear that the main beneficiaries of these enterprises,
aside from their owners, will be the middle and upper-middle
classes of large cities. The volume of this new activity is thus
far small, less than one percent of the national income. But
some Soviet economists predict that if the growth of the private
sphere continues at the present rate, by the late 1990s it may
account for more than ten percent of the national income.

The Soviet privatization of agriculture, agricultural production, and marketing is, to be sure, extremely modest in comparison with the radical steps taken in China under Deng
Xiaoping. This is the result of the differences in the political
situations confronting the two leaders. Deng's reprivatization
of farming came directly after the Chinese Cultural Revolution, which destroyed much of the party bureaucracy in the
countryside. Gorbachev, on the other hand, confronts a strong
rural party apparatus whose power would be seriously threatened by more radical agricultural reprivatization. Be that as it
may, the trend toward the expansion of private enterprise will
increase if Gorbachev has his way; and it is part and parcel of
a liberalized society.

GLASNOST

The most startling developments of the Gorbachev era so far, which bear on the creation of a more hospitable political and social climate for human rights, have come not in the economy but in culture and politics. Unless Gorbachev is forced to reverse them, these measures will profoundly change the nature of the Soviet system. In one of the world's most secretive countries, there is talk of openness. In a society that throughout its history has not known a single day of democratic order, the leadership preaches democratization and grass-roots participation. A state that has put a premium on homogeneity is now trying to shift toward innovation and individuality. Authorities promote the clash of views where a single truth was once proclaimed self-evident. While stressing patriotism, they no longer equate it with the cult of the military. They are retreating from the notion of the "perfect society," from the goal of a secular utopia in the future that was once continually invoked to justify the imperfections of the present. They are starting to take account of the past so as to avoid repeating it.

These policies are summarized by the word *glasnost,* which denotes greater openness and public accountability on the part of the authorities and wider political and cultural self-expression by the people of the Soviet Union. *Glasnost* was initiated, and is promoted, from above. It has gathered momentum from the courageous activities of some members of the intelligentsia who are active within the system. It is increasingly supported by broader circles of the educated classes. It is finding at least some resonance among working people in the large metropolitan centers.

The embrace of *glasnost* reflects a growing affinity between the educated classes, especially the intelligentsia and the professionals, and what was best in the critical and searching spirit of the old democratic intelligentsia. For the first time, a central principle of the Communist Party's rule is being seriously challenged—the principle of *partiinost,* according to which the worth of anything depends on its contribution to the advancement of Communist Party policy.

Today people in the Soviet Union are searching for the meanings of good and evil. They are trying to define, from the point of view of social health, what is abidingly moral and what is not. They are attempting to find the meaning of justice. They declare the search for truth as the highest social value. Questions that are almost religious in their intensity, that would have been asked only at the questioner's peril just a few years ago, are now becoming the focus of attention, indeed the passion, of many in the intelligentsia.

Glasnost covers a number of activities. The speeches of Party leaders at the top and the level directly below do not on the whole avoid difficult questions, such as problems with consumer supplies. They are moving away from what the Russians call *paradnost,* from the word *parade,* which means showing everything in rosy colors that do not reflect reality.

Glasnost is expressed most importantly in the actual elimination of censorship in many newspapers and journals, in the theater, in the cinema. Many issues that were previously taboo —such as drug abuse, hooliganism, corruption, the exemption of some children of the powerful from compulsory military service, and to some extent even the war in Afghanistan—are discussed at Party and non-Party meetings and find their way into print and radio and television. Difficult, sometimes even hostile questions are published in newspapers, and attempts are made to answer them seriously and at length. Private freedom—immunity from persecution for honest, unrestrained discussions among friends and in the family—is beginning to be recognized as a citizen's right.

By far the most visible, effective, and important expression of *glasnost* is the new freedom of the media. Programs about the seamy side of Soviet life, critiques of the bureaucracy reaching the level of deputy ministers of the central government, timely information on natural and man-made catastrophes, and programs for young people that borrow extensively from the West fill the press and the airwaves. Soviet journalists have discovered investigative reporting and are becoming very good at it. The political class is no happier about this than is its American counterpart.

The Soviet Union is very far from being or becoming an open society on the Western model. But the cult of secrecy is in retreat. The country is much more open today than it has ever been since the moment Joseph Stalin took control of it. The most innovative feature of the INF treaty that the U.S. and the USSR signed in Washington in 1987 is the opening of the Soviet Union to American inspection of its missile storage, deployment, and productive facilities.

A highly critical attitude toward the Soviet past is another important component of *glasnost*. The reevaluation of Soviet history has only just begun. There are indications that the revisionism will not limit itself to the period of full-blown Stalinism, between 1930 and 1953, but will include NEP and even the Revolution and Civil War, at one end, and the Brezhnev period at the other. Although this historical revisionism got underway only recently, it has already gone further than it did in Khrushchev's day. Khrushchev criticized Stalin; Gorbachev rejects Stalinism.

Gorbachev's policy of *glasnost* is the most important component of the process of liberalization. It creates the atmosphere necessary for elements of liberty to grow. Official openness, freedom of inquiry, and liberty of the political process are basic human rights in the Western tradition. These are far more accessible in the Soviet Union today than at any time in the last fifty years. The expansion and institutionalization of this policy would provide guarantees against the reversal of liberalization.

DEMOCRATIZATION

Along with economic reform and *glasnost,* the third pillar of Gorbachev's program of reform is what he calls the democratization of the political and social order. This, too, bears directly on human rights in the Soviet Union. Since at least the Tenth Party Congress in 1921, authoritarianism has been the ruling principle within the Party. With the transformation of the institution of soviets (councils) from representative into administrative bodies, a harsh authoritarianism, and then totalitarianism, became the dominant form of rule in the society. It is Gorbachev's aim to alter or modify the authoritarian nature of both the Party and the political system, by fostering the growth of grass-roots democracy. There are to be elections from among multiple candidates in some economic enterprises, in local soviets, and in lower Party organizations. The purpose of grass-roots democratization, in Gorbachev's eyes, is to produce feedback to the upper-level institutions that will in turn respond to criticism from below and rectify their errors.

What may emerge in the Soviet Union is something that might be called "inverted democracy." In capitalist democracies the most visible and important democratic institutions generally exist at what might be called the "macro-social" level. These are parliamentary and local assemblies that are democratically chosen. At the "micro-social" level, especially in entities concerned with economic life, the units are in most cases not democratic. The leaders of corporations and enterprises are not elected as presidents and prime ministers are.

Gorbachev's "democratic" vision seems the reverse of the model of capitalist democracy. He apparently envisages elements of a grass-roots democracy at the lower levels of society —election by the workers of enterprise directors, the election of members of the local soviets, perhaps even the genuine election of local trade union leaders, the accountability of industrial micro-management to the workers and of local officials to their constituencies, and probably also genuine election of leaders in primary Party organizations.

In the society at large, however, Gorbachev's initiatives do not imply democratic patterns of behavior in either state or party institutions, either now or in the foreseeable future. While the government is already practicing greater openness in dealing with its people and is trying to curb abuses of official power, the basic thrust of Gorbachev's program is not in the direction of full-scale democracy on the Western model.

Gorbachev seems to be conscious of the unusual character of the "democracy" he is trying to bring to the Soviet Union. He has spoken of the pioneering, innovative role of his efforts in this area and of his hopes that the Soviet Union will become a unique international model deserving of emulation. It must be acknowledged, however, that on the basis of past experience with efforts to install this sort of "inverted democracy" either in capitalist or in socialist states—such as Yugoslavia—Gorbachev's concept would seem to have little chance of success.

How far does Gorbachev intend to democratize the life of the Soviet Communist Party itself? "Democratic centralism" has been the guiding principle of Soviet rule. The principle itself, even if truly adhered to, has nothing in common with the Western understanding of democratic order. It is often forgotten, however, that the perniciousness of democratic centralism is associated with its breach in practice. In Lenin's time there was at least a measure of democracy within the Communist Party even if not in the society as a whole. Stalin snuffed it out, and imposed undiluted centralism. Genuine "democratic centralism" in Party life would make the system much less rigid, although not fully democratic. This seems to be what Gorbachev is aiming for.

Gorbachev is also trying to establish the rule of law in the relationship between the citizen and the state, and in dealings between state and private institutions. A new criminal code is being prepared, which is apparently less harsh in its prescribed punishments, narrower in the range of punishment considered for particular crimes and therefore less capricious, and much more precise in defining categories of crimes. A new code of criminal procedures is also being prepared, which apparently grants the accused more rights than the procedural code now in effect. It strives to strengthen the position of the public defender and gives him at least some measure of autonomy vis-à-vis the judicial authorities. The issue of the independence of the courts themselves is being hotly debated.

The ferment in legal activity is far from ended. The leadership considers it a major part of the new course. It is meant to introduce predictability into the law and legal proceedings, and greater rights for the citizen in his relationship to the state. Just as important, it is meant to create a strict legal base for future relations among government institutions, among enterprises, and between the consumer and the producer. These reforms will have momentous consequences for the status of human rights in the Soviet Union: for the essence of rights is law.

In Gorbachev's program the traditional and total supremacy of "order" is being diluted. The supreme idea of order, it is now claimed, is not what is necessary for a party and a society to be dynamic. Gorbachev is trying to legitimize the idea of wide-ranging conflicts as necessary for the dynamic progress of the society even if they impinge on the kind of order that prevailed under his predecessors. In his vision of Russia, conflicts and clashes of ideas over a wide range of issues that concern the past, the present, and the future will facilitate modernization.

An important part of the Western conception of political liberty is freedom of association. In pre-Gorbachev Russia, this was not available. The normal form of organization and association, indeed the only kind that was tolerated, was of a "vertical" nature, connecting the populace with the authorities. In the past few years organizations and associations of a "horizontal" nature have begun multiplying. These associations link individuals or groups with one another outside the supervision of the state or Party. From jazz clubs to stamp collectors' circles, organizations of veterans of the war in Afghanistan and motorcycle "gangs," their very existence is itself a political statement, and they cannot but become actively involved in political questions.

THE NATIONAL QUESTION

Crucial for the future of Gorbachev's program of reform and for the prospects for liberalization is the national question. The Soviet Union is a multinational state; Russians constitute only 51 percent of the total population. The rest consists of over one hundred "nationalities," non-Russian ethnic groups of which twenty number more than one million.

Many of the non-Russian nationalities are nations in the full sense of the word. As recognizable groups Georgians and Armenians go back centuries or even millennia, well before the existence of the Russian nation. In recent history, Latvia, Lithuania, and Estonia were independent states. The largest of these nations are organized into separate administrative units called union republics, autonomous republics, and regions. The largest of them, the Ukraine, is almost twice the size of France. A few ethnic groups, most notably Jews, Poles, and Germans, are dispersed among other national administrative units.

Gorbachev has certainly not intended to raise the question of independence of the non-Russian nations. He is no less committed than his predecessors to preserving a unitary multinational state with a central government in Moscow. But he will not be able to avoid the task of democratizing relations among the different nations of the Soviet Union and especially their relations with the dominant Russian nation. The policies of Stalin and his successors discriminated harshly against non-Russians. Moscow Russified their education, falsified their history, subordinated their economic development to the goals of the Russian elite, promoted Russian immigration to their cities, imposed powerful Russian officials to supervise their bureaucracies, and blocked the promotion of non-Russians to the central Party and state institutions in Moscow.

Gorbachev's reforms have inspired hundreds of petitions, requests, and demands for redressing national injustices. The non-Russian intelligentsia, and even members of the communist elite, have addressed them to the central authorities in Moscow. In February 1988, animosities suppressed for many decades between Muslim Azerbaijanis and Christian Armenians, in the Caucasus region in the southern Soviet Union, surfaced violently. They were encouraged by the growing expectations of justice and the climate of greater permissiveness the general secretary had created. This conflict, between two nations of the Soviet Union, is far from over. It is thus far the most dramatic and important, but not the only, unintended and unwelcome consequence of reform. In addition, Tatars have demonstrated to regain the Crimean homeland from which Stalin brutally evicted them in World War II for allegedly collaborating with the German invaders. And in the early summer of 1987 Muslim Kazakhs in Alma-Ata protested the replacement of their Muslim Party boss by a native Russian.

Nationalist ferment is growing. This was in fact predicted by Western analysts and expected by the authorities. Gorbachev evidently hopes that the new spirit of non-Russian nationalism can be controlled and dealt with gradually as a part of the long process of reform. He certainly hopes that nationalism can be managed through nonviolent channels. In the light of the riots in the south, however, he may have to reassess these hopes and expectations. His policies must respond to two simultaneous but contradictory needs. He is trying first of all to reassert Moscow's control over the elites in the non-Russian republics, which was sharply weakened during the last years of Brezhnev's rule. He is attempting to destroy the cliques that were formed in the leaderships of the non-Russian republics. At the same time, in the spirit of reform, he must grant greater political, cultural, and economic autonomy to the people, the intelligentsia, and the elites of these republics. It will be difficult to accomplish both together.

The course of reform is uncertain. The process of change has only started, and the process seems likely to make the Soviet Union a less harsh and repressive country, one where human rights, as they are understood in the West, have greater scope. But there are limits to how far, even in the best of circumstances, the Soviet Union will move in a Western direction, limits established in no small part by the nationalities issue.

THE EVOLUTION OF THE SOVIET SYSTEM

Economically, the Soviet Union is not becoming a capitalist country. Markets and capitalist economic instruments existed before the advent of capitalism and are potentially compatible with diverse economic models. Moreover, although there will be greater use of Western economic technologies and more room for private economic activity, the Soviet economy will remain, on the whole, centrally controlled.

Politically, as noted above, the Soviet Union is not becoming a Western democracy. Nor are there any indications that this is a goal toward which the leadership is moving or wants to move. Perhaps some institutions of a Western democratic system will develop, but in the foreseeable future they will not lead to an evolving democracy in its Western meaning. What is taking shape in the Soviet Union does not transform the key political institutions. The Western democratic model is more likely to thrive in some societies than others. The odds of a Western-style democracy developing in an immense, multinational country, with a strictly authoritarian political history, are extraordinarily long.

Socially, the Soviet Union is not becoming an open society permitting a generally free flow of information. It is not about to turn into a country in which the relations between state and society are largely bridged by authentic participation and where the prerogatives of the state are sharply curtailed. Freedom of religious belief and practice is not being restored, or rather created, in the Soviet Union. The freedom to abstain from participation, to develop legal forms of employment free of state control, to earn private incomes that will provide an additional alternative to the present choice of public service and conformity or dissent and public irrelevance—these are as yet only marginally enhanced by the reforms. Nor is the dominance of the Russians and to some extent other Slavs in almost all fields of endeavor being challenged.

Despite these limitations, the changes Gorbachev has set in motion could have enormous historical significance. *Glasnost* marks the beginning of a process of political and professional emancipation of the Soviet creative intelligentsia. Its significance can be compared to the emancipation of the Russian peasants from serfdom in the 1860s.

Gorbachev's reforms could well lead to the development of elements of civil society, that is, of social groups and political and economic life independent of the Party and the state. Units of trade unions, professional groups, cultural associations, and other similar institutions may gain a significant degree of independence from the political authorities.

Considering the school of Soviet politics from which Gorbachev and his closest associates graduated, and the experience of the Russian and Soviet past, is it really possible to believe in the authenticity of his even limited commitment to libertarian policies and structural changes? It is, for one cardinal reason: libertarian policies and structural changes serve both his shorter-range political interests and his longer-range goals. Gorbachev's overriding aim is the modernization of the Soviet Union, so that it can, to use his own words, "enter the twenty-first century as a great and respected power."

His shorter-range interests and political strategy to make *perestroika* work require that he consolidate his power, surmount the fierce resistance of the administrative bureaucracy, and overcome social inertia and mass apathy. The cluster of policies that are incorporated in *glasnost* are instruments to serve those interests. They are part of Gorbachev's political strategy of combining pressure from above, emanating from the powerful office of the general secretary, with direct application of force from below that the media will create or catalogue. Yet the process of emancipation of the intelligentsia, for example, and the other changes he is proposing, serve not only Gorbachev's needs of the moment but also the long-term interests of reform and liberalization, and of human rights as well.

THE FUTURE OF HUMAN RIGHTS

For the first time since the advent of Stalinism, a major improvement in the Soviet record on human rights is possible. Does this mean that the Soviet-American conflict over human rights will fade? The answer to this question must distinguish between long-term prospects and short-term realities.

Over the long term, the way the Soviets treat their own citizens may well improve significantly, and the concept of inalienable rights may become a norm of political life. A number of factors and trends make this at least possible.

First of all, the nature of change in the Soviet Union is itself changing. The reform started, like other such movements, as a "revolution from above," but, in contrast to past Soviet patterns, its success depends fundamentally on its attracting voluntary mass support. It needs a virtual "revolution from below" that will activate significant social strata in the service of modernization. This cannot be achieved simply by economic bribery, and even less by naked coercion. It will require greater individual and group autonomy, greater respect for individual rights, and ultimately greater freedom for the society overall.

Moreover, almost unobserved, the new Soviet leadership is starting to accept the legitimacy in principle of the human rights issue, rather than seeing it merely as a matter for tactical concessions in the service of its foreign policy. Some leaders have begun to accept the validity of the Helsinki process and the concept of universal standards governing the way governments treat their citizens.

Psychological factors are important. Gorbachev may lose his temper, and complain bitterly about the Western press's incessant questioning about human rights in the Soviet Union. But his anger is at least partly motivated by a conscious or unconscious acceptance that a country's record on human rights is a valid standard by which to judge it. For Gorbachev and other members of the elite, the Soviet human rights record may become, whether they admit it or not, an important element in their political self-esteem.

Moreover, Gorbachev intends for the Soviet Union to become increasingly a part of the international community, which for him means the economically advanced capitalist democracies. The Soviets have started to recognize that many significant problems require broad international cooperation. Gorbachev's program also envisages a Soviet retreat from economic, scientific, and technological autarky. In addition, for the success of the reform program the Soviet Union requires stable relations with capitalist countries. All this cannot help but make the leadership more conscious of the costs of human rights violations at home.

Nonetheless, everything that permits a measure of cautious optimism about human rights in the Soviet Union is of long-term relevance. In the immediate future the Soviet-American conflict over the Soviet human rights record is not likely to disappear, perhaps not even to wane. In some respects it may even expand and intensify.

The American preoccupation with human rights in the Soviet Union is likely to continue. Even if progress on arms control and regional issues moves the American government to adopt a lower public profile on human rights issues, private feeling about human rights is so strong that interest in and reactions to Soviet behavior will remain intense.

Gorbachev's years in office have produced some positive steps. A large number of political prisoners have been freed from labor camps and prisons. The status of others, it is said, is being reviewed on a case-by-case basis. Some of the most famous exiles and prisoners of conscience have been freed, for example Sakharov, or permitted to leave the Soviet Union, like Shcharansky. The emigration of Jewish refuseniks and of divided families has picked up. A law is being enacted that will make it much more difficult to send individuals to psychiatric wards and will make it a crime to commit a sane person to an insane asylum.

The improvement in Soviet official attitudes toward human rights, however, will probably go hand in hand with a radical expansion of the human rights struggle within the Soviet Union and with a much greater and more detailed flow of information to the West about Soviet violations. The more information that becomes available, the more concerned Americans will be.

The program of radical reforms in all fields of endeavor is an unpredictable process in which major forces collide. It will not be entirely directed and planned. Even its intended, let alone unintended consequences, involve clashes of ideas, interests, emotions, and power. While in the 1960s and 1970s human rights issues, aside from the questions of Jewish emigration, involved thousands of individuals who were isolated and relatively easy to suppress, in the late 1980s and 1990s they will surely touch tens of thousands, perhaps even millions, of Soviet citizens. The range of issues over which the battles for human rights are fought will expand, as will the breadth of the demands being made. The struggle will also acquire a stronger organizational base, with the development of thousands of voluntary associations and clubs that are already springing up everywhere and quickly becoming politicized.

American expectations of what Gorbachev's government will do on human rights issues will be much higher than before, partly because his government has promised to do so much more than its predecessors and partly because the American public has to some degree misread Gorbachev's intentions and harbors illusions about what he wants to do and can do. In addition, the Soviets may be more sensitive to foreign public opinion, and thus by better performance and responsiveness to effective pressures may raise expectations still higher.

The question of Jewish emigration must be considered separately. There is a case to be made that under the new regime this issue will pose less difficulty than in the past, for at least two reasons: Gorbachev may be more willing to permit emigration, and Soviet Jews may be less eager to leave if their lives as citizens improve in a liberalized environment. It is also possible, however, that this issue will follow a different path. In the 1970s, Jewish emigration was for Russia's rulers primarily an international issue, bound up with their policy of détente with the United States. Its domestic consequences were negligible in the harsh authoritarian environment of Brezhnev's Russia, with no other groups making comparable, or at least comparably insistent, demands. Under the new conditions, with the general relaxation of controls, Jewish emigration becomes more of a domestic problem, with its internal consequences much more difficult to control. In advocating a liberal approach to Jewish emigration, Gorbachev works under a double handicap: permissiveness in the case of Jews will encourage demands for emigration from other nationalities with a large demographic base abroad such as Armenians, Ukrainians, Germans, Estonians, Latvians, and Lithuanians; and any special rights for Jews will be used as a weapon against Gorbachev by the vocal Russian chauvinist opposition to his programs.

Though it is possible that domestic liberalization will make emigration less attractive to Soviet Jews, their alienation from the system is deep. A more or less definite answer to the question of how many Soviet Jews want to emigrate would require the recognition of the right to emigrate without punitive consequences such as losing one's job or endangering the education of one's children. That would be very difficult for Gorbachev to accept, because it is precisely these consequences that serve to discourage emigration.

NUCLEAR WEAPONS AND NEW THINKING

The issue of human rights has profound implications for Soviet society as a whole and for Russian and Party control. Nuclear weapons, by contrast, affect foreign policy, and are the province of a handful of people. The general secretary has more leeway to change policy. Gorbachev and the new leadership have begun to rethink the role of nuclear weapons in their foreign policy. They appear to have come to three main conclusions.

• First, the Soviet Union cannot achieve strategic superiority over the U.S. Superiority may be defined in either of two ways: the ability to strike first and limit retaliation to acceptable losses; or strategic preponderance of such proportions that it will undermine the credibility of American deterrence in Europe and render indecisive any American response in an international crisis involving the Soviet Union;

• Second, the continuation of the arms race with the U.S., and especially its expansion into space, where Western technological advantages over the Soviet Union are immense, presents the danger of a possible American "breakout" that could endanger strategic parity between the two superpowers;

• Third, a continuing arms race will require greater expenditures than in the past. Such a competition will require more and more scarce high-quality human and material resources. It could sidetrack Gorbachev's economic reforms. These reforms therefore require taking priority away from the military-industrial sector and accumulating reserves for the difficult transition period from the old to the new managerial system.

Gorbachev has adopted the idea of "nuclear sufficiency," which proclaims that nuclear buildup beyond mutual assured destruction is meaningless and that a lower level of weaponry than the current one will lessen psychological tensions, diminish the danger of accidental war, and increase the security of both superpowers and the world.

He has also embraced the concept of common security (or mutual security), which expresses in Soviet thinking a major departure from the practice of traditional Soviet defense policies. The idea is both simple and, in the Soviet context, revolutionary. It proclaims that if the United States feels militarily insecure this does not serve Soviet interests; indeed, American insecurity can endanger Soviet security. Therefore, one side has to consider probable effects of its military power on the defense policy of the other. This concept, like sufficiency, also implies an end to the nuclear arms race—if it is implemented.

Gorbachev has redefined national security to include factors that are not strictly military. The most obvious is economic power. In addition, domestic morale and order, the vitality of the society, and the state of alliances all find a place in the general secretary's understanding of national security. Gorbachev has postulated nothing less than the proposition, which flies in the face of Soviet tradition, that a Russia that participates in a strict arms control regime, that reduces its nuclear forces significantly, that devotes more attention to its civilian economy, that is flexible and ready for compromises in its foreign policy, will be more secure than it is now, or than it would be by deploying thousands of new weapons. This reconceptualization of national security is crucial for the success of his domestic program. He has to convince the political elite and persuade or force the military elite to accept his view. Without it, the reordering of national priorities implicit in his thinking about security, and necessary for his program of reform, will be impossible.

Also key to Gorbachev's new thinking about nuclear weapons is his attitude toward nuclear deterrence. Officially, the Soviet political-military establishment has never accepted the American concept of nuclear deterrence. They have castigated it as American blackmail directed against the Soviet Union. This was connected with the Soviet refusal to accept its rationale on the American side, namely that there exists a danger of Soviet nuclear attack against the United States or Western Europe. Yet, obviously, the concept of deterrence has been the fundamental principle on which both American and Soviet strategic policies have been based.

On the surface, Gorbachev's critique of nuclear deterrence is grounded in Soviet tradition. In fact, however, his attack on the idea is quite different from the line taken in the past. Gorbachev understands the psychological nature of the concept of deterrence, and he objects strenuously to two of its consequences. First, the internal logic of deterrence leads to an unending arms race between the two superpowers, since neither side can ever be certain that its own strategic weapons forces are perceived by the other side as sufficient to deter a nuclear attack. Second, that same internal logic also requires the integration of nuclear forces into the structure of the armed services and contingency planning for a nuclear war. Without the mutual belief that, in case of an attack by one power, the other will use its nuclear forces, deterrence will not deter.

Gorbachev argues for a retreat from the concept of deterrence to a plan for the total elimination of strategic nuclear forces. He sees arms control as the process through which the ultimate elimination of nuclear weapons will be achieved. This final goal is utopian, even if his intent in announcing it was more than propagandistic. It is said in Moscow that only two people in Russia and America believe in the elimination of nuclear arms—Mikhail Gorbachev and Ronald Reagan. Nonetheless, arms control is clearly now a matter for serious negotiations. It fits the general conclusions about security matters reached by the new leadership. It is increasingly influential in Soviet foreign policy thinking.

No matter how sweeping his reforms, Mikhail Gorbachev

will not abolish the Soviet nuclear arsenal. The nuclear threat —to both sides—will remain. But, as with human rights, his approach to nuclear weapons offers the prospect, though not the certainty, of an easing of a principal source of tension in the global rivalry.

6

THE ARENAS OF CONFLICT: THE THIRD WORLD AND THE STRATEGIC QUADRANGLE

The Soviet-American rivalry began in Europe with the forcible imposition of communist regimes in the countries the Red Army had occupied in its drive westward. This raised the fear of Communist conquest or subversion of Western Europe. But the American Marshall Plan stabilized and reinvigorated the Western European economies. The decision to rearm West Germany and the creation of the Atlantic Alliance and NATO in 1949 constituted an effective bulwark against further Soviet pressures on Western Europe. So Stalin turned eastward.

By 1949 a momentous historical and strategic change had taken place in China. The communists, led by Mao Zedong, established their control over mainland China and created the People's Republic. China and the Soviet Union entered into an alliance that combined the resources of the largest country in the world with that of the most populous country in the world. The pendulum of history seemed to be moving decisively toward communism.

Stalin decided to continue the postwar expansion of communism in Asia by arming and training the North Korean communist forces and permitting them to invade South Korea in June 1950. Initial communist success was reversed by the growing commitment of American forces under the UN flag. They routed the North Korean armies and pushed northward toward the Yalu river, the border between Korea and China.

The Chinese communists, who apparently were not a part of the Soviet decision to unleash the North Korean forces, intervened against the Americans because of their fear that the counteroffensive against North Korea would develop into an all-out war to topple them. In the middle of 1951 the Korean War settled into a stalemate. With the deadlock in Korea, and the defeat by Britain of communist guerrilla forces on the Malay peninsula, Stalin's probe of the Asian continent was stymied.

The initial Soviet political and military sorties beyond Europe, to East Asia and what would come to be known as the Third World, were therefore modest and halting. Moreover, Stalin's drive to the east, such as it was, had about it a provincial, regional flavor. Far from being global, it was limited to areas adjacent to the Soviet Union. After its initial successes and strategic probes of further opportunities for expansion, it acquired a defensive quality. The key maxim of the prewar Stalin, "Socialism in one country," was succeeded by "Socialism in one empire." Stalin's ingrained caution and aversion to risk-taking, his awareness of Soviet economic weaknesses after a devastating war, and his healthy respect for American power left the Soviet Union at the time of his death isolated and on the defensive.

During the Khrushchev era, the dream of international revolution reawakened. The disintegration of the colonial empires and the nationalist strivings of the former colonies kindled the hope that these countries would select a revolutionary road to development, which might make them Soviet allies or even dependents. Khrushchev's hope for the creation of a revolutionary postcolonial world was reinforced by the Marxist-Leninist ideas and vocabulary embraced initially by many leaders of newly independent countries—Nkrumah in Ghana, for example, and Sékou Touré in Guinea.

In the Khrushchev period the leadership invented the concept of the "noncapitalist road of development," which was to account for the peculiarities of the newly independent states. From the Soviet point of view, this road was not yet socialist. The expectation was that its trend of development would be toward socialism, with an inevitable alliance with the Soviet Union.

After Khrushchev's ouster in 1964 these attitudes remained, but were tinged with growing disenchantment. Brezhnev's views on revolutionary and pro-Soviet development in the Third World, and particularly Africa, were much more sober. Perhaps he and his colleagues remembered the verdict on the Third World revolutionary movements in the 1920s of one of the most prominent agents of the Communist International, Mikhail Borodin: "They come to us," he said, "and cry 'Revolution, Revolution.' What they really want is arms." For the sake of whatever influence they could bring, however, Brezhnev's Soviet Union was willing to provide arms to Third World countries, especially those that could pay with hard currencies.

THE GORBACHEV REASSESSMENT AND THE FUTURE

In the last years of Brezhnev's rule, particularly after the invasion of Afghanistan, the community of experts and advisors on the Third World started to reevaluate the Soviet experience and began to reach negative conclusions.

The Soviet leadership and foreign policy establishment are developing a different assessment of the Third World, and the appropriate policies toward it. This revisionist point of view consists of several conclusions:

• The dominant problems of most Third World countries stem not from domestic class warfare or external political domination but from internal factors.

• The socialist revolutionary potential of most of these countries is very limited. Genuine revolutions are unlikely.

• The attractiveness of Marxist-Leninist ideology to the leadership and elites of these countries is declining. Even when they use communist terminology, more often than not this serves simply to camouflage a corrupt and cynical political dictatorship.

• The Soviet strategy of transforming a backward economy through forced industrialization is inapplicable to most of these countries. Moreover, the present economic predicament makes the Soviet economic model unattractive elsewhere. It is "Confucian capitalism," as represented by the newly industrialized countries of Asia, that is likely to appeal to these countries.

• Soviet economic aid and military assistance through arms and advisors, even if extended on a large scale, will not assure steadfast and reliable support for pro-Soviet policies, let alone Soviet control of other countries' domestic and foreign policies, as the Soviet experience in Egypt, for example, vividly demonstrates.

• The direct projection of Soviet military forces, or those of Soviet proxies, while sometimes profitable in political terms, is economically expensive, and subject to major unexpected difficulties. This is the sobering lesson of Afghanistan.

• To be a global power requires diversified foreign policy resources—economic, political, and cultural, as well as military. Soviet resources are primarily military.

• Supporting a Third World country engaged in a regional conflict or engulfed in a civil war can lead to a backlash, that is to resistance. Especially if the resisting forces receive help from the United States, this increases the economic and political costs to the Soviet Union of such support and renders its outcome questionable. The Soviet Union no longer has a monopoly on the so-called national liberation movements, and the Reagan Doctrine, as practiced in Asia, Africa, and Latin America, has affected Moscow's calculations.

• Soviet expansion in the Third World, and particularly direct military involvement, can endanger more central and important relations with the United States, with China, and with Western Europe and Japan. The 1970s and

1980s established beyond doubt the linkage of Soviet world-wide expansionist policies with arms control negotiations and political and economic relations with other great powers. Soviet policies in southern Africa weakened, and the invasion of Afghanistan effectively killed, the détente of the 1970s.

• Direct Soviet involvement in regional conflict and civil wars can even carry with it the danger of direct confrontation with the U.S. or China. Lebanon could have been the site of a dangerous Soviet-American confrontation in the early 1980s, for example, with Soviet antiaircraft troops stationed in Syria and American naval task forces near the Lebanese shores and a contingent of Marines inside Beirut.

• Some conflicts outside Europe, for example the one in the Middle East, have ceased to be zero-sum games in which one side's losses are necessarily gains for the other. The rivals may share an interest in stability.

The reassessment of the Soviet approach to the Third World has occurred on the analytical level. It is a long step from a fresh analysis to different policies. Moreover, while concentrating on domestic reconstruction, the leadership does not want to abdicate the role of a global power. The Gorbachev generation that now holds the reins of power in Russia is extremely ambitious and nationalistic. But there are already signs that the reassessment is affecting policy in some international trouble spots, although not in others.

The Soviet invasion of Afghanistan was by far the most blatant and, for Moscow, the most expensive case of Soviet expansion. It was the first time since the Second World War that Soviet troops invaded a country that was not a part of the Soviet empire. It was also the first place where large-scale deliveries of American arms were used to combat Soviet forces. But the Soviet adventure failed, and in 1988 the leaders decided to withdraw.

Central America is a small, backward region, economically and militarily of little consequence. It looms large in American eyes, however, because of its proximity to North America and because since the nineteenth century the only outside power with influence there has been the United States, in accordance with the Monroe Doctrine. The American concern with the dangers of communism in Central America is buttressed by the fear that what happens there may influence developments in Mexico, where social and economic instability threaten.

The key country in the present turmoil in Central America is Nicaragua, ruled by leftist revolutionaries, the Sandinistas. Soviet (and Cuban) support for the Sandinistas is both crucial and marginal. It is crucial because without it, in the face of American economic pressures, political isolation, and military action by the well-armed and -trained anticommunist Contras, the Sandinista regime might well collapse. It is marginal because the Soviet commitment to the Sandinistas and their cause (although not Cuba's) is of low priority. Even an American invasion of Nicaragua would evoke only a hostile propaganda response from Moscow. Moreover, the material support for the Sandinistas is highly calibrated. It is sufficient to prevent their military defeat by the Contras, but limited enough to avoid a confrontation with the United States. Soviet economic aid is minimal. The Soviet Union does not provide enough oil to a country with a population of a large Soviet city to ensure the uninterrupted flow of electricity, nor has it given enough food to prevent hunger. In the military area, the supply of heavy weapons such as tanks and heavy helicopter gunships is limited. Moscow is unlikely to envisage the transformation of Nicaragua into a Soviet military base; it has not accomplished such a goal in Cuba, where the communist regime was established thirty years ago. Moreover, in 1988, the Soviets were apparently advising the Sandinistas to accept a compromise settlement, and such a settlement was concluded in March.

In Angola, Soviet involvement dates back to 1976. The Soviet role was unprecedented, involving as it did the introduction into the civil war of a 20,000-man contingent of Cuban expeditionary forces and, later, limited Soviet air power. The Soviets saw Angola as a crucial member of the so-called front-line black African states that border South Africa. Soviet involvement in Angola escalated the civil war there. With time it brought substantial American support for the forces opposing the pro-Soviet government in Luanda.

Angola is one country in which reassessment, if it has taken place, has not led to new policies. There is no serious sign that Gorbachev is ready to terminate arms deliveries, withdraw advisors and pilots, and send home the Cuban troops. The price of Angola is not high because, ironically, the costs are paid by the Angolan government from oil revenues accruing from Western companies. Moreover, because of increased South African military pressure and internal turmoil in front-line black states like Mozambique, and because of the Soviet decision to cut expenditures to support the governments of these states, the importance of Angola for the Soviets has, if anything, increased. The negative political consequences of the involvement are tempered because the Soviet Union (and Cuba) is opposing South Africa. The continuous commitment to the Angolan regime provides Moscow with a base in any future struggle against the South African government. The chances that Gorbachev will eliminate the Soviet enterprise in Angola in the foreseeable future are therefore not high.

The Soviet presence in Ethiopia bears some similarity to the Angolan venture because it includes an expeditionary Cuban military force, which took part in the victorious war against Somalia in the 1970s and helps keep in check secessionist activities in the province of Eritrea. But otherwise the situation is quite different. On the one hand, the costs of Soviet and Cuban participation in this disastrously poor country have to be borne exclusively by Moscow. On the other, the Eritrean rebels do not receive much Western help and their aim is independence for one province rather than control of the entire country as in Angola.

The Ethiopian regime, moreover, is the only authentic Marxist-Leninist outpost in Africa. It is therefore quite likely to be a loyal ally of the Soviet Union even if the Cuban troops are withdrawn. It is also possible that the Ethiopian regime's strength could in the near future be sufficient to deal with its domestic political and military problems without the presence of substantial Cuban forces. The Soviet alliance with Ethiopia is unlikely to expire anytime soon. But while Ethiopia is a strategic asset for the Soviet Union, it is not likely to become a matter of contention and discord with the United States.

The Indochinese conflict, instead of subsiding with the end of the Vietnamese civil war and American withdrawal, has heated up. The Vietnamese goal of gaining predominance in Indochina is opposed by the Chinese, who consider Indochina their own sphere of influence and are concerned about Vietnam's role as a Soviet military ally. Soviet support for Vietnam in its occupation of Kampuchea is an obstacle to the improvement of Soviet relations with China. Even so, despite Vietnam's heavy dependence on the Soviet Union—there is no other country to which it can turn—Moscow's influence on Vietnam's policy toward Kampuchea seems to be strictly limited. The Vietnamese communists, like the Chinese, the Yugoslavs, and the Cubans, won by themselves the wars by which they came to power. They will not become a Soviet satellite. Still, the United States is virtually uninvolved in Indochina. Once central, the area is now marginal to the global rivalry.

The most complicated regional contest is in the Middle East. At the outset of the 1970s the Soviets had an alliance with Egypt and a stable relationship with Iran, despite the American alliance with the Shah. Moscow was the main supplier of Iraq's weapons, had better relations with this country than any other power, and was the main non-Arab international champion of the Palestine Liberation Organization (PLO).

In the 1970s and early 1980s, the Soviet position in the Middle East deteriorated. Moscow's only good relations were with Syria. Libya was an embarrassment, albeit a hard-currency customer. The importance of the PLO declined. There was turmoil on the U.S.S.R.'s southern borders, and the U.S. increased its military presence in the Indian Ocean and in the Persian Gulf.

When the Soviet position was strong in the Middle East, its preference was for neither war nor peace between Arabs and Israelis. This state of affairs secured it a strong political base in the region and assured Arab dependence on Moscow. With the deterioration of the Soviet posture, however, and particu-

larly with the emergence of Islamic fundamentalism, this position ceased to serve Soviet interests. The Soviet leaders are
wary of an unintended confrontation with the United States.
They are unhappy with the military efforts of the Arab states
against Israel and particularly embarrassed by the poor performance of the weapons they have supplied the Arabs. Moreover, after the Camp David agreements and the peace treaty
between Israel and Egypt, a large Arab-Israeli war seems unlikely. The Syrian monopoly of close relations with the Soviet
Union gives Damascus the upper hand in dealing with Moscow.
The instability of their own southern borders, particularly
after the withdrawal from Afghanistan, cannot but worry the
Russians. In the event that Iran overcomes Iraq, the Arab
states would likely request a larger American military presence in the area, which the Soviets would prefer to avoid.

Moscow obviously wants to increase its power and influence
in the Middle East. But it seems to have decided that the best
prospects for doing so lie in transforming the present triangle,
consisting of the Arab states, the United States, and Israel, into
a quadrangle in which the Soviet Union participates. This
would require the resumption of diplomatic relations with Israel. Both Israel and the United States may become more interested in an active Soviet role. Secretary of State Shultz's
initiative of March 1988 called for an international conference
in which the Soviet Union would take part, and was welcomed
by the Labor members of the Israeli cabinet, although not by
the Likud coalition. In general, therefore, there is some convergence in Soviet and American interests in the Middle East.

THE FUTURE OF THE RIVALRY IN THE THIRD WORLD

The Soviet Union will remain a global power for the rest of this
century and beyond but, if the Gorbachev reforms proceed, one
with a lower military profile. The leadership will be less receptive to opportunities for political gains in the Third World. The
political elite will turn inward to concentrate on domestic reform. This is a task, if taken seriously, for an entire generation.
It is likely that the United States will also be less involved

in political and military conflicts in the Third World, with the exception of the Middle East. This will be in part a response to the lower Soviet profile. But it will also be the result of a reassessment of the proper American international role. The costs of international commitments have risen and the growth of American resources has not kept pace.

Outside Europe it is likely that the two superpowers will face dangers that do not pit them against each other, and that sometimes draw them closer together. The acquisition of nuclear weapons by Third World countries is in the interest of neither, indeed is dangerous for both. International terrorism is at present directed against the West, but the Soviet Union and its allies may not remain immune to it.

The force of Islamic fundamentalism may grow, threatening the interests of both rivals. Its spread to Egypt, for example, would deal a devastating blow to the American position in the Middle East. An Afghanistan from which Soviet troops are gone could become another Iran, dominated by militant fundamentalists. Soviet Central Asia may be susceptible to fundamentalist sentiments on a large scale—a nightmare for its Russian rulers but not necessarily an advantage for the West.

This future of Soviet-American rivalry in the Third World is one of partial disengagement, but it is not the only possible future. It is sometimes argued that Soviet expansionism in the Third World is inherent in the system itself and particularly in its Marxist-Leninist doctrine. This doctrine, the argument goes, is necessary for the survival of the regime because it provides domestic legitimacy. The impulse for expansion is further reinforced by Russian nationalism, which is even stronger in the ranks of the Gorbachev generation than among its predecessors.

The argument has some merit. Marxism-Leninism does imply expansion, and it—and Russian nationalism—are powerful forces in Soviet political culture. But expansion is not inevitable. Ideologies can change, and such change is even now taking place in the Soviet Union. Gorbachev is promising to build a better society, one more efficient and better able to satisfy the needs of its citizens. The legitimacy of his own leadership and of the Party rests on their ability to fulfill this promise, rather than, as with their predecessors, on promises to build a utopia in the future. This is an ideological change.

Moreover, it is important not to confuse the use of doctrine to justify policies with its operational role in determining such policies. For the Soviet Union, Marxism-Leninism continues to perform the first task but not always the second.

Furthermore, the present expansion in the Third World is hardly popular with the Soviet population, the almost 20-million-member Communist Party, or even the Party elite. The population, including the Party, sees little glory in overseas adventures. Every observer of the Soviet Union encounters, in his conversations with Russians, complaints about the use of the country's resources to help some "uncivilized" people or other gain or hold power, when the money spent could be better used at home. (The popular attitude toward Soviet control of Eastern Europe is quite different. This, it is widely thought, belongs to them, having been paid for with the fearful human price of the victory over Nazi Germany.)

Most important, the domestic crisis dampens the Soviet appetite for foreign adventure. In addressing it, Gorbachev is already starting to encounter unintended consequences, such as nationalist unrest in the Soviet south and the demands of the non-Russian republics for greater autonomy. He will have to concentrate his attention, and that of the Party, on these challenges. It was after all Gorbachev himself who said upon attaining power that if the Soviet Union did not reconstruct itself "we will even lose what we have already attained."

It is quite possible that for many leaders the policy of limiting their expansion and presenting a lower profile in the Third World is intended to be only temporary, to be replaced at some future point by a new offensive push. Even if this is so, the present policy could last for a long time, and strategies that endure for prolonged periods tend to become firmly established. Nothing endures, as the saying goes, like the provisional.

What the United States does will affect Soviet policies in the Third World. Responding favorably to more accommodating Soviet policies will fortify these policies. Resisting further aggression and expansion will discourage them. The United States needs to preserve and even increase its resolve to raise the price of Soviet expansion by all means available, including military aid for indigenous groups that oppose Soviet causes. Pressure against Soviet Third World expansion and American willingness to reach accommodation with Moscow are not contradictory but complementary policies to encourage Soviet moderation.

THE STRATEGIC QUADRANGLE IN ASIA

Outside Europe, it is not the Third World that increasingly plays a decisive role in the Soviet-American rivalry but rather the relations between the Soviet Union and the United States with China and Japan. The relations among these four powers may be called "the strategic quadrangle."

The Soviet Union occupies a subordinate and defensive position in the quadrangle. While its relations with the other three countries are improving, and may improve even further, its power position will in all probability weaken. The quadrangle revives old Soviet fears of encirclement and inspires new fears connected with the prospects for China.

After the Sino-Soviet split in the early 1960s, relations between the two countries deteriorated sharply. There were violent border skirmishes in 1969. China demanded Soviet recognition that tsarist Russia had illegally annexed large territories. Anti-Soviet demonstrations took place during Mao's Cultural Revolution. Competition broke out within the international communist movement and in the Third World. The Soviet Union and China each came to regard war between them as a possibility.

The Soviet Union built up substantial nonnuclear forces on the Sino-Soviet border. In the 1970s these forces were modernized almost to the standard of the units facing NATO in Europe. The Soviet armies in Asia constituted about one-third of the country's strength. At the same time, the Soviets quadrupled the number of their missiles targeted at Asia, primarily at China. At some point in the late 1960s the Soviet leadership seems to have contemplated a preemptive strike against Chinese nuclear facilities.

In the wake of Mao's destructive Cultural Revolution and international isolation, China resumed relations with the United States in the early 1970s. The specter of a fanatically anti-Soviet China supported by powerful America generated fears in Moscow not only about the security of Soviet eastern borders but also about its overall strategic position. The fear of a de facto Sino-American alliance was one of the reasons that the Soviet Union moved to a policy of détente with the United States in the 1970s.

After the death of Mao in 1976 and the purging of the radical "Gang of Four," Sino-Soviet relations started to improve. The improvement has continued. The short-term danger to the Soviet Union from China is slight. Yet the potential long-term strategic threat has increased. The fanaticism of the Cultural Revolution has been replaced by a pragmatic program of modernization that, still in its initial stages, shows promise of achieving extraordinary success. Certainly China is, in comparison to Russia, still a backward country for which the task of industrial development will be monumental and protracted. But its chances for successful modernization are probably better than those of the Soviet Union. China's development strategy seems more realistic than Russia's. The experience of the newly industrialized Asian nations will be easier for China to tap. China's ethnic homogeneity is an advantage that the Soviet Union does not share. Even a limited Chinese success, given the sheer size of its economy and population, could create in one or two decades a high-technology power with a major impact on the world economy.

China's international political achievements have also been impressive. Beijing has managed friendly and improving relationships with the United States despite occasional dissatisfaction with American policy toward Taiwan. The leadership succession in Taiwan did not lead to the reemergence of a "two Chinas" policy either in Taiwan itself or in the United States. China has also developed good relations with Japan, especially in economics and education. Though the Chinese are far from enamored of the Japanese and complain bitterly about some of their trading practices, the links between these two key Asian countries are based on the solid foundation of common short- and long-term interests. China needs Japanese help in technology and managerial know-how. Japan needs China as a military counterweight to the Soviet Union and hopes for a growing Chinese market. While the Soviet Union has no single major country as a reliable friend, China has no single major country as an enemy—with the possible exception of India, with which it has unresolved border disputes. China's global aspirations are presently modest.

The long-term strategic implications for the Soviet Union of China's present course are alarming. Military improvement is last on the list of China's "Four Modernizations," after economy, science, and education, and in fact China has demobilized over one million troops. Yet Chinese military modernization is proceeding. The country has developed close military relations with the United States. The exchange of intelligence information, regular meetings of high-level military officials, the sale of weapons, and other forms of military assistance have become routine. China and the U.S. are not allies but they do coordinate closely in many areas. Chinese capabilities are growing.

Sino-Soviet relations have improved under Gorbachev, who, in a speech delivered in Vladivostok in the summer of 1986, made peaceful overtures to China. China's fear of the Russians has declined. But there is not the slightest hint that the Soviets and China are moving toward a resumption of their alliance of the 1950s. What is happening can be best described as the normalization of relations; they are establishing the sort of ties characteristic of nonhostile powers. Moreover, China has stipulated conditions for further improvement: unconditional withdrawal from Afghanistan (where a Chinese ally, Pakistan, has important interests), a significant cut in the Soviet forces deployed on the Chinese border, and the withdrawal of Vietnamese forces from Kampuchea. The first Chinese condition is, according to the Soviets, to be fulfilled. As for the second, Moscow may make gestures of more than symbolic importance but is unlikely to decrease the size of its troop deployment to the

1955 level as the Chinese demand. On the other hand, Soviet leverage on the Vietnamese is limited, and the withdrawal of their troops from Kampuchea is unlikely in the foreseeable future. The conflict between China and Vietnam over Indochina (and Soviet bases in Vietnam) is a constant irritant to Sino-Soviet relations.

In the Brezhnev era, the Soviet Union's relations with Japan were bad. Soviet policies toward Japan, combining virulent propaganda and pressure with no attempts at a rapprochement, were used by Western analysts as an example of an unimaginative and counterproductive foreign policy. The natural complementarity of the Soviet and Japanese economies—one poor in technology and rich in raw materials, the other rich in technology and poor in raw materials—suggests that Moscow should have a considerable interest in a rapprochement with Tokyo at a time of internal reconstruction.

After Gorbachev assumed power, Soviet anti-Japanese propaganda declined in volume and virulence but did not disappear. Gorbachev has made overtures to Tokyo, and hinted at a Soviet-Japanese summit meeting, but nothing concrete has come of this. Japan has a low priority in Soviet foreign policy. This is partly shortsightedness toward a country that the Soviet leaders both fear and dislike, but it is also based on a realistic assessment of the possibilities in the near future.

To improve the situation with Japan substantially, the Soviet Union would have to return to Japanese sovereignty what Japan calls its "northern territories," four small islands annexed after the Second World War. This is a domestic issue in Japan, one that is highly charged emotionally. Any Japanese government will resist Soviet approaches unless it is resolved. Even the compromise that Khrushchev considered in 1958, of returning the two southernmost islands, will not satisfy the Japanese.

The military importance of these islands is considerable. Soviet naval forces in the adjacent Sea of Okhotsk are at present the fastest-growing element of Soviet might. Giving back the islands would not be popular at home among the forces of Russian chauvinism. Furthermore, yielding them could create

a costly precedent. Japan is hardly the only country with irre-
dentist claims against the Soviet Union.

Still, Gorbachev might be willing to give up the islands but
for his calculation that Japan is unready to reward the Soviets
sufficiently for such a concession. Japan will not invest on a
large scale in the Soviet Union if America does not become a
partner in such a venture. Protectionism in the United States
is on the rise, and those who oppose it are primarily conservatives whose support would vanish if Japan is seen as helping
Russia strengthen itself. The American market is central to
Japanese prosperity, and Japan will do nothing to risk access
to it. The effect on American public and congressional opinion
of the recent disclosure that Toshiba sold to the Russians high-
technology products related to submarine warfare suggests
that close Japanese economic ties with the Soviet Union could
pose that risk. Despite the changed direction of Soviet-American relations under Gorbachev, the United States is not ready,
for political and also purely economic reasons, to invest with
Japanese partners in joint ventures in the Soviet Union on a
large scale.

The alliance with the United States is the cornerstone of
Japanese security. If the belief in extended American deterrence is declining in Western Europe, its viability is not in
question in Japan. The United States is the counterweight both
to Soviet military forces in the Far East and to the growing
weight of China. Japan's nightmare is to be left alone facing
these two giants. A major improvement in Soviet-Japanese relations is therefore unlikely in the near future.

Japan does play a considerable, and growing, military role in
the region. One percent of the world's second-largest GNP goes
to military purposes—in absolute terms, an appreciable
amount. Most of it is spent on actual fighting capabilities, while
in the United States the defense budget includes major sums
for other things such as veterans' pensions and hospitals. Not
included is the Japanese financial support for U.S. bases in
Japan. The Japanese military forces rank high in arms and in
training, motivation, and discipline. Japan is close to being able
to defend itself against a conventional invasion and can provide

significant support for American naval and air power in the
Western Pacific. The importance of the American bases in
Japan is increasing owing to the instability of the Philippines,
where American bases can no longer be taken for granted, and
to the presence of Soviet naval and air facilities in Vietnam.

Japanese military growth may increase in the next decade,
but it is unlikely that the increase will change the country's
military status significantly. The United States is pressing for
greater military development, and Japan will probably share
more of the American economic burden in the Far East. But
domestic opposition to the militarization of Japan (let alone its
acquisition of nuclear weapons) is considerable, primarily for
psychological but also for economic reasons. China, too, is opposed to any major expansion of Japanese military power.
There will probably be an increase in Japanese financial and
technological contributions to the strength of both the United
States and China, with the growth of its own combat power
limited to the present rate.

The American position in the strategic quadrangle is and
will probably remain comfortable, but the time when the
United States was the only one of the four powers capable of
conducting full-scale relations with the other three has passed.
The perception of a declining threat from the Soviet Union
makes American security commitments, to Japan directly and
to China indirectly, of decreased value. America's weakening
control over the political use of economic resources of Western
Europe, and in the future probably those of Japan as well,
diminishes the importance of the American connection for the
Soviet Union. Yet at the same time rising Chinese power that
is not associated with a radical change in Sino-Soviet relations,
the continuing dependence of Japan on the American security
shield, and the declining aggressiveness of the Soviet Union
under Gorbachev all serve long-range American interests.

In summary, if the outlook for Soviet-American relations in
the Third World favors a measure of disengagement, the prospect in the strategic quadrangle is for stability.

The role of China remains central. China's present policy of
leaning toward the United States while lessening its enmity

with Russia helps to moderate the Soviet-American conflict. A Sino-Soviet alliance would be disruptive and, for the West, dangerous.

The long-term danger stemming from the modernization of China provides an incentive to the Soviet Union to improve its relations with the United States, in order to counterbalance China and perhaps to slow the American contribution to the military modernization of China. The Soviet Union cannot afford a flare-up with China. As long as East Asia is stable, Soviet policies are likely to be moderate and opportunities for increasing their influence will be negligible.

While the Soviets may become more willing to make concessions to Japan in return for economic benefits, and while Japan may become more disposed to improving its relations with the Soviet Union, the basic limitations of Soviet-Japanese rapprochement—the Japanese dependence on the American security umbrella—will remain in place for a considerable time.

All in all, therefore, the trends within the strategic quadrangle, as in the Third World, are compatible with improvements in relations between the two global rivals.

....

7

THE ARENAS OF CONFLICT:
EUROPE

....

In the 1950s and 1960s the United States fought two wars against Soviet allies in Asia. In the 1970s relations between the superpowers foundered on Soviet activities in the Third World. Yet the region that is central in the Soviet-American rivalry is Europe. Since the beginning of the 1960s Europe has been tranquil.

But this does not mean that the continent has become unimportant. Despite the postwar growth of American economic, political, and military power, despite the emergence of the Pacific region as the most dynamic area of economic growth, despite the redirection of Soviet expansionist ambitions away from Western Europe, the old continent continues to be the heart of the international system. Direct or indirect domination of Europe still constitutes the ultimate stake in the global rivalry.

The establishment of the Soviet East European empire was and continues to be the most important cause of the Cold War. The Soviet commitment to the preservation of this empire is the greatest obstacle to ending it.

Periodic outbreaks of unrest in East European countries, and Soviet military intervention or Soviet-sponsored internal repressions in response to such unrest, are incompatible with lasting détente. Turmoil and repression in Eastern Europe re-create in the American body politic the conditions that started the Cold War—mistrust and fear of the Soviet Union.

The continuous Soviet domination of Eastern Europe nurtures the Western anxiety that a serious imbalance in East-West military power, even if it does not invite an outright Soviet assault on Western Europe, may lead to the erosion of its resistance to Soviet pressure and to its isolation from the United States.

Soviet subordination of Western Europe, or even its neutralization, would dramatically alter the balance of power between the superpowers. The American commitment to Western Europe represents the first and main line of American defense against Soviet expansion. The continuing Soviet dominance of Eastern Europe, regardless of strategic and tactical zigzags in Soviet-American relations, is a permanent reminder of Moscow's expansionist appetite and of its aggressive tendencies if its military power is not firmly confronted.

As the Red Army moved westward during World War II, liberating the countries of Eastern and Central Europe from the Nazis and their allies, the Soviets imposed communist regimes by force of arms and through secret police activity. By 1949, Poland, Czechoslovakia, Hungary, Romania, Bulgaria, and East Germany had been transformed into one-party communist systems and satellites of Moscow. In most of these countries at the end of World War II there were revolutionary situations that, if left to run their course free of outside interference, would probably have toppled the existing governments, and might even have brought radical, or communist, or pro-Soviet governments (or all three) to power. Communism, however, was imposed on each by the Soviet Union.

In the history of Soviet expansion there is no greater or more important achievement than the establishment of the East European empire. Along with the internal empire—the non-Russian republics of the Soviet Union—Eastern Europe is today the only surviving empire in the world. Much of Soviet domestic, foreign, military, and economic policies can be explained by the felt need to preserve hegemony there. The existence of this domain was and is perceived by the leadership as the basis for the future expansion of Soviet rule and of communism, and as confirmation of the historical trend toward the "inevitable" victory of socialism over capitalism. Leaders from Stalin to Gorbachev, despite major differences in their specific policies toward the region, have been steadfast in their determination to preserve Soviet rule in Eastern Europe.

However, neither security interests—Eastern Europe as a buffer zone and as a military and economic counterbalance to NATO—nor the usefulness of Eastern Europe for advancing Soviet global ambitions suffices to explain the depth of the Soviet determination to maintain the empire regardless of the cost. Considerations of security and political utility alone do not require the present level of Soviet control over social and political developments in Eastern European countries.

The explanation lies beyond practical considerations. Soviet rule provides one of the ideological foundations of Great Russian and Communist Party control within the Soviet Union itself. It also contributes to the credibility of Soviet foreign policy.

Victory in World War II was the central legitimizing experience of Soviet rule at home and is intimately associated with control over Eastern Europe. As the major spoil of war, the empire serves to legitimize the Kremlin's rule in Russia. In particular, it has helped to form a bond of common interest between the government and its Great Russian and other Slavic populations. It is important to remember that the creation of the empire made permanent the unification of the Ukraine and Byelorussia with the eastern parts of Poland annexed in 1939. It also led to the division of Germany, the historic threat to the Eastern Slavs.

The Soviet leadership hoped that the dubious origins of the regimes in Eastern Europe and their lack of nationalist bases would cease to matter over time and that they would attain legitimacy in the eyes of their populations. In the 1950s and the 1960s these hopes were based on the belief in the malleability of the younger generations in these countries and their attraction to communist ideals. The hopes were not fulfilled. In the 1970s, these regimes were expected to achieve legitimacy on the strength of their economic performance, a type of legitimacy much more fragile than that based on traditional values and national identity. Indeed, in Hungary and East Germany this goal may have been at least partially achieved through credible economic performance and improved living standards. But the stagnant Czech regime, the chaotic, despotic, and spiritually empty Romanian government, and the facsimile of communist government that exists in Poland cannot even make this claim. Further decay during the 1990s is likely. Economic problems tend in Eastern Europe to lead to social unrest and political turmoil directed at local leaders and their Soviet masters. Yet the Soviet Union is in no position to help Eastern Europe economically.

The dilemma of the communist elites in Eastern Europe is insoluble. On the one hand, they can gain popular support only by advocating the cause of national independence, with the accompanying risks of Soviet military intervention. On the other hand, they can retain power only through unqualified Soviet support and, if need be, military intervention. Communism has been victorious in places like Cuba, China, and Vietnam primarily because the regimes that were forged in communist revolutions managed to identify themselves with nationalism and independence. It is the crucial flaw of the Soviet-controlled Eastern European regimes that they cannot do so.

In this empire, unlike others in the modern era, the dominant power is superior to the dominated in only one attribute —military power. It lags behind in standard of living, economic development, educational levels, and cultural achievement. Soviet military superiority has so far sufficed to preserve the empire. Historically, empires do not disintegrate when the imperial power is at the peak of its military strength. But if apocalypse does not threaten the Eastern European empire in the next decade, serious instability surely does.

More than ever, conditions in its Eastern European empire are a source of critical vulnerability for the Soviet Union. For forty years it has had the good luck to confront a crisis in only one Eastern European country at a time. This luck may hold in the 1980s, but even if successive explosions fail to rock the region during the remainder of this decade, serious tensions will certainly persist, both within the client states and between them and the imperial center. And these tensions will affect Soviet-American relations. If the internal changes underway in the Soviet Union and the likely circumstances in the Third World and East Asia all promise a moderation of the global rivalry, the portents in Eastern Europe are different. There the trend toward improvement, and indeed Gorbachev's entire program of reform in the Soviet Union, could come to grief.

THE CONDITIONS IN THE 1990S

Mikhail Gorbachev may be willing to permit far-reaching, liberalizing, economic reforms in East European countries. Most of them need market-oriented reforms to improve their economies. But the key problem for Eastern Europe has to do with purely economic factors, specifically the resources available to these countries, and their positions in the international economy in the years ahead.

Hungary, for instance, is in serious economic straits. Yet it is the most "reformed" of all the Soviet satellites. It is a model of market socialism, which Gorbachev wants partly to emulate. Yugoslavia, a fully independent country outside the Soviet bloc, has an economy that is liberalized and marketized far beyond anything that the satellite nations have achieved. Unlike them, it has a convertible currency. Yet Yugoslavia in the 1980s has been in a very serious economic plight.

Perhaps Hungary and Yugoslavia did not make sweeping enough reforms to reap the benefits of free enterprise. But neither government can move much further without renouncing its control over the economy and its socialist character. In Hungary, moreover, such steps would be opposed by even the most liberal Soviet leader. What dogs Hungary and Yugoslavia, in addition to the fact that their economic models may have reached the upper limits of their effectiveness, is economic reality. The two countries suffer from a lag in productivity growth, limited incentives, and inflation that is magnified by social policies. Quality control is poor. Neither has been able to expand its foreign trade with hard-currency nations. Both have made irrational investment decisions and provide subsidies that allow unprofitable enterprises to survive for the sake of keeping unemployment low. In the Hungarian and Yugoslav cases, the major changes in the conditions of the international market and economy—from the 1970s, when they were propitious for their rapid development, to the 1980s, when they are restrictive—are the most important reason for their economic decline. These changes include the greater internal cohesion of the European Common Market, increased competition from Japan and the newly industrial Asian states, and the shift from a buyer's to a seller's credit market. These difficulties demonstrate that Soviet permissiveness with regard to reforms in Eastern Europe is at present not crucial.

To be sure, economic reform is necessary in Eastern Europe. But for the moment it has little to do with Soviet permissiveness. The Polish government, for example, desires reform and is supported in Moscow, but is so mistrusted by its people that it cannot introduce changes. The rulers of Czechoslovakia are determined to stick to their economic command system, not because of Soviet pressures but for their own reasons. In Romania, what is missing is not economic reform but simply elementary rationality in public policies. Moreover, all East European countries need not just reform but also economic assistance, technological modernization, and increased trade. Here the Soviet Union cannot help. It is irrelevant to the basic economic needs of its satellites. Aid can only come from the West. The one Eastern European country that does receive substantial assistance from the West, the German Democratic Republic, is much healthier economically than the others. Soviet client states require economic help and have to get it from the West. This is not only an East European but also a Soviet problem, and it is primarily a political one.

THE SOVIET APPROACH

Beset by its own domestic problems, the Soviet leadership underestimates the seriousness of its long-range imperial prob-

lems. Gorbachev himself may not want to think through to the
end the dismal prospects for Eastern Europe and to face
squarely the dangers to his domestic reform that may arise
there. It is worth recalling that in the years immediately following Khrushchev's ouster in December 1964 the Soviet leadership seriously considered and even experimented with
economic reforms like those that Gorbachev has launched. This
reformist mood was, however, decisively terminated by the Soviet invasion of Czechoslovakia in 1968.

A Soviet official who supports Gorbachev's *perestroika* and
concedes the connection between the invasion of Czechoslovakia and the regression to conservatism in Brezhnev's Russia
made the following remark: "In case of need we will defend our
security interest in Eastern Europe by all necessary means.
But we will never again be deterred from pursuing our domestic reforms and renewal by whatever happens there." This is
probably unrealistic. Major turmoil in Eastern Europe, let
alone explosions that will require direct Soviet intervention,
will stifle changes in Russia, especially if they occur at the early
stages of reform. The new Soviet leadership may permit East
European developments similar to Dubček's Prague Spring,
but will certainly not hesitate to intervene militarily in the
event of a repetition of the Hungarian revolution of 1956 or of
Polish Solidarity. Given the choice of losing Eastern Europe or
of downgrading reform in the Soviet Union, Moscow is likely
to opt to preserve its empire.

Is there an alternative policy that the Soviet Union can adopt
toward Eastern Europe to avoid the worst case there? The
truth is that it is probably already too late. Soviet policies
toward Eastern Europe can be better or worse, and Gorbachev's
are clearly better than those of the past, but if the fundamental
Soviet approach to its empire in the east does not change,
confrontation and dangerous conflict cannot be avoided in the
long run. Despite the innovative character of Gorbachev's leadership and programs for Russia, it is still too early for Moscow
to rethink the basic notion of preserving the empire. Gorbachev's policies toward Eastern Europe, therefore, can at best
delay confrontations and win time for the gradual movement

away from fundamental Soviet approaches and assumptions that may be possible later.

The Gorbachev leadership clearly appreciates the potential for serious instability in Eastern Europe. It is also beginning to be aware of the dangers that turmoil there will present for the new Soviet policies. Yet the main lines of its policy toward Eastern Europe are only starting to take shape and still contain many uncertainties. After Stalin's death the Soviet leadership adopted a policy toward Eastern Europe of tolerating "different roads to socialism": The new Soviet leadership may be ready, within limits, to accept different roads *from* socialism.

Gorbachev plainly takes Eastern Europe seriously. He has made frequent visits there and expanded consultations with the leaders of these countries. His proclamation on Eastern Europe in November 1987 is a charter for more permissive and liberal Soviet–East European relations. The Politburo has instructed Vadim Medvedev, the Central Committee secretary responsible for Eastern Europe, to develop a new set of guidelines for these relations.

Gorbachev's evolving policy toward Eastern Europe contains diverse and not always compatible goals. The first priority is to preserve Soviet domination. In practice this means perpetuating the communist nature of regimes, ensuring foreign policies in the service of the Soviet Union, and setting the limits to domestic reform and relations with the West in the satellite countries. The second aim is to preserve social and political stability as a necessary condition of pursuing reform at home and détente with the West, particularly the United States. Gorbachev's third goal is to increase the contribution that the East European countries make to the modernization of the Soviet Union itself.

The first goal requires the retention of strict Soviet control over the domestic and foreign policies of the East European states and continuous intervention in their leadership politics and policy-makings. The second goal presupposes a tolerant attitude toward internal reforms in these countries and a wider margin for political and cultural autonomy, as long as these contribute to stability and do not undermine loyalty to the Soviet Union. The third goal envisages an end to Soviet subsidies to Eastern Europe, which include the low pricing of raw materials delivered to these countries and the low quality of goods received from them, and a greater integration of Soviet and East European economies not only through trade and the division of labor but also by direct East European investment in the development of Soviet energy and raw materials. Policies toward Eastern Europe, in short, aim to combine continuous Soviet domination through the preservation of loyal communist regimes, on the one hand, with the promotion of political stability and domestic peace, on the other. Moscow wants to have it both ways.

In his pursuit of these goals, Gorbachev confronts stark dilemmas. His short-range problem in Eastern Europe is not unlike the one that he faces at home—how to reconcile the need to reassert control by the metropolitan center over the provinces with increased liberalization in the spirit of *perestroika*.

Gorbachev inherited an empire in a state of disarray. The last years of the slack Brezhnev rule and the power vacuum created by the ensuing interregnum left the East European communist leadership with a greater degree of independence from Russia than ever before and with a growing appetite for autonomy. Gorbachev's first priority after he assumed power was to make it clear that the Soviet Union would remain the ultimate arbiter of what is acceptable in Eastern Europe. A number of steps served this purpose: two summit meetings with the leaders; a conference with secretaries of the East European parties responsible for economic affairs in the fall of 1985 at which warnings were issued against excessive reliance on market forces; visits of East European leaders to Moscow; Gorbachev's trips to the German Democratic Republic, Hungary, Czechoslovakia, and Romania; Soviet intervention in the process of succession in Hungary and Czechoslovakia; and the forced cancellation in 1986 of the planned visit of the East German leader Erich Honecker to West Germany.

Yet at the same time Gorbachev showed that he was aware

that Moscow's domination of and frozen opposition to change in Eastern Europe were as dangerous as the decline of Soviet control before his ascension to power. The revision of Soviet–East European relations became an integral, if not yet clearly defined, part of his reform. Gorbachev seems fully aware that revolutionary transformations in the Soviet Union itself cannot but have an impact on developments within East European countries.

Reform in Russia will inevitably fuel the aspirations of the intelligentsia and workers in Eastern Europe countries for greater freedom and material improvements. It will also reinforce the desire of the communist rulers and elites for greater autonomy from Soviet tutelage. If there were any doubts in Gorbachev's mind about this they should have been dispelled by his 1987 trip to Czechoslovakia, where he encountered an open outpouring of the hopes of the Czechoslovakian people that his radical reforms would be adopted in their country.

The most authoritative and extensive statement of Gorbachev's liberalized approach toward the East European empire was his declaration of November 10, 1987. This statement promised less Soviet intervention in East European domestic affairs and greater political and cultural autonomy for its ruling elites. It held out hope for economic liberalization and hinted at a desire for lessened repressiveness. These themes were also openly voiced by Gorbachev during his visit to Romania—aside from Albania, the most brutally repressive and mismanaged state in Europe. The essence of Gorbachev's program of *perestroika* for Eastern Europe can be reduced to two simple propositions: the promotion of liberalization within the most conservative East European regimes such as Czechoslovakia and Romania, and the limitation or prevention of further liberalization within the most liberal East European regimes such as Hungary. This policy might be described as centrist.

Gorbachev's attitudes toward Poland and the German Democratic Republic are of particular significance. These are the largest and, from the strategic, political, and economic points of view, the most important countries for the Soviet Union. Both exemplify the inherent contradictions and dilemmas of his policies and of the dangers to *perestroika* originating from Eastern Europe.

The Polish leader, General Wojchiek Jaruzelski, is by all accounts the closest to Gorbachev in Eastern Europe. He was able to stifle the most massive and dangerous challenge to communist authority in East European history with Polish forces and thus prevent an immensely costly and unpredictable Soviet military intervention. In his own way he is a Polish patriot, who has, however, proven his loyalty to Moscow and accepts the inevitability of Soviet domination. He has been able to establish a semblance of political stability, a kind of balance among Solidarity, the church, and the regime. At the same time, his government permits greater freedom for its citizens than any other province of the Soviet Empire. It accepts—out of necessity, to be sure—what amounts to a de facto organized opposition with its own press, as well as a powerful, independent church. His vision of a reformed economy is closest to Gorbachev's own vision.

Poland is, however, the weakest link of the Soviet empire. So estranged are the Poles from the regime that Poland has, in effect, a people without a government and a government without a people. It is a country where the balance of political power is extremely fragile, economic conditions are disastrous, and the chances for successful economic reform are minimal because of popular distrust of the government. Poland is a country without hope, where the forces of repression are strong enough to preserve social peace, to prevent or suppress localized outbursts of deep-seated hate and dissatisfaction. Yet it is also a country where the regime could, given a sufficient catalyst, actually be swept away by a national explosion.

Erich Honecker is the East European leader most distrusted by Gorbachev, and his country, East Germany, the most disliked. Yet only fifteen years ago, the East German elite was the most servile of all ruling satellite governments. It was normal for the East Germans to refer routinely, in public and in private, to the Soviets as "older brothers." The East German attitude toward the Prague Spring and Polish Solidarity was the most negative in all of Eastern Europe and the most supportive of the Soviets. The East German economic contribution to the Russians has been the most reliable and most highly valued by Moscow. East German participation in arms deliveries, military advisors, and security forces in support of Soviet objectives in the Third World is greatly appreciated by the Russians.

In recent years East German attitudes have changed radically, however. Arrogance has replaced servility, barely hidden contempt has surfaced in place of deference. Gorbachev's reform plans have been greeted in the East German press and in the speeches of its leaders either with silence or with simple factual reporting without the praise of former days. As to the relevance for East Germany of Gorbachev's reforms, the prevailing attitude in East Berlin may be summarized as: "We are doing fine and don't need foreign models. The Soviets cannot offer us anything; we have nothing to learn from them, but they have a lot to learn from us."

The Soviets are well aware of East German attitudes. They are uneasy at the growth of German nationalism in both parts of Germany. They are clearly distrustful of the closer relations between them. The historic week-long visit of Honecker to West Germany in the winter of 1988 was covered in the Soviet press by a single paragraph, and never mentioned on Soviet television. Moscow fears the growing West German preoccupation with their brethren, and the East German conviction that the Soviets have nothing to offer them.

And yet, at the same time, the GDR is the most stable and most prosperous country of Eastern Europe—the very model of what Gorbachev would wish for the rest of the Soviet empire. East Germany stands out as the exception to the economic failures of the empire, both in Europe and elsewhere. Its relative success is in part the result of the German national character, which stresses the work ethic, orderliness, and respect for authority and can thus overcome even the monstrous inefficiencies of the communist economic system. The regime has managed to preserve stability in the communist country most exposed to Western influence—West German television is viewed by about three-quarters of the East German population and in 1987 alone three million East German citizens (15 percent of its population) visited the Federal Republic. East Germany's relative prosperity and stability are supported by very large West German subsidies and by intra-German trade. For all practical purposes, East Germany is a member of both Comecon and, through its West German connection, the European Common Market.

This, then, is one facet of Gorbachev's dilemma in Eastern Europe. Stability can be attained only by close ties with the West. Yet such links move the East European states away from the Soviet Union. As Poland demonstrates, the loyalty of local communist rulers to Moscow and a policy preserving the communist system by a combination of repression and concessions is an inherently unstable mixture, lacking as it does the necessary economic basis for prolonged stability.

THE ATLANTIC ALLIANCE

Soviet-American relations are inexorably intertwined with the Western alliance in Europe. This alliance and its military arm, NATO, were created to defend Western Europe against Soviet aggression by ensuring American support of West European resistance to Soviet pressures of all kinds, military and political. Three key elements of the original basis for the Atlantic Alliance are now undergoing change.

First, the West European feeling of threat from the Soviet Union is diminishing, particularly in the Federal Republic of Germany. Franz-Josef Strauss, the most conservative figure in that country's ruling Christian Democratic Party, traveled to Moscow in the winter of 1988 to meet with Gorbachev, and proclaimed that the Soviet Union had ceased to be a military threat to Western Europe. This denotes a significant change. The Soviet perception of military threat from the Western alliance and NATO is also declining, as was demonstrated by the authoritative Soviet article stating that "the United States and NATO do not plan aggression against the Soviet Union."

Secondly, at the same time the West Europeans' faith in American "extended" deterrence—an American commitment to go to nuclear war with the Soviets if Western Europe is attacked—is weakening. The French have always doubted the seriousness of this extended deterrence, but now, for a number of reasons, some mutually exclusive, other Europeans are beginning to share the French skepticism.

Oddly, both liberals and conservatives in the United States have contributed to the doubts about American extended deterrence. President Reagan's rejection of nuclear deterrence as unacceptable mutual nuclear terror and his desire to substitute for it a defensive shield (SDI) reinforced them. Although the INF agreement of December 1987 does not change militarily the balance in Europe, its psychological impact on Western Europe may be considerable. The treaty removes American nuclear weapons deployed in Europe capable of reaching Soviet territory. Deterrence itself is a psychological concept that depends for its effectiveness on the conviction of friends and foes alike.

Europeans' uneasiness about the American commitment to their defense also stems from the growing rapprochement between the two great global rivals. This syndrome is not new: Whenever Soviet-American relations have been bad, the West Europeans have worried that the Americans would blunder into a confrontation with the Soviets with devastating consequences for them. Whenever Soviet-American relations have moved toward reconciliation, the West Europeans have worried about a bilateral deal that would ignore their interests.

Thirdly, the American economic position in the world, so exceptional just after the Second World War, has eroded significantly. While the idea of a West European union achieved through directly political channels declined in the 1970s, Western Europe has moved haltingly toward economic unity. The plans for very significant deepening of economic interconnections among the countries of the Common Market could conceivably result by the end of 1992 in an unprecedented economic convergence that would have major political, and perhaps even military, consequences. As now envisaged, the new Common Market would constitute an integrated economy with a population of 320 million, creating throughout Western Europe an almost free flow of capital and labor, unified prices and taxes, tightly linked currencies, and highly coordinated activities in science, applied research, and technology.

All three trends will have important consequences for American and Soviet relations with Western Europe, and with each other. Western Europe, with West Germany as its core, will represent much greater economic power. While its individual countries will surrender elements of their economic sovereignty to the larger entity, collectively they will become more powerful. Western Europe's willingness to give credit to Russia on favorable terms and with government guarantees will increase. Episodes like American opposition to the German-Soviet gas pipeline deal in 1982 that provoked resistance from allies will be politically more costly to all concerned, and therefore less likely.

While the West Europeans' economic strength will increase, this will not make them more willing to raise their military expenditures. Such increases were politically difficult even in the early 1980s, at the height of the post-Afghanistan tensions with the Soviet Union. In an atmosphere of détente, expectations of growth of European military budgets are unrealistic. Europe long ago abdicated the role, and the cost, of mounting a global defense against the Soviet Union to the United States. This is unlikely to change, but its consequences for West European–American relations may change. Public resentment in the United States of what appears to be the inequitable sharing of the costs of mutual defense may become sharper. While a total withdrawal of American troops from Western Europe is unlikely, some reduction in the American contribution to Europe's defense may be unavoidable. This will complicate the negotiations with the Soviets on conventional forces in Europe and may also result in a degree of West European–American estrangement that is unprecedented in the postwar period.

The West European countries are likely to move closer together in their foreign and military policies. For France, ties with West Germany will acquire ever-greater importance. Great Britain's longstanding special relationship with the United States is apt to erode further and perhaps even become a hindrance to the British position in Europe rather than an advantage.

The anti-Soviet and anticommunist spirit that has always been weaker in Western Europe than in the United States will surely decline even further there, especially if Eastern Europe remains at least relatively stable. This decline will gain force from Europeans' hopes for liberalization of the Soviet Union itself and also from the altered status of the major West European communist parties—disintegration in France and Spain, and integration into the establishment in Italy.

The European socialists are apt to become less moderate in their international, political, and particularly military positions. The West German SPD has already developed direct party-to-party ties with the East German communist party. British and Spanish and Greek socialists are tilting not so much in pro-Soviet as in anti-American directions. Simultaneously, the center of gravity of centrist and right-of-center West European parties has moved, on foreign policies, to the left.

Developments of particular importance are occurring in West Germany. There is a preoccupation with the fate of East Germany, and a not entirely realistic hope that with the liberalized atmosphere Gorbachev has introduced in the Soviet Union, and his "new thinking" in foreign and security policies, ever-closer ties between the two Germanys will become possible.

All this does *not* mean that NATO will dissolve. It does, however, foreshadow less cohesion within the Alliance. It may become more difficult for the United States, and easier for the Soviet Union, to influence Western Europe—although the West Germans, French, and British will remain within the Western camp. Bilateral Soviet-American relations, and bilateral Soviet–West European relations will be of growing importance. These two sets of bilateral relations are likely to develop with less coordination than in the past.

THE PLAUSIBLE FUTURES

Fundamental changes in Soviet–East European relations are possible, but only if Gorbachev remains in power and continues his reforms. The general secretary frequently refers to his program as Russia's "last chance" to become a truly modern country. Similarly, liberally inclined leaders in Eastern Europe often remark in private that Gorbachev's rule represents the last chance for changing Soviet–East European relations and beginning a gradual process of domestic transformation in their countries. Gorbachev's policies do represent the first potential opportunity ever to break out from the confines imposed by the Soviet commitment to preserve its East European empire. If he fails, the possibilities for gradual changes in the fundamental Soviet approach to Eastern Europe will die. The likely alternative to him will be a harshly authoritarian and chauvinistic Soviet regime that will seek to preserve Soviet imperial domination over Eastern Europe at any price.

Assuming, however, that Gorbachev enjoys at least moderate success, what futures are within the realm of possibility for Eastern Europe? Three issues will be crucial: Soviet security concerns, East European economic and political relations with the West, and domestic changes in Eastern Europe.

Soviet security concerns regarding Eastern Europe, and particularly the German Democratic Republic and Poland, are based both on the experience of the past and on current relations with the West. They may ease with the progress of arms control, particularly conventional arms control. Yet, short of disbanding the opposing military blocs in Europe, Soviet security preoccupations will probably require the deployment of battle-ready, elite forces in East Germany, the stationing of some Soviet nonelite forces in Poland and Czechoslovakia and Hungary, and Soviet operational control and administrative supervision of Eastern European armed forces.

The Soviet armed forces deployed in Eastern Europe can be divided into three categories: the front-line troops facing NATO, which are concentrated in East Germany and are present as well in Poland and Czechoslovakia; lower-quality troops deployed in these three countries whose mission is to secure the lines of communications and supply between the Soviet Union and their front-line troops; and other forces whose purpose is to intimidate the countries of Eastern Europe and provide a quick response if crises endanger communist rule in these countries.

The first category of Soviet forces will probably remain in place even if the Soviets' fundamental approach to Eastern Europe changes. But there may be fewer of them and, if conventional arms negotiations with the West succeed, their structure and mode of deployment will shift from an offensive to a defensive orientation. The presence of these troops in East Germany, and of their supporting logistical formations in Poland and Czechoslovakia, are not necessarily incompatible with the erosion of the imperial ties between the Soviet Union and Eastern Europe. Even the stationing in Eastern Europe of special Soviet units whose purpose is quick response to dangerous domestic turmoil does not rule out fundamental changes in Soviet–East European relations. After all, the Soviet Union has more than enough forces stationed on its western borders to intimidate the East European countries and to mount a rapid invasion if it decides to do so. Thus, the continuation of the military dimension of Soviet–East European relations (including the operational and administrative Soviet supervision of the armed forces of East European countries) can at least in theory be reconciled with a trend away from the Soviet subordination of Eastern Europe.

The greatest promise for the transformation of the nature of Soviet–East European relations lies in Eastern Europe's relations with the West. As noted, stability in Eastern Europe depends on economic performance, which in turn depends heavily on East European relations with the West. Thus both the East European *and* the Soviet leaders have a deep interest in expanded economic relations with the West.

But it is clear that expanded East European–West European economic relations cannot be separated from political relations. Almost all leaders of Eastern Europe (with the possible exception of Czechoslovakia) seem to be eager to move closer to the West. The Soviet Union is ambivalent, torn between the economic benefits to Eastern Europe (and to the Soviet Union itself) from closer political contacts with the West and the dangers of the greater East European independence that such relations will encourage. Overall, however, as long as the Soviets understand that the best hope for stability in Eastern Europe lies in expanding ties with the West, the possible benefits are likely to outweigh the fear of possible dangers.

Moreover, as we approach the end of the 1980s, Eastern Europe has ceased to be an asset to Soviet foreign policy. The Soviets' main concern about Eastern Europe is the preservation of Marxist-Leninist regimes there. The Soviets tolerated a degree of foreign policy independence on the part of Romania because it remained authoritarian at home. Changes in the foreign policies of East European client states will not necessarily have a major impact on the fundamental principles of their domestic order.

East European relations with the West are primarily relations with Western Europe, not the United States. The American interest in Eastern Europe is almost entirely conditioned by Soviet-American relations. But the evolving West European and East European foreign policies display a remarkable convergence. In both, the increasingly popular attitude is to avoid getting too deeply involved in the conflict between the two superpowers. In its extreme form, this is the attitude of "a plague on both your houses." Both the left and the center of the political leadership and the elite, the business community and the important social classes in both Europes, consider the Soviet-American rivalry less and less relevant to their principal concerns.

The spread of this kind of attitude in Eastern Europe may not be to Moscow's liking, but it does not yet pose a major threat to Soviet power, especially because it dovetails with the trends of Soviet foreign policies under Gorbachev. The general secretary's first priority is to lower the temperature of the Soviet-American conflict and pursue far-reaching reductions in all types of armament. His second priority is to develop stable relations with all the other major capitalist countries and with China. His third priority is to secure Western help in the task of modernizing Russia.

While Soviet-American relations remain the centerpiece of Gorbachev's foreign policy, Western Europe is of increasing importance especially with regard to the second and third tasks. The Soviet Union would like to see the loosening of the Atlantic Alliance and the emergence of a Western Europe more independent from American policies. This desire stems not only from political calculations but also from economic requirements. Gorbachev's hopes for expanded Soviet economic cooperation with capitalist countries rests primarily not with Japan and America but with Western Europe.

For the moment, then, Soviet foreign policy priorities and the West and East European preferences complement each other. The concept of "One Europe" reflects the growing commonality of East and West European interests. At this point, the East European attraction to Western Europe does not conflict with Soviet goals. If, however, at some point in the future, East European–West European *political* relations become too close for Soviet comfort, the Soviet dilemma of fostering social stability in Eastern Europe through freer association with the West at the risk of undermining East European loyalty to the Soviet Union will again emerge. Relations between the two Germanys would be the object of particular Soviet concern. Still, it may well be that sustained interaction between East and West Europe will expand the latitude of East European foreign policy, especially if this interaction has a limited impact on the domestic regimes.

The greatest difficulties in a fundamental change in Soviet–East European relations concern the domestic transformation in East European countries that such a change will entail. These problems are further complicated by the interests and attitudes of the communist leaderships of the East European countries. While the main barrier to such a transformation remains Moscow's attitude, the domestic difficulties are far from negligible.

There can be no doubt that the peoples of the Soviet bloc are opposed to their regimes. Of course, they differ in their historical traditions and their experience under communism. Their social structures are diverse. Their aspirations for their economic and political systems are not uniform. But all desire some form of democratic rule. The people of Eastern Europe do not have political elites whom they trust and who could make the changes they desire. Their leaders can achieve a modicum of support if they partly fulfill popular economic aspirations by providing improvements in the standard of living. This will become more and more difficult, except in East Germany. Some regimes (Romania is an exception) can achieve broader and deeper support if they are perceived by their citizens as being anti-Soviet, and display some independence from their Soviet rulers.

But even if that were possible, the indigenous communist leadership groups would still face a basic problem. If they move away from the Soviet Union, the danger to their leadership is not only that they might be ousted by the Soviets, but also that a liberalizing process could lead to their replacement by new, and more popular, leaders. This is an unresolvable problem.

The most likely development in Eastern Europe is not that the present leaders will embark on radical democratization, but that competing communist leadership groups will challenge them under the banner of far-reaching reform and greater independence from Moscow. The Prague Spring of 1968 in Czechoslovakia, under the leadership of Alexander Dubček, is a precedent for such a change. Ironically, in the most conservative countries of Eastern Europe, like Romania and present-day Czechoslovakia, such a development is plausible primarily if Gorbachev exerts pressure to bring it about—as he may.

The present East European leaders, or their successors, will probably seek somewhat greater independence from the Soviets in foreign policy within limits—notably, remaining in the Warsaw Pact—and they may achieve grudging acceptance for such a course from Moscow. In domestic affairs it is reasonable to expect Gorbachev to be ready for political, cultural, and economic democratization and liberalization in East European countries similar to the trends in the Soviet system itself. But his support for such an evolution in Eastern Europe poses a number of problems, and it raises major difficulties.

To begin with, Hungary and Poland have attained a level of liberalization that probably goes far beyond what Gorbachev wants to see in Russia; they have reached the limits of what he considers prudent for Eastern Europe. In Hungary, there are signs that the Soviets do not want the post-Kádár leadership to move beyond the existing reforms. In Poland, de facto freedoms are already more extensive than in any other East European country. Movement beyond what already exists would be tantamount to the recognition of an official institutionalized opposition, something that no Marxist-Leninist regime can tolerate. For neither Gorbachev nor Jaruzelski is this an acceptable prospect. In the economic area, the question is not the extent of Soviet permissiveness but the ability of Jaruzelski to gain sufficient support among the intelligentsia and the workers for highly liberal economic policies that will require initial sacrifices.

In the most conservative East European regimes, particularly Romania and Czechoslovakia, liberalization depends not only on Soviet permissiveness but also on the attitudes and orientation of their own leaderships. Romania may explode in a way that the Soviets will not accept. The future of Czechoslovakia depends on the willingness of the present leadership to change its ways and promote liberalizing reforms, on Soviet effectiveness in pressing Czechoslovakia in this direction, and on the ability of the intelligentsia and workers to exert strong pressure on their government to adopt different policies.

Finally, throughout East Europe, the crucial question for the Soviets is whether liberalization and reforms can be calibrated and controlled. In his own country, Gorbachev is already facing spontaneous and unintended consequences of *perestroika*—for example, the unrest and riots in non-Russian republics. Yet in the Soviet Union, and particularly in Russia, the task of controlling the process of reform is much easier than in Eastern Europe. Longevity of communist rule, the lack of democratic traditions, the very modest identification with Western culture and civilization, the merger of the goals of communist rule and Russian nationalism—all contribute to the capacity of Soviet leaders to keep reform within desired limits.

In Eastern Europe, things are different. A process of change, once it starts, will be difficult to keep within preset limits.

Russian reform will inevitably encourage the East European populations. Gorbachev's preferred response to this possibility seems to be what can be called "preemptive liberalization" of conservative regimes and limitation on further reforms in the relatively liberal governments.

But in both cases, the possibility of uncontrolled developments must be haunting the Soviet leader, especially when he considers their likely disastrous effects on *perestroika* at home. Gorbachev will probably pursue a twofold policy: support for liberalizing reforms that is cautious and measured, along with the preservation of the credibility of Soviet intervention and support for security crackdowns like the one in Poland in 1981. For the German Democratic Republic the Soviet attitude toward reforms will be particularly cautious. The relative prosperity, order, and stability in this country, combined with its strategic importance and the unpredictability of West German reaction to massive unrest in the GDR, suggest that Erich Honecker, or his successor, will get his way in preserving the status quo—if the East German people will permit it.

In conclusion, if Gorbachev survives, the prospects for greater independence of East European countries in the foreign policy area are promising. The liberalization of the conservative regimes and the preservation of the liberal regimes are likely. In the longer run, more basic change in the East European regimes seems much more possible than before Gorbachev came to power in Russia. He seems to be willing to entertain the idea that liberalization in Eastern Europe need not impinge on the security interests of the Soviet Union. He may even be convinced that such liberalization is a necessary condition of the preservation of the Soviet strategic position in the region and the development of stable and beneficial relations with Western Europe and the United States.

Even so, communist Eastern Europe will probably retain one-party systems. These might, however, be inclusionary, enlightened authoritarian regimes that will tolerate economic and social activity independent of the government. Such an evolution would require the continuation and deepening of Gorbachev's revolution in the Soviet Union in concert with growing domestic popular pressure in Eastern Europe that is encouraged by the Gorbachev experiment. It may also depend on popular unrest, or at least the threat of it, in response to economic hardship there. It may require divisions within the ruling communist elite, with important groups emerging committed to significant liberalizing reforms and Soviet support of these reformist groups as the alternative to violent crises. On the other hand, uncontrollable unrest in any of the main East European countries will almost certainly provoke a harsh Soviet response and will also restrain or even reverse the Soviet program of domestic reform.

What role can the West play in promoting the most desirable evolution in Eastern Europe? American and Western European policies toward Eastern Europe have ranged from impotence to inactivity. The chance for influence on liberalization is greater today than ever. Stability throughout Eastern Europe depends on economic performance and is endangered by the region's grim economic prospects. Beset by their own gigantic economic problems, the Soviets can offer almost nothing in this respect. Western economic help and intensified economic relations with Eastern Europe are the only lifesaver available. Western assistance can therefore create leverage both on the Soviet Union, which desires stability there, and on the East European regimes themselves.

Such aid should be clearly conditional. The East Europeans should not get something for nothing. The "something" in this case should be Soviet relaxation of control over Eastern Europe and liberalization in these countries. American help for Eastern Europe—if there is any—will almost certainly be conditional. The chances that Western Europe, particularly West Germany, will mount an economic rescue operation for Eastern Europe are much higher; but there is the danger that such assistance will be given unconditionally, squandering the considerable leverage that it could otherwise bring. The Atlantic Alliance, and particularly the United States, ought to put forcefully on the agenda a plan of coordinated Western policy toward Eastern Europe. Nothing of the sort is yet in sight. But the existing opportunity is too important to waste.

8

THE FUTURE
OF THE RIVALRY

The next decade has the promise of being a calmer period in Soviet-American relations than any since 1945. The global rivalry will not disappear, but there is for the first time a chance that it will be considerably less acute, less dangerous, and less expensive than in the past. This is so because substantial progress in resolving the political issues that underlie the conflict are possible, for the first time since it began. There are three reasons for this: the world has changed, the United States has changed, and, most importantly and most dramatically, the Soviet Union is changing—in ways that may make that huge country easier for the United States and the rest of the world to live with than has been the case since 1945, indeed since 1917.

The basis for change in the Soviet Union is nothing less than the exhaustion of the fundamental precepts of governance—the ways of organizing political, economic, and social life—that have come down to Mikhail Gorbachev and his colleagues from the man who established them a half-century ago, Joseph Stalin. The Stalinist order, as modified after his death, has proved inadequate to cope with the conditions that Gorbachev inherited upon coming to power. The Soviet leadership has recognized its shortcomings. In response they have set in motion changes that, although their aim is to revitalize the Soviet Union itself, carry with them the prospect of a less taxing, less acrimonious rivalry with the United States.

Although the focus of Gorbachev's reforms is internal, they

are likely to affect the Soviet Union's relations with the United States. This is so because the rivalry between the two rests, in part, on the character of the Soviet system. The West, and particularly the United States, objects, among other things, to what the Soviet Union is. To the extent that the Soviet system becomes less objectionable, the rivalry will be less intense.

Already some of the worst human rights abuses have been curbed. Many prisoners of conscience have been released. The use of psychiatric hospitals to imprison and torture dissidents has apparently declined. With the wider, livelier public discussion that the policy of *glasnost* has sanctioned, with the prospect of a modest range of political choice at the lower levels of the system, with the beginnings of legal private economic activity and the effort to introduce the rule of law into relations between citizens and the government, some elements of the civil freedom that is the hallmark of the West are now appearing in the Soviet Union.

The process of reform, it is important to repeat, will not make the Soviet Union a Western country in this century or in the first decades of the next one. Nor will it become as Western as Hungary had turned out to be by the end of the 1980s. But reform can make Soviet society less harsh, the political system less repressive, and the economy less rigid than they have been for fifty years. Reform will not eliminate the differences between the Soviet Union and the United States, but it can make those differences appear more the result of distinctive patterns of historical, cultural evolution and less the product of a concerted effort to construct a world separate from and hostile to the West.

The consequences, in some cases unintended ones, of Gorbachev's changes thus may make the Soviet Union, from the Western point of view, a less forbidding and so less threatening place. The reforms could conceivably, however, have the opposite effect. Gorbachev's aim, after all, is to make the Soviet Union a vibrant, powerful, attractive country. Such a development could worsen the global rivalry by making Moscow better able to pursue the goals that the United States opposes. A more powerful Soviet Union would present a more effective challenge to the United States and the West than can be posed by the crisis-ridden country of today, formidable though it is in military terms. Indeed, Gorbachev's leadership has already made his country a more flexible, dynamic, appealing presence in the world than it has ever been in the postwar period.

His diplomatic skill, however, camouflages the weaknesses of the society over which he presides. And his program of reform will not eliminate them. There is no possibility of his remaking the Soviet Union into a Slavic Japan, or an eastern, multinational Germany. The obstacles his program faces are immense. The most ambitious goal that is realizable by the end of the century is to prevent the gap with the West from widening further. Closing it is out of the question.

Nor would the complete failure of Gorbachev's program necessarily serve Western interests. For the result could be a harsher form of authoritarian rule at home and perhaps more belligerent policies abroad. From the point of view of the United States, therefore, a partial success for the Gorbachev reforms is the best of all possible outcomes—and it happens as well to be the best that it is actually feasible for Gorbachev to attain. The Soviet leader no doubt hopes for much greater success than the United States would welcome; but there is no way to achieve it.

Gorbachev has set in motion a process. The end product that he envisions is a more powerful Soviet Union. The United States does not share his interest in that product, but does have an interest in the process because it has the potential to make the Soviet Union a less forbidding country. That process may also have a direct impact on the foreign policy of the Soviet Union.

THE RETHINKING OF SOVIET FOREIGN POLICY

The very existence of an ambitious program of domestic reform will moderate Soviet policies abroad. Internal matters will preoccupy the leadership. The reconstruction of society, Gorbachev has made clear, must take precedence over any and all international goals. He is convinced that his country needs a calm international environment in order to concentrate on that reconstruction, and this is the major reason for his vigorous pursuit of détente with the United States as well as of better relations with China.

The policy of *glasnost* bears on Soviet foreign policy, and therefore on Soviet-American relations as well. Within the country, discussion about foreign policy still is more restricted than it is on internal Soviet affairs, but it has begun. Public criticism of Soviet policy in Afghanistan has appeared. Several prominent academicians have questioned the military strategy of the Warsaw Pact forces in Europe. If and as debate on these and related issues broadens, and if this helps to change Soviet policies, the global rivalry will become less acrimonious.

Foreign policy itself has started to change. Some minor and tentative but nonetheless significant signs can be detected of a full-scale challenge to the established methods of dealing with other countries. Those methods have come down to Gorbachev and his associates from the Stalinist period, although their roots reach far back into the tsarist past. Soviet foreign policy has rested on three basic precepts. Each is firmly embedded in the Russian and Soviet experience, and each has in fact been vindicated by much of that experience, including the postwar history of the Soviet Union. In the late 1970s, however, each began to seem not only not to advance but actually to undercut the interests of the Soviet Union. Since Gorbachev came to power, there is evidence that each is being reconsidered.

The first of these basic precepts is the imperative to control territory. It is an axiom that the tsars followed faithfully, as the kingdom of Muscovy expanded to encompass huge chunks of Europe and Asia. Whatever they conquered they ruled directly.

In the wake of their victory in the Civil War, the Bolsheviks reclaimed much of the territory the tsars had acquired. In the aftermath of World War II, they added more of the former tsarist possessions and also parts of Eastern Europe the Romanovs had never dominated. Moscow did not annex Poland, Czechoslovakia, and Hungary directly, although under Stalin these countries were governed as if they were republics of the Soviet Union. But the Soviet Union followed the principle of territorial control all the same. The Red Army was stationed throughout the region and in the Soviet western military districts, standing ready to move wherever needed to guarantee the continuation of communist rule.

In the 1950s and 1960s, Moscow tried to extend its influence abroad without Soviet troops, by establishing friendly relations with nationalist leaders in the Third World. The results were disappointing. When, therefore, in the 1970s the Soviets launched another effort at expanding their influence in Africa and Asia, they relied on more familiar methods. They sent troops to Afghanistan and sponsored the dispatch of Cuban military forces to Africa. Instead of relying on the friendship of non-communist leaders in these countries they encouraged, to the extent possible, the creation of Soviet-style regimes, with ruling Parties enjoying a monopoly of power, state ownership, and management of the economy, and most of all the familiar security apparatus. Of these pro-Soviet regimes perhaps only Ethiopia could qualify, by the end of the 1980s, as a genuinely communist regime. Nonetheless, during this period the emphasis of Soviet policy plainly shifted from cultivating influence to exercising control.

The result of Russian and Soviet fidelity to this first precept of international policy is visible on any map of Europe and Asia. By following it, the Soviet Union attained its present size and acquired its current empire. But the policy of trying to exert control wherever possible has drawbacks, which became increasingly apparent in the 1970s and 1980s. The people of Eastern Europe, never enthusiastic citizens of the Soviet orbit, grew increasingly restive. In Poland, the largest and strategically the most important Soviet satellite, a huge national grassroots anti-Soviet movement of the working class appeared, the free trade union Solidarity. National liberation movements, once a favored Soviet weapon for attacking pro-Western regimes in the Third World, arose to challenge governments aligned with the Soviet Union in Afghanistan, Angola, and Nicaragua. Soviet ties to client states also weighed on relations with other countries. The occupation of Afghanistan alienated much of the Islamic world. Its sponsorship of Cuba made Moscow suspect in Latin America. Its alliance with Vietnam prevented cordial relations with the rest of Southeast Asia and with China.

The European empire became expensive. The abrupt rise in the price of oil in the 1970s, while the Soviet Union, an oil exporter, was supplying petroleum to its satellites at much lower cost, meant that Moscow was providing a healthy subsidy to these countries. Similarly, the pro-Soviet governments of Cuba, Vietnam, Angola, and Mozambique required subventions of one kind or another. To be sure, the purpose of the Soviet empire had never been economic gain. Still, as the economic and political costs of having them rose, the string of clients beyond its borders that the regime had collected by the tried-and-true method of imposing direct Soviet or at least communist control began to appear less and less attractive.

The changes that this growing disenchantment with empire have produced are thus far modest. But the leadership has openly expressed displeasure with Vietnam for wasting its money, and with Syria (a country that is not controlled by Moscow or its proxies), for political inflexibility and adventurism. Articles in official journals have questioned the value of the clients that the Soviet Union has acquired and have proposed improving relations with large, important Third World countries in which there is no chance that communist parties will come to power, countries like Brazil, Mexico, Indonesia, and Nigeria. In the 1980s the Soviet Union had good relations with only one such country—India.

Although Gorbachev shows no sign of being willing to abandon the clients acquired in the 1970s, let alone the Eastern European empire, the Soviet appetite for bringing more countries into its sphere by conquest and control is plainly muted.

The second precept by which Russian and Soviet foreign policy has steered is the imperative of amassing as much military force as possible. For a country with no natural frontiers, which had to be ready constantly to defend its borders and that was, as well, by the terms of its first guiding precept, constantly seeking to expand its reach, the impulse to be as strong as possible in military terms came as second nature. It scarcely needed to be stated and was certainly not a subject for debate. This impulse was not unknown to other countries with less relentlessly expansionist histories. It is the kind of behavior that membership in the international system, in which states have to protect themselves, encourages.

Moreover, the Russian state and its Soviet successor consistently lagged behind the Western powers in military technology. The quality of the Russian army was almost always inferior to that of its neighbors and potential adversaries. Russia, and later the Soviet Union, had to compensate with superior numbers. All apart from expanding, the task of sustaining a balance of power with the rest of the world and so defending the motherland depended on accumulating large armed forces. This has been especially true in the postwar period, for much of which the United States has enjoyed a substantial and, to Moscow, threatening advantage in nuclear weaponry.

Most of the history of the Soviet period is a testimony to the wisdom of this second precept. Having been defeated by Germany in World War I, Russia, in the form of the Soviet Union, overcame the Germans, at great cost, in the war of 1941–45. After the war, again at considerable expense, the Soviet Union succeeded in matching the military might, including the nuclear weapons, of the Western coalition, led by the United States. Soviet military power secured the country itself, its wartime gains in Europe, and its postwar acquisitions beyond the European continent.

The open-ended accumulation of military force seemed all the more important at the end of the 1960s, when relations with China deteriorated sharply, leading to armed clashes on a small scale. The Soviet general staff had to cope with the prospect of a two-front war, against NATO in the west and China in the east.

In the late 1980s, however, this second precept, like the first, has begun to appear something other than a formula for unambiguous international success. The military buildup, especially in nuclear weapons, reached the point of diminishing political returns. Having attained military parity with the United

States, it began to be apparent to the Soviet leaders that they had no hope of achieving military superiority over their rival. Brezhnev and his colleagues had believed that when the Soviet Union became the military equal of the United States it could expect to exercise comparable political influence throughout the world. This did not happen. Instead, the limits to the gains that military force could bring, and the handicaps that a stagnant economy and an obsolete ideology imposed on the Soviet quest for international influence, became increasingly clear.

The accumulation of more and more armaments not only was not necessarily an asset for the Soviet Union, it turned out to be a liability. It acted as a drain on the economy. With a substantial fraction of the gross domestic output—perhaps as much as 20 percent—going to military uses, and with the best scientists, technicians, workers, and machines assigned to the military sector, the civilian economy suffered. Gorbachev made clear his belief that the emphasis on military production was one of the reasons for the economic backwardness of the Soviet Union, and not the least important reason.

In addition, the continual accumulation of military hardware provoked a reaction from the West. The Soviet buildup alarmed the United States. It helped to trigger, in the early 1980s, the largest peacetime increase in defense expenditures in American history. Moscow began to understand that the perpetuation and acceleration of the arms competition had something to do with its own policies, and that its continuation did not necessarily serve Soviet interests.

The signs that the second precept of Soviet foreign policy is being rethought, and perhaps modified, are abundant. The general secretary's rhetoric suggests such changes. In place of Leonid Brezhnev's favorite slogan, "Equal security," which denotes the Soviet drive for military and political equality with the United States in all aspects of international relations, Gorbachev and other spokesmen use the term "common security," which expresses the recognition that the security of each country depends on the policies of the other, and that neither can be secure in the nuclear age at the expense of the other. Indeed, Gorbachev has explicitly said so.

Revised attitudes toward the second fundamental precept of Soviet foreign policy have also been evident in the arms control proposals that the Soviet Union has made to the United States since Gorbachev came to power. There have been many more than in the past. While some rehashed familiar positions, others have broken new ground. The Soviet side has been more interested in concluding agreements, more agreeable to giving up its own armaments to achieve them, and more willing to enter into arrangements for verifying compliance with them since 1985 than was the case in previous years. The new Soviet approach made possible the treaty eliminating intermediate-range nuclear forces that the two countries signed at the Washington summit in December 1987.

The third basic feature of Soviet foreign relations is the practice of economic autarky. The Soviet Union, with its satellites, has been a more or less self-contained economic order, with few ties to the rest of the world.

Russia had always stood apart from the rest of Europe. Under the tsars the same aversion to foreigners that thrived under Stalin was widespread. Once it was clear that revolution was not going to sweep through Europe, the regime sought to create a society free of the corrupting taint of the capitalism practiced beyond Russia's borders.

To be sure, neither Russia nor the Soviet Union has ever been entirely cut off from the rest of Europe and the world. Toward the end of tsarist rule foreign investment in the country was appreciable. On several occasions the Soviet government decided that an economic opening to the West would serve its interests. In the period of the New Economic Policy in the 1920s, trade increased and Westerners made capital investments in Russia. During the war, Lend-Lease shipments of war matériel were crucial to the Soviet Union's survival and ultimate victory over Germany. In the 1970s, during the first period of détente, the regime once again invited foreign capitalists to build factories in the Soviet Union, such as the Fiat automobile plant in Togliatti, a city named for the former leader of the Italian Communist Party. Still, for most of its history the Soviet economy was more or less self-contained. Once Stalinist

economic practices became established, to the political reluctance to become entangled with world capitalism were added
more strictly economic obstacles created by the sharp differences between the liberal and the communist economic orders.
It was difficult for trade and investment to take place even
when political leaders on both sides desired it.

The Soviet version of autarky was at first a successful economic policy. The Soviet Union became an industrialized country with only episodic assistance from the rest of the world. The
economic gap with the West narrowed steadily. In the early
1960s Nikita Khrushchev could boast that the Soviet Union
would soon overtake its capitalist rivals. In the 1970s that no
longer seemed imminent and by the 1980s the gap between the
communist and the capitalist worlds was growing. Autarky was
one of the reasons. The Soviet economy stagnated for want of
the stimulus that foreign competition could provide. The failure to master the production and assimilation of high technology, especially computers, was due in large measure to the
organization of the economy and the political restrictions imposed on society; but the country would have done better with
greater exposure to, and thus greater opportunity to learn
from, the economies that made and used those machines.

There are signs that Gorbachev is not as fully committed to
economic autarky as his predecessors. He has promulgated a
new law on joint ventures, which offers the opportunity for
foreigners to make equity investments in the Soviet Union, to
own 49 percent of the resulting enterprise, and to exercise a
degree of managerial control over them. Gorbachev is person-
ally enthusiastic about attracting foreign investment. He has
frequently met with Western businessmen in Moscow and held
a special meeting with American business leaders during the
Washington summit.

As it happens, the role his program of economic reform envisions for foreign investment and international trade is more
modest than the grandiose—and, as it turned out, wildly unrealistic—hopes Brezhnev and his colleagues held for the expansion of economic ties with the West during the 1970s. The
potential for expanding such ties in the Gorbachev period is,

however, ultimately greater now than it was then. For Gorbachev is presiding, as Brezhnev emphatically was not, over what he hopes will be a sweeping reform of the Soviet economic system. The reform, if it takes hold, will make the Soviet economy more compatible with those of the West, and so reduce the economic obstacles to trade and investment between the capitalist and communist worlds.

As with the reform of Soviet society, changes in the basic directions of foreign policy have just begun, and are not guaranteed to continue. To the extent that these changes are sustained, and do continue along the lines that Gorbachev has charted, they make the present moment a better opportunity for composing some of the differences between the United States and the Soviet Union than the occasions in the past when American hopes for an end to the Cold War rose, only to be disappointed. Unlike previous occasions, the Soviet Union is not seeking to catch up with the West in military terms. By the 1980s it had caught up but had ruled out, or at least set aside temporarily, the aspiration to surpass the Western coalition militarily. Unlike in the 1970s, the Soviet leaders do not presently aspire to expand their influence abroad. Gorbachev and his colleagues are much less sanguine about the prospects of acquiring more power and influence through traditional Soviet methods than was the Brezhnev generation. Indeed, they are concerned about revitalizing the domestic basis of Soviet power so as to avoid losing what they already possess.

The United States has made several important contributions to the leadership's desire for change. It has been America that has offset the increases in Soviet military might with an arms buildup of its own, thereby helping to persuade Moscow that further accumulation of hardware is not likely to yield political payoffs. The United States has given assistance to opponents of Soviet-sponsored regimes in Afghanistan, Angola, and Nicaragua, raising the costs of empire to Moscow. Most important, the United States has served as the anchor of a dynamic, liberal, international economic order that, despite its difficulties, has so decisively outpaced the communist system that the Soviet authorities have felt compelled to introduce reforms to try to catch up.

Still, the United States is not entirely the beneficiary of the Soviet Union's travails. Some of the trends that have subverted the traditional precepts of Soviet politics, economics, and foreign policy have reduced American power as well. If the Soviet Union is a less formidable presence in the international arena than it once was, or at least than its leaders wish it to be, this is also true of the United States, and for some of the same reasons.

Third World countries have resisted American as well as Soviet efforts to influence the way they govern themselves. Before Afghanistan there was Vietnam. The same global economic trends that have left the Soviet Union far behind have weakened the American position. Formidable economic competitors have arisen in Western Europe and East Asia. The United States no longer dominates the international economy as it did from the 1940s to the 1960s. It is further burdened by imbalances between the commitments it has made and the resources that are available to carry them out, an imbalance that found expression, in the 1980s, in a growing federal deficit.

The Soviet Union discovered, in the 1980s, that the effort to sustain a huge military establishment and a far-flung empire was draining the economic strength on which its foreign policies ultimately had to rest. The United States, too, suffered from what the historian Paul Kennedy has called "imperial overstretch." Moscow felt the pinch, for example, of providing aid on a large scale to Vietnam; Washington had difficulty in finding the resources to support Corazon Aquino's newly democratic government in the Philippines.

If both global rivals have experienced difficulty in playing their postwar roles as great powers, however, the Soviet difficulties are much more acute and, from the Soviet point of view, considerably more dangerous. For the United States, but not for the Soviet Union, the principal economic competitors are also political allies. These allies could, and did, assume political responsibilities that the United States could not carry out. France, for instance, has long been the dominant Western presence in West Africa. In the 1980s the Federal Republic of Germany began to play an important economic role in Southern and Eastern Europe. Japan has supplanted the United States as the principal donor of economic aid to Southeast Asia. By contrast, no country other than the Soviet Union is prepared to finance Fidel Castro's regime in Cuba or to police Poland.

Just as important, the competitors of the United States share the American commitment to a liberal economic order. The rising powers of Western Europe and East Asia are, by and large, capitalist democracies. They have prospered through the practices that the United States has been trying, for four decades, to spread around the world. Soviet political and economic institutions and procedures, by contrast, are causes of Soviet failures.

Others' successes may reduce the power at Washington's disposal, but they advance the principles to which the United States is committed. This is not at all the case for the Soviet Union. The relative American decline is, in this sense, a victory for liberal principles; the decline of the Soviet Union is a defeat for communist ones.

The Soviet Union is not resigning from its role as a great power. If anything, Gorbachev and his colleagues are more ambitious for power and influence than their predecessors. Having inherited a country that is a military giant but an economic weakling, they seek to make it a "full-service" superpower with an international presence equal to that of the United States in all respects. It is that ambition, and the fear that even what has already been achieved is in jeopardy because of economic stagnation and technological backwardness, that motivates the Soviet elite. The aspiration to play a great role in the world is one of the driving forces behind the reforms.

It is precisely this aspiration that has brought the Soviet Union into conflict with the United States since 1945. Its persistence is not, therefore, necessarily a good sign for the moderation of the rivalry. But in order to pursue that aspiration over the long term, Gorbachev and his colleagues seem prepared to conduct a more restrained, less belligerent foreign policy in the short term. It must be the hope of the West that policies of restraint, moderation, and cooperation undertaken for tactical purposes will become established as more fundamental expressions of the Soviet Union's conception of its role in the world. It is the hope of the West, as well, that reform within the Soviet Union will lead to a gradual redefinition of the nature of the influence to which the Soviet Union aspires, to bring it more into line with what is acceptable to other countries.

THE FUTURE OF THE MILITARY COMPETITION

Changes in Soviet foreign policy, of the sort that would be acceptable, indeed welcome, in the West, are possible. They are in fact already occurring. How far will they go? The question is more than an academic one. For where the global rivals are directly engaged, the United States has some capacity to shape the evolution of Soviet policy—and vice versa. The most important of the issues on which each side has some influence over the other are military ones. The United States and the Soviet Union negotiate directly on the structure of their armed forces. Negotiations cover nuclear armaments, on which several major treaties have been signed, and the no less important, although less publicly visible, nonnuclear or "conventional" weapons as well.

The size and the composition of these forces are determined principally by unilateral decisions on both sides. Neither the United States nor the Soviet Union shapes its army, navy, and air force to suit the wishes of the other. Moreover the geographic and political determinants of the two forces differ. The United States places greater emphasis on naval power than the Soviet Union, separated as it is from its principal allies by the Atlantic Ocean. The Soviet Union must prepare to face two formidable adversaries—NATO and China—while the U.S. confronts only the Soviet Union. But negotiations—on nuclear and nonnuclear forces—do give each country the opportunity to exert some modest influence on the armed forces of the other.

In these negotiations there is a feasible goal at which American military policy has intermittently aimed. This is an end point, progress toward which can serve as a standard for evaluating proposals and agreements on the control of armaments. This end point is a defensive orientation on both sides.

In general, and with notable exceptions such as naval forces, the United States has developed and deployed nuclear and conventional armaments to defend rather than to attack. Soviet forces have generally, although not always, had a more offensive cast. If both sides were devoted exclusively to defense, if neither had the means to launch an attack, war would be even less likely than it is now. An extremely stable balance of military power between the two coalitions would exist.

For nuclear weapons, the balance is stable when neither side can hope to launch an attack that would deprive the other of the capacity to retaliate, known as "assured destruction." When both sides possess it, when there is mutual assured destruction—often abbreviated by the grim acronym MAD—the nuclear balance is stable. Assured destruction is not, to be sure, a purely defensive military posture; but when the capacity is mutual the result is a purely defensive one. It discourages attack, not by proposing to ward off that attack but by promising to retaliate in decisive fashion in response to it.

The chief American strategic concern since the beginning of the 1970s has been the Soviet capacity to destroy part—although not all—of the American nuclear retaliatory force. Successive American administrations have worried about the political disadvantages to the West that this imbalance might create, and have tried to correct it through negotiations.

During the Brezhnev period, the Soviet Union was unwilling to conclude agreements that relieved this threat to American land-based nuclear forces. The Gorbachev regime has been much more forthcoming on this subject. The strategic arms reduction agreement that began to emerge in 1988 went some distance toward striking a stable balance between the two main nuclear arsenals.

The goal of nuclear stability through mutual assured destruction, it should be noted, is not compatible with three aims that enjoyed particular prominence in American strategic policy—or at least President Reagan's rhetoric about that policy —in the 1980s. The first is the abolition of all nuclear weapons. This is a goal that both the American president and the Soviet general secretary have embraced, although in different ways. Reagan has sought to abolish all offensive nuclear weapons; Gorbachev to eliminate all such weapons of any description. Abolition is simply not feasible. Nuclear weapons cannot be disinvented; and to remove all incentives for states to have them would require dispelling all the reasons for mutual suspicion. That, in turn, would require eliminating the circumstances in which states can attack each other. It would mean a world government to enforce order among sovereign states, a development far beyond the realm of current possibility.

Stability through mutual assured destruction is also incompatible with the deployment of full-scale defenses against nuclear attack, of the kind that President Reagan's Strategic Defense Initiative (SDI) is supposed to develop. The SDI's goal is one with which it is difficult to disagree: the protection of the continental United States against nuclear attack. This is, moreover, a defensive goal. And if both sides had foolproof systems of defense, nuclear stability would truly rest on mutual defense—that is, on mutual assured *protection* rather than on the guaranteed threat of annihilation, mutual assured destruction.

Unfortunately, perfect defense is not technically feasible. Each side has so many nuclear weapons—both have more than 10,000 separate explosives—that neither could hope to protect itself completely in a full-scale attack by the other no matter how sophisticated and extensive its systems of defense. A few bombs, at least, would get through any such system. Each nuclear weapon is so powerful that those few bombs would cause enormous, unprecedented destruction.

The two sides could move from mutual destruction to mutual protection only by cooperative measures. Thus far, however, the Soviet Union has refused to contemplate such an approach. Moscow has denounced SDI as an American effort to upset the nuclear balance and achieve nuclear superiority over the Soviet Union, and has vowed to take measures to defeat any

space-based defenses that the United States may deploy. Over
the coming decades the Soviet leadership may change its mind.
The two sides may begin to explore ways to provide themselves
with defenses against nuclear attack—by third countries if not
by each other—in cooperative fashion. Unless and until the
commitment to defense is mutual, however, MAD will remain
the only available basis for nuclear stability.

The third aim of the Reagan administration that is not entirely compatible with the goal of constructing stability in the
nuclear balance is substantial reductions in the levels of offensive nuclear forces on both sides. The American public evidently shares President Reagan's enthusiasm for such "deep
cuts." High force levels, however, make it easier for both sides
to feel comfortable with the nuclear balance. The more weapons each side possesses, the less worried each will be about
differences, inequalities, and possible changes in the composi-
tions of its arsenals.

High force levels also set the global rivals apart from Britain,
France, and China, which all have smaller nuclear forces. The
further the two reduce their own stockpiles, the closer they will
come to nuclear equality with the other three, a development
that the Soviet Union, at least, against whose territory French,
British, and Chinese nuclear weapons are targeted, can be expected to resist. In the years ahead, therefore, no matter how
dramatically political relations between the United States and
the Soviet Union improve, no matter how strong the Soviet
commitment to nuclear equilibrium becomes, there will be limits to the reductions in their nuclear forces that they will be
willing to make.

As nuclear arms control proceeds, the negotiations on nonnuclear weaponry in Europe will grow in importance. With fewer
nuclear weapons, nonnuclear armaments will play a greater
role in protecting Europe. In conventional forces the Warsaw
Pact is widely thought to have an advantage over NATO. That
advantage is likely to loom ever larger in Western military
calculations, and give rise to efforts to address it—by negotiations if possible, by additional Western military deployments if
necessary.

Conventional forces are likely to attract increasing attention from both the Soviet and the American governments as well because they are costly. It is considerably more expensive to develop, deploy, and maintain the tanks, troops, and airplanes that are poised to wage a nonnuclear conflict on the European continent than it has been to acquire nuclear arsenals. Reducing those conventional forces offers the prospect of saving money, which both great powers are likely to find increasingly attractive.

For negotiations on conventional armaments, as with nuclear weapons, the ultimate goal is stability through mutual defense. The goal will be harder to achieve for nonnuclear forces, however. Precisely because the Soviet Union does enjoy an advantage, arranging an even balance will require the sacrifice of more forces by the East than by the West. The problem is further complicated by the fact that the Soviet high command will insist on retaining forces large enough to cope with both NATO and China. By contrast, the two sides came to the nuclear arms talks with roughly equal forces. Furthermore, the differences between offensive and defensive forces are not as clear-cut with conventional as with nuclear weapons. Whether an army is poised for attack or devoted to defense depends not only on what weapons it has but also on how many there are, how they are deployed, and the manner in which its forces are trained and exercised. All this is complicated. Agreements will not be easy to reach.

Moreover, while nuclear arms control accords have covered a handful of weapons that could be easily counted, conventional arms control will have to encompass thousands of troops and weapons that cannot be monitored with the same confidence. In addition, the nuclear arms talks have concerned the United States and the Soviet Union and those two countries alone. The weapons at issue belong to them. The weapons and the soldiers that will be the subjects of conventional arms talks, by contrast, are provided by all of the members of the two military blocs. Each will therefore have to be included in the negotiations. The members of the Warsaw Pact may or may not follow Moscow's lead obediently; the European members of

NATO will certainly assert their independence of the United States on a variety of issues.

Still, Gorbachev has expressed interest in giving new life to the negotiations on conventional forces, which have dragged on inconclusively since the early 1970s, and has hinted at a willingness to give up more forces than the West does as part of such an agreement. With conventional forces, therefore, as with nuclear weapons, the possibility now exists for, in effect, ending the arms race. It is at least conceivable now, as it certainly was not for the first four decades of the global rivalry, that the two sides will, in the years ahead, enter into agreements to promote stability through the common possession of military forces whose main purpose is defensive. With such agreements, both would retain large military establishments but each would be confident that the other had no imminent intention of using them to try to make political gains, and neither would feel particularly compelled to add to its forces.

POLITICAL ACCOMMODATION

The military competition between the United States and the Soviet Union is an outgrowth of the global rivalry and an irritant to it. Arms are not, however, the fundamental causes of the rivalry; the political differences between the two powers are. It is these that must be addressed in order to improve the relationship between them.

The geopolitical conflict can, for the sake of convenience, be divided into three main theaters: East Asia, the Third World, and Europe. In all three the principal requirement for conciliation is a change in Soviet policy, involving concessions, accommodation, and even withdrawal. Such measures are seldom easy for any government and have never come easily to the Soviet Union. Still, in the Third World and in Europe, although not in the same way in East Asia, the Gorbachev foreign policy offers the hope—although not the certainty—of more substantial improvement in relations between the two countries than at any time since the conflict began.

The Far East might seem a promising place for the Gorbachev regime to adopt conciliatory policies. The Soviet Union is at odds with the two most important countries there, Japan and China. Each has a specific issue or set of issues that it demands Moscow address as a precondition of normal relations.

Japan demands the return of the four southern islands of the Kurile chain, which it calls its "northern territories." China insists that the Soviet Union leave Afghanistan, that Moscow's ally, Vietnam, quit Kampuchea, and that Soviet forces on China's border be reduced. It is possible that the Soviet Union will go some way toward meeting some—conceivably even all —of these demands over the next decade. A dramatic change in Moscow's relations with either Japan or China is not, however, likely.

There is now a rough balance in the strategic quadrangle that includes these three countries and the United States. There is a very loose alignment among Washington, Beijing, and Tokyo against Moscow. The alignment serves as an effective check on Soviet expansionism. But it is loose enough so that it does not constitute a pressing threat to the Soviet Union. A dramatic change in Soviet relations with either of the Asian powers could upset that balance, with unpredictable consequences for each of the four powers. The risks of such a shift are likely to outweigh the potential gains for both China and Japan. Relations between the Soviet Union and the two of them are likely to improve gradually; indeed they have already done so since Gorbachev came to power. Sweeping changes are unlikely, and would not necessarily serve the interests of the United States.

Soviet-American relations have been most difficult over the past two decades in the Third World. It is there that Soviet policies have annoyed, indeed alarmed, the United States. The recurrent friction in Africa, Asia, and Latin America has inspired efforts to devise a code of conduct for bilateral relations in these regions. The conflicts in the Third World have also inspired proposals for active cooperation to resolve political disputes into which the two might be drawn on opposite sides. Throughout the 1970s the Soviet leaders were attracted to the idea of establishing a kind of "condominium" with the United States to manage the international system; this fit in with their drive for full political equality with the other superpower.

Neither is a promising way of composing the two countries' differences outside Europe. Any rules of conduct to which they might subscribe would either be too vague to be meaningful—such as a commitment to behave "prudently"—or too specific to be acceptable—like a division of the world into officially delineated spheres of influence. Formal rules are also, in a sense, superfluous. The two sides have been extremely cautious in their dealings with each other. The prudence that has been the hallmark of their relations has required no written constitution.

As for cooperation, the differences between the two rivals exist because their interests are opposed in most regions of the world. They have taken opposite sides in the Middle East, in Central America, and in Southeast Asia. Prudence dictates that neither allow these regional differences to engulf it in a nuclear war with the other; nor, however, is either side likely to give up its support for a client or ally for the sake of good relations with the other.

There is another reason that the two superpowers are unlikely to be able to cooperate to settle regional conflicts. The control each can exercise over the main parties to these conflicts has steadily diminished, and will no doubt continue to do so. It is precisely this trend, however, that is the basis for believing that Third World conflicts will have a less disruptive effect on Soviet-American relations in the future. Because each great power can do less, each will attempt less, and the two will therefore not be so prone to come into conflict with one another.

Vietnam for the United States and Afghanistan for the Soviet Union were defeats. Each failed to prevail over a stubborn Third World country. The experience of Vietnam made the United States more wary of committing military forces outside Europe; the outcome of its war in Afghanistan is likely to have a similar effect on the Soviet Union. This common reluctance to become involved in such conflicts will limit the opportunities for friction.

If one lesson that the United States learned from Vietnam was that victory was not available at what Americans considered a reasonable price, another was that the consequences of defeat were less catastrophic than had been feared. Indeed, the consequences for American interests of the loss of Indochina to communists, while not favorable, have been modest. The United States therefore emerged from the Vietnam war with not only a lower estimate of its own capacity to determine the outcome of Third World conflicts but also with a much lower estimate of the need to do so. Political conflicts in the Third World became less salient. The trauma of Afghanistan and the disappointing performance of Soviet clients in the Third World in the 1980s have made the Soviet model of political and economic organization appear less and less suitable for export. If Moscow decides that this does not threaten the basic purposes of the state, the effect will be to reinforce the tendency to pass up the opportunities for engagement outside Europe.

Whatever happens in Europe itself the two military blocs will not dissolve. The idea of a single undivided European community free of the military forces and the political tutelage of the two great non-European nuclear powers may well become an increasingly attractive aspiration for the people in both parts of the Continent, but it will not become a reality. The Soviet Union will not release its grip on its East European satellites, nor will the West be powerful enough to break that grip by force.

The military deployments in the two Europes may, however, be somewhat reduced in size, and the fate of the arms control negotiations will certainly affect the political climate on the Continent.

Although the division of Europe will not disappear, the breach in the wall separating east from west is likely to continue to widen. The proliferation of contacts—social, cultural, and economic—between liberal and communist Europe that has taken place since 1953 and that accelerated during the détente of the 1970s will likely gain momentum in the future. So, too, will the pace of economic reform—with important differences among the various countries of the region. But it remains very much to be seen whether the expansion of contacts, the acceleration of reform, and such economic assistance from the West as may be available will suffice to forestall anti-Soviet explosions, which would set back reform in the Soviet Union and chill Soviet-American relations.

To affect the global rivalry the new approach to the Third World and to Europe must shape Soviet policies toward particular countries. Afghanistan and Poland each offers a test of the Soviet capacity to conciliate neighboring countries by putting an end to policies that have poisoned relations for decades, sometimes for generations and even centuries. Each country is important not only in and of itself but also as the representative of a class of countries with grievances against the Soviet Union, grievances that in turn affect Soviet relations with the United States.

Afghanistan qualified as the most pressing problem of foreign policy that Gorbachev inherited upon assuming power. In his speech to the Twenty-sixth Party Congress in February 1986, he called the war there "an open wound." In 1988, the signs multiplied that the Soviet Union was prepared to pull its troops out of the country completely, even if that meant—as it surely would—that the Soviet-sponsored regime would fall, to be replaced by a government dominated by forces that had fought the Russians since the invasion.

Although poor and backward, Afghanistan is an important country for the Soviet Union; the decision to leave it is therefore a momentous one, and a sign of serious change in Soviet foreign policy. Soviet involvement there is often compared with the American role in Vietnam. The differences, however, make Afghanistan much more consequential for the Soviets than Vietnam was for the United States. Vietnam is distant from North America; Afghanistan is situated on the Soviet border. It is a place where militant Islam is a potent political force, an important consideration for the rulers of a country that harbors over 40 million Muslims who are susceptible to its political appeal, and that already has one aggressively Islamic state—Iran—on its southern border.

Afghanistan is also important to the Soviet Union because of the major investment in blood and treasure that has been made there since 1979. Fifteen thousand Soviet soldiers are estimated to have died there. The greater the costs that have already been sunk in a policy, the more difficult it is for any country to abandon that policy unless forced to do so. The Soviet Union has not been forced out of Afghanistan. It could have stayed, if it were determined to do so, for decades.

Afghanistan, finally, represents the application of the Brezhnev Doctrine, according to which once a country has a communist government that government must remain in power at all costs. The Soviet leadership invented this doctrine to justify the invasion of Czechoslovakia in 1968. It was a declaration that communist gains were irreversible. In Afghanistan, if the Soviet Union does withdraw, a gain will be reversed. A Soviet-style regime, which was once kept in power, like those in Eastern Europe, by Soviet bayonets, tanks, and helicopters, will fall. The collapse of the Afghan regime will hardly be encouraging to other communists whose rule depends on Soviet military support. Moscow's willingness to risk their anxiety in order to cut its losses and remove significant obstacles to the improvement of its relations with the Third World and the West would suggest a genuine change in the way that it calculates its interests.

If Afghanistan is an important country for the Soviet Union, Poland is still more important. It is the largest nation in Eastern Europe and the keystone of the Soviet empire there. It is the place where the global rivalry began. Poland remains the first and in many ways the foremost victim of the Cold War. A change in its status would have an enormous impact on the Soviet Union's standing in Europe and the world and its relations with the United States.

The change that would be acceptable to the Poles is in one sense easy for Moscow. All it has to do is leave the Poles free to work out their own destiny. The result would not be the communist system that exists, in an enfeebled form, in Poland today. But to permit Poland to determine its own destiny would be extraordinarily difficult for even Mikhail Gorbachev.

To abandon communism in Afghanistan is to call into question the Brezhnev Doctrine. To abandon communism in Poland would have serious consequences for the Party's rule in Russia. It would undermine the greatest single international achievement of the Soviet state, which in turn serves as the basis for its claim to universal validity and historical inevitability. Even so determined a reformer as Gorbachev is unlikely to permit the kinds of arrangements in Poland that the Poles themselves would find wholly satisfactory.

Nonetheless, the elements of such arrangements are not difficult to sketch. They would re-create, with some modifications, the relationship between the Soviet Union and Finland. Poland would pursue no course in foreign policy that would jeopardize the security of its neighbor to the east. If Soviet troops continued to be stationed on Polish soil, their mission would be to resist an attack from the West, not, as is now the case, to enforce an unwanted political and economic regime on the Poles. The people of Poland would be free, as are the Finns, to govern themselves and organize their economy however they desired. There is little doubt that, like the Finns, they would opt for liberal rather than communist forms.

If they were allowed to do so, this would remove the largest cause of the global rivalry. The United States is in Europe to protect Western Europe against Soviet aggression. Soviet aggression against Western Europe seems possible precisely because it has already occurred against *Eastern* Europe. The reversal of Stalin's policies through the "Finlandization" of Poland would make the Soviet threat seem considerably less menacing.

This will hardly take place overnight. But it is possible that the Soviet Union will eventually come to make a distinction, as it does not at present, between the requirements for its security and the internal governance of the countries of Eastern Europe. They may ultimately conclude that their interest in Eastern Europe is in preventing the governments of the region from carrying out foreign policies hostile to the Soviet Union, but that this need not require that those governments be communist ones.

The movement toward the independence of Eastern Europe,

or more precisely the evolution of regimes there that are acceptable to the people whom they govern as well as to Moscow, will be a long, slow process—if it occurs at all. If it does happen, nothing will do more to moderate the Soviet-American rivalry.

THE END OF ARMS CONTROL

The next decade may see more cordial, less conflict-ridden relations between the United States and the Soviet Union than these two great powers have enjoyed since the beginning of their global rivalry. What would a new relationship between them look like? One way of expressing it is as an end to the central place in Soviet-American relations of what may be called the arms control paradigm.

The dominant role of the arms control negotiations was scarcely intended when the negotiations began, at the outset of the 1970s. Then the two sides had modest expectations for them. They were designed simply to make adjustments in the nuclear balance at the margin; that, in fact, is what the arms treaties that have been concluded have accomplished.

But the negotiations came to play a central political role in the rivalry. Their status became a barometer of the relationship: when agreement seemed imminent, this heralded a warming trend; when the positions of the two sides were far apart this was taken as evidence that they were at odds politically. The negotiations also affected the political relationship. A successfully concluded treaty became a cause of more cordial ties.

Arms control has been important because nuclear weapons are important. They are visible, powerful symbols of the Soviet-American rivalry. Arms control has been crucial as well because the nuclear competition has turned out to be the one area where agreement between the two has been possible, where common ground has existed. They could agree on modest limits to their nuclear arsenals but not on solutions to the political conflicts that divided them. Thus better relations between the United States and the Soviet Union came to depend upon arms control.

Arms control has had several basic features: it has involved direct, bilateral negotiations between the United States and the Soviet Union; it has concerned military issues; its goal has been specific agreements, covering nuclear weapons, on the basis of equality. In the next phase of Soviet-American relations, improvement may be measured by the extent to which these elements are missing.

Treaties on conventional armaments will lack the last two features. Not only will they not cover nuclear weapons, they will not affect the two sides equally. The Soviet Union will give up more than the United States. Conventional forces may also be reduced without benefit of formal negotiations, through the unilateral reconstruction of each of the two military establishments. Nikita Khrushchev tried to thin out Soviet ground forces in Europe in the late 1950s. It is possible that Mikhail Gorbachev will seek to follow his example, without even seeking reciprocal measures from the United States.

More important, the focus of the rivalry may shift away from military matters. Hubert Humphrey was once asked what had happened to the liberal social and political agenda to which he and other Americans had been devoted in the 1950s and 1960s. "We passed it," he replied. It may someday be appropriate to say the same thing about the arms control agenda. There is, at least, a logical goal for the negotiations on both nuclear and nonnuclear weapons: equilibrium through a common orientation to defense. It is conceivable that the negotiations over the next ten to twenty years could establish military equilibrium between the two sides, thereby making further negotiations unnecessary.

The military conflict, it bears repeating once more, is not the heart of the global rivalry. The Soviet Union and the United States are in conflict over political issues. The advent of Gorbachev holds out the hope that these political differences, which have been intractable since the Cold War began, may at last be susceptible to resolution. The most important political disputes, however, are not between the Soviet Union and the United States but between the Soviet Union and a whole host of other countries, which, because of their grievances against Moscow, have allied themselves with the other great nuclear power.

The bipolarity of the international system, the dominant place of relations between the United States and the Soviet Union, is itself the result of the historical primacy of military issues. These have been important because political questions have not been susceptible to settlement; each side has been concerned above all to prevent the other from imposing its preferences by force. Since military matters have dominated East-West relations it has been natural for the United States, as the leader of the Western military coalition, to take the lead in relations with the Soviet Union. If other countries' relations with Moscow have less to do with armaments and more to do with issues of which arms are the product, the American role will diminish.

The primacy of the United States, or at least its political monopoly on relations with the Soviet Union, has not gone unchallenged within the Western coalition. Charles de Gaulle of France was the first to strike out on an independent political course toward Moscow, in the 1960s. In the 1980s the Federal Republic of Germany's policy toward the eastern bloc has been more conciliatory than the one the United States was pursuing.

Mikhail Gorbachev and his policies increase the incentives for America's allies to deal with Moscow on a bilateral basis. It seems to be one of the aims of his foreign policy to encourage such a diplomatic trend. This has given rise in the West, and especially in the United States, to fears of a Gorbachev "charm offensive." There is a danger, it is thought, that the Europeans and others will be swept off their feet by the vigor and seeming liberalism of the general secretary, and will make unwise compromises and dangerous concessions.

America's allies, some of whom have been dealing with Russia since well before the founding of the American republic, may not take kindly to nervous warnings from North America. Moreover, the United States is not well placed to try to prevent what it has been a major purpose of American foreign policy to ensure. It is precisely the independence that its friends and allies are beginning to practice that it has been a declared goal of the American presence throughout the world to foster and protect.

In the postwar era the American role in the world has been determined by the perceived need to contain the Soviet Union. This has generally seemed a large task, requiring vigilance and exertion all over the world. American foreign policy has been active, costly, and sometimes dangerous. To the extent that Soviet policy changes and the task of containment becomes an easier one, the American role will correspondingly become more modest. Better relations with the Soviet Union, therefore, will lead to a lesser, although hardly a minor, American role in the world.

The summit meetings between the American president and the Soviet general secretary have stood as symbols of conciliatory moments in Soviet-American relations. The world has watched as these two powerful men have met, discussed, and decided issues that affect the destiny of the entire planet. The staging of a summit meeting has sent a message that the global rivalry is in a benign phase. Yet in one sense it conveys the opposite message.

The annual economic summit meetings of the leaders of the industrial democracies began in the 1970s because economic relations among them had become strained. The practices that governed the world economy since the end of World War II had broken down. The gatherings of the Western leaders symbolized their common commitment to preserve as much of that order as possible, but were at the same time a sign that the future of that order was in doubt and that strenuous efforts were needed to preserve it.

So it is with Soviet-American summits. They take place because both sides feel the need for them. They are needed because the United States and the Soviet Union are rivals. It would be a sign that the relationship had been transformed, and the rivalry muted, if the convention of summitry were to go out of fashion. For that would mean that such encounters were no longer needed. Where once the absence of summit meetings signified the inability to agree on important issues, in the best of all possible worlds the two leaders would not meet because there was nothing serious on which they disagreed.

INDEX

ABM (Antiballistic Missile) system, 101; 1972 Treaty, 60, 63

Afghanistan, 28, 29, 100, 107, 114, 175; Soviet invasion of, 60, 61, 71, 79, 88, 132, 133, 134, 176, 192–5; Soviet withdrawal, 72, 134, 138, 143, 191, 194–5; U.S. aid to rebels, 72, 134, 182

Africa, 4, 37, 38, 100; U.S.-USSR rivalry in, 6, 34, 37, 56, 61, 65–6, 131–2, 133–4, 135–7, 176, 191

agriculture, Soviet, 75; collectivism, 23–4; reprivatization of, 112

Albania, 157

Alexander I, Tsar, 29

American Revolution, 30

American system (of liberalism and individualism), 11–13, 29–32, 39–40, 70, 94; criticisms of, 31–2; roots and evolution of, 14

Angola, 61, 65, 135–6, 176–7, 182

antiballistic missile system, *see* ABM

anticommunist regimes, 102

antinuclear movements, 100–1, 102

Aquino, Corazon, 183

Arab states, 65, 137–8; *see also* Egypt

Armenians, 68, 103, 118–19, 125

arms control, 6, 9, 44, 59–60, 103, 127–8, 180, 185, 197; ABM Treaty, 60, 63; basic features of, 197–8; INF Treaty, 115, 161, 180; Limited Test Ban Treaty, 41, 57, 58; SALT I, 60; SALT II, 59, 60, 61, 71

arms control negotiations, 71, 72, 81, 95–6, 99–100, 102, 134, 185–90, 197; conventional arms, 164, 165, 185,

188–90, 198; defensive orientation, 186–90, 198; linkage with human rights issue, 103–6; Reagan resistance, 102; Reagan support, 187–8; START, 186; verification issue, 105–6, 115, 180, 189; "window of vulnerability" problem, 64

arms race, 5–6, 8, 55, 60, 126–7, 190; nuclear, 46, 48, 50–2, 57, 62–3, 93–4, 102–3, 178–9; *see also* military aid; military rivalry; nuclear weapons

art, in Soviet Union, 24–5

Asia, 4, 37, 38; economic development, 77–8, 133, 148, 153, 183; Soviet armies in, 141; Soviet missile deployment, 71, 141; U.S.-USSR rivalry in, 6, 34, 37, 56, 65–6, 99, 130–1, 133, 137, 141–7, 176, 191

association, freedom of, 118, 125

Aswan Dam, 56

Athens, ancient, 10

Atlantic Alliance, 130, 160–3, 167, 171, 199

Atlantic Charter, 34

atom bomb, 51; in World War II, 52, 54

Austria, 49; 1955 Treaty, 54

authoritarianism, 19, 170; in anticommunist regimes, 102; Russian tradition of, 18, 19, 94–5, 109, 115–16

Azerbaijanis, 68, 119

Baruch Plan, 45, 50–1

Berlin, Germany, 45, 46, 99; blockade and airlift, 46, 56; crises, 56, 58

Bolsheviks, 17–22, 23, 26, 28–9, 39, 175

Borodin, Mikhail, 132
Brazil, 177
Brest-Litovsk, Treaty of (1918), 26
Brezhnev, Leonid, 22, 71, 86, 93, 110, 111, 115, 120, 125, 154, 156; foreign policy under, 50, 53, 59–62, 64–70, 71, 89, 107–8, 132, 144, 179, 182, 186; "pre-crisis" era, 73–4
Brezhnev Doctrine, 195–6
British Campaign for Nuclear Disarmament, 100
Bulgaria, 45, 149
bureaucracy, Soviet, 40, 74, 84–5
Byelorussia, 150

Cambodia, *see* Kampuchea
Camp David agreements, 138
capitalism, 12, 20, 24, 25, 30, 40, 53, 107, 181; "Confucian," 133; "counter-revolutionary designs" alleged for, 23; excesses of, 32; industrial, 14, 15, 16, 83; Marxist overthrow projected, 16, 17, 25–6, 89, 150; technological progress under, 76–8
Carter, Jimmy, 59, 61, 71
Castro, Fidel, 58, 184
censorship, Soviet, 114
Central America, 134–5, 176–7, 192
Central Committee, Soviet Communist Party, 80, 155; Plenum, 73, 75, 83
centralism, 86; democratic, 117; economic, 24, 53, 86, 120; vs. liberalization, as Gorbachev's reform dilemma, 86–7, 156
Chernenko, Konstantin, 79
Chile, 36
China, People's Republic of, 27, 28, 38, 54, 88, 90, 130, 137, 141–4; military growth, 143, 146–7; modernization, 112, 142, 143, 147; Nixon détente with, 36; nuclear capability, 99, 188; Soviet relations with, 130–1, 133–4, 137, 141–4, 146–7, 166, 175, 177, 178, 185, 189, 191; in strategic quadrangle, 141–4, 145, 146–7; and Vietnam, 137, 144
Churchill, Sir Winston, 45, 47
civil liberties, 29–31, 94, 99, 109; denial of, 36, 102; denial in USSR, 20, 21–2,

36, 67–9, 92–3, 103; Soviet gains, 114, 118, 121–3; Soviet redefinition of, 94–5; *see also* human rights issue
civil war, 39; American, 30; Russian, 21, 22, 26, 29, 115, 175
coexistence, 25, 38–9; peaceful, 89–91
Cold War, 6, 8, 38, 43, 58, 59, 70, 72, 88, 182, 195, 198; lost opportunities to end, 41–2, 44, 53–4, 56–7, 59–62; origins, 44–53, 70, 148–9
collectivism, 11, 12, 14, 15; in Soviet agriculture, 23–4
Comecon, 160
Comintern, 27, 132
command economy, 76, 83, 153
"common security," concept of, 179
communications revolution, 77, 97
communism, 11, 13, 19, 107; Brezhnev Doctrine, 195–6; in Central America, 28, 58, 135, 137, 151; in China, 27, 28, 130, 151; in Eastern Europe, 28, 48–9, 149–51, 155–60, 167–8; East European resistance to, 48, 55, 60, 71, 79, 104, 151, 157, 167–71, 176; international, 25–7, 28, 48–9, 137 (*see also* expansionism, Soviet); vs. liberalism, 11–13, 20, 40, 184; roots of, 14, 15–17; Soviet Russian, 18–25, 40, 169; in Vietnam, 28, 137
Communist International, 27, 132
communist parties, 12, 27; in Western Europe, 35, 163
Communist Party, USSR, 7, 11, 18, 20–5, 39–40, 74, 76, 82, 85, 86, 88, 91, 111–16, 140, 150; alienation in, 74, 76; democratization of, 117; privileges, 95; Tenth Congress (1921), 115; Twentieth Congress (1956), 54; Twenty-sixth Congress (1986), 194; *see also* Central Committee
competition, 83–4, 95, 109
conservatism, American, 36, 61
Contras, Nicaraguan, 135
conventional weapons, 164, 165, 185–6, 188–90, 198
"correlation of forces," 66–7
cruise missiles, 71
Cuba, 33; communist, 28, 58, 61, 135–6, 137, 151, 176–7, 184
Cuban missile crisis, 41, 56–8, 99
cultural exchanges, 60, 90–1

cultural life, in USSR, 24–5, 68, 74; *glasnost*, 113–14
Cultural Revolution, in China, 112, 141, 142
Czechoslovakia, 49, 56, 151, 153, 156–7, 165, 168–9; Prague Spring and Soviet intervention, 48, 50, 154, 168, 195; Soviet domination of, 45, 49–50, 149, 156, 175; Soviet forces in, 164–5

Declaration of Independence, 30, 40
de Gaulle, Charles, 199
democracy, 4, 20, 29, 31, 102, 121; "inverted," 116–17; lack of tradition in Russia, 19, 94, 95, 109, 113, 169; U.S. promotion, 32, 33–4
democratic centralism, 117
democratization in USSR, 7, 84–5, 86, 113, 115–18, 121
Deng Xiaoping, 112
détente: of 1970s, 9, 36, 41, 58–62, 65–7, 69, 78–9, 89, 107–8, 125, 142, 180, 193; of 1970s, U.S. disenchantment with, 61, 108; of 1980s, 8, 41, 72–3, 88, 175
deterrence: extended (in Europe), 126, 145, 160–1; mutual, 43–4, 94, 128
dissent, right to, 9; denial in USSR, 21–2, 93, 103, 107–8
Dubček, Alexander, 50, 154, 168
Duvalier, Jean-Claude, 4–5, 102

East Asia, 191; economies of, 77–8, 133, 142, 145, 183, 184; strategic quadrangle and rivalry in, 141–7, 190–1
Eastern Europe: economies of, 152–3, 156, 159, 165; future of, 152–60, 163–71, 196–7; liberalization in, 156–8, 164–71; Red Army in, 45, 48, 149, 164–5, 176; Soviet domination of, 28, 45, 46–50, 52–3, 55–6, 69, 88, 104, 140, 148–52, 155–60, 164–5, 175–6, 177, 195–6; unrest in, 48, 55, 71, 79, 104, 148, 151, 157, 167–71, 176; *see also* Europe
East Germany (German Democratic Republic), 151, 153, 158–60, 168, 170; 1953 uprising, 48; relations with West Germany, 156, 159–60, 163, 167, 170; as Soviet client state, 45,

49, 149, 156, 157, 158–9; Soviet forces in, 164–5; *see also* Germany
economic aid to Third World, Soviet, 56, 133, 135, 177, 184
economic autarky, 52–3, 90, 123, 180–1
economic cooperation, east-west, 123, 167; in Europe, 153, 160, 165–7, 171; postwar failure of, 46, 48, 52–3, 180; U.S.-USSR agreements, 36, 53, 60, 104
economic systems: East Asia, 77–8, 133, 142, 145, 183, 184; Eastern Europe, 152–3, 156, 159; Gorbachev's market socialism and reform, 76, 83–4, 95, 111–12, 123, 126–7, 152, 181–2; liberal vs. communist, 12, 15, 20, 76–9, 181, 184; Stalinist, 75–6, 83, 180–1; U.S. vs. other Western, 31; Western Europe, 161–2, 183, 184; *see also* capitalism; global economy; market economy; planned economy
efficiency, American emphasis on, 95
egalitarianism, in USSR, 95, 109, 110
Egypt, 56, 60–1, 65, 133, 137–8, 139
Eisenhower, Dwight D., 54
Engels, Friedrich, 16, 24
environmental cooperation, 104
"equal security," concept of, 179
Eritrea, 136
Estonia(ns), 119, 125
Ethiopia, 61, 65, 136–7, 176
Europe, 4, 96–7, 100; antinuclear movements, 100–1, 102; conventional forces in, 162, 164–5, 188–90; and détente of 1970s, 58, 60, 79, 193; division of, 37, 45–50, 55, 70, 193; east-west relations in, 153, 155, 159–60, 162–3, 165–7, 171, 184, 193; eclipse of imperialism of, 4, 37, 38–9; Helsinki accords of 1975, 59, 69, 104–5; Marshall Plan in, 46, 52–3, 130; missile deployment in, 71, 101; nuclear deterrence in, 126, 145, 160–1; postwar boundaries, 69, 104; U.S.-USSR rivalry in, 3, 6–7, 34–5, 37, 45–50, 52–3, 55–6, 58, 70, 78–9, 88, 99, 130, 148, 160, 162–7, 170–1, 190, 192–6; *see also* Eastern Europe; Western Europe
European Common Market, 153, 160, 161–2

expansionism, Soviet, 26–8, 35, 48–9, 51, 56–8, 64–7, 78–9, 131–8, 139–41, 148–9, 175–7, 183

Fascism, 38
Finland, 54, 196; Finlandization, 196
Ford, Gerald, 59, 61, 66
Four Freedoms, 34
Fourteen Points, 33, 34
France, 4, 16, 17, 37, 161, 162–3, 184, 199; communists, 35, 163; nuclear capability, 99, 188; socialists, 15
free enterprise, 32, 111–12; *see also* capitalism; trade
French Revolution, 4, 14, 16, 19, 96–7

geopolitical conflict, 99, 100, 175–7, 190–7; *see also* Europe; Middle East; Third World
Georgia(ns), 28, 68, 118
Germans, in USSR, 119, 125
Germany, 16, 17, 19, 26, 56, 96; defeat of 1945, 37; division of, 49, 150; *see also* East Germany; West Germany
Ghana, 56, 131
glasnost, 7, 84–5, 113–15, 121–2, 173, 175; in media, 114–15
global economy, 90–1, 182–3
Gomulka, Wladyslaw, 55
Gorbachev, Mikhail, 7–8, 9, 80–7, 95, 163, 198, 199; as catalyst for change, 73, 75–6, 79, 81, 139–40, 172–4; and democratization, 7, 84–5, 86, 113, 115–18; dilemma of centralization vs. democratization for, 86–7, 156; and Eastern Europe, 154–60; economic reform goals, 83–4, 111–12, 123, 126–7, 152, 154, 181–2, 184; foreign policy of, 73, 81–2, 87–91, 126–9, 132–4, 136, 143, 144–5, 146, 154–60, 164–71, 175, 177, 179–80, 181, 184–5, 190–1, 194–6; *glasnost* of, 7, 84–5, 113–15, 121–2, 173, 175; and human rights, 113, 115–18, 123–6; and non-Russian nationalities question, 118–20, 140; nuclear and arms control policy of, 126–9, 179–80, 186–8, 190; opposition to, 84–5, 112, 125; *perestroika* of, 7, 81, 82–7, 90, 122; at summit meetings, 41, 72, 200

Gorbachev, Raisa, 82
Gorky, Maxim, 24
government: authoritarian, 18, 19, 94–5; liberal vs. communist traditions, 12–13; parliamentary, 19, 20, 95; socialist, 14–15, 22–3
Great Britain, 4, 14, 16, 17, 37, 131, 162–3; Labour Party, 15; nineteenth-century rivalry with Russia, 29; nuclear capability, 99, 188
Greece, 46, 56, 163; ancient, 10, 14
Guinea, 131

Haiti, 4, 102
Hegel, Georg Wilhelm Friedrich, 16
Helsinki summit and accords (1975), 59, 69, 104–5, 123
Hiroshima, 52, 54, 92
historical revisionism, 115
historiography, Soviet, 24–5, 119
Hitler, Adolf, 47, 48, 53, 56, 67, 71
Honecker, Erich, 156, 158, 170
human rights issue, 67–70, 92–8, 99–108, 173; linkage with arms control, 103–6; projected future, 113, 115–18, 122–6; Soviet redefinition of rights, 94–5
Humphrey, Hubert, 198
Hungary, 49, 90, 151, 152–3, 157, 168–9, 173; 1956 uprising, 48, 55, 154; as Soviet client state, 45, 49, 156, 175

ideological conflict, 34–5, 36–40, 41, 48–9, 53, 64, 69, 90
imperialism: European, eclipse of, 4, 37, 39; Soviet, 28, 148–51, 175–7, 183 (*see also* expansionism, Soviet); U.S., 33; U.S. "overstretch," 183
India, 5, 56, 143, 177
individualism, 11–12, 14, 94, 113
Indochina, 103, 137, 144, 193; *see also* Southeast Asia; Vietnam
Indonesia, 56, 177
industrialization, USSR, 21, 23, 24, 75, 89, 181
Industrial Revolution, 14, 16–17; Third, 77, 90
INF (Intermediate Nuclear Forces) Treaty (1987), 115, 161, 180
intelligentsia, Soviet, 21, 85, 113–14, 121, 122; non-Russian, 119, 120

intercontinental ballistic missiles, 99
intermediate-range ballistic missiles, 71, 72, 101, 180; *see also* INF
internationalism: American, 33–6, 42, 47, 65, 79, 139; communist, 25–7, 28, 48–9, 51, 137; Marxist, 25–7, 51; Soviet Russian, 26–8, 48–9, 51, 56–8, 64–7, 78–9, 131–4, 148–50
Iran, 4, 56, 102, 137, 138, 139, 194
Iraq, 137, 138
iron curtain, 45–6, 53
Islamic fundamentalism, 88, 138, 139, 194
isolationism, American, 32
Israel, 60–1, 65, 68, 137–8
Italy, communists of, 35, 163

Jackson, Henry, 68
Jackson-Vanik Amendment, 68–9, 96
Japan, 19, 78, 133, 153, 184; defeat of 1945, 37, 52; military growth, 145–6; Soviet relations with, 144–6, 147, 167, 191; in strategic quadrangle, 141, 142–3, 144–7
Jaruzelski, Wojciech, 158, 169
Jews, Soviet, 67–9, 92–3, 103, 119, 124–6

Kádár, János, 169
Kampuchea, 137, 143, 191
Kazakhs, 68, 120
Kennedy, John F., 34, 57–8
Kennedy, Paul, 183
Khrushchev, Nikita, 22, 25, 40, 85, 109–10, 154, 181; foreign policy under, 54–8, 64, 89, 131–2, 144, 198; Stalin rejected by, 54, 115
Kipling, Rudyard, *Kim*, 29
Kissinger, Henry, 36, 61
Korea, 78, 130
Korean War, 42, 45, 47, 130–1
Kurile Islands, 144, 191

Latin America, 176–7; economic exploitation of, 32; U.S.-USSR rivalry in, 6, 34, 58, 133, 134–5, 191
Latvia(ns), 119, 125
law, rule of, 20, 33, 117, 173
League of Nations, 33, 34

Lebanon, 134
Lend-Lease program, 52, 180
Lenin, Vladimir Ilyich, 11, 17, 18, 20–1, 22, 23, 24, 76, 81–2, 107, 117; internationalism of, 26–8, 64, 89
Leninism, 18, 85, 90; *see also* Marxism-Leninism
liberalism, 11, 13, 20, 29, 42; American, 29–33, 40, 41–2, 53, 184; vs. communism, 11–13, 40, 184; roots and evolution of, 14, 19; tempered by socialism, 15
liberalization, Gorbachev's, 82–7, 115, 122–6; vs. centralism, as dilemma, 86–7, 156; in Eastern Europe, 156–8, 164–71; *see also* democratization; *glasnost*
Libya, 137
Limited Test Ban Treaty (1963), 41, 57, 58
linkage, arms control and human rights, 103–6
literature, in Soviet Union, 24–5
Lithuania(ns), 119, 125
Lysenko, Trofim, 25

MAD, *see* mutual assured destruction
Malay peninsula, 131
Manchuria, 54
Mao Zedong, 27, 139, 141, 142
Marcos, Ferdinand, 4–5, 102
market economy, 12
market socialism, 76, 83–4, 111–12, 120, 152
Marshall Plan, 46, 52–3, 130
Marx, Karl, 11, 15–17, 22, 24, 53; internationalism of, 25, 26, 27, 28
Marxism, 14, 15–17; Bolshevik adaptation of, 17–18, 19–20; as international creed, 25–7
Marxism-Leninism, 18, 24, 27–8, 53, 90, 140, 169; fading of faith in, 39–40; goal of spreading, 51, 64–5, 131–2, 136, 139, 166
McKinley, William, 33
medium-range missiles, 71, 72, 101, 180
Medvedev, Vadim, 155
Mexico, 135, 177
middle class, 16; absence in Russia, 19; new Soviet, 76, 109–11, 112

Middle East, 134, 139, 192; 1967 war, 68; Soviet policy in, 56, 60–1, 65, 137–8

military aid to Third World, 56, 60, 72, 131–8, 141, 143, 147, 182

military rivalry, 3, 5–6, 8, 39, 45–6, 50–2, 55, 56–7, 60, 62–4, 71–2, 92–8, 99–108, 126–9, 160, 162–5, 178–80, 182, 185–90, 197–9; defensive vs. offensive posture, 186; parity attained, 65, 126, 178, 189; Soviet precept of military force, 177–80

MIRVs (multiple warheads), 63

monopoly, Russian norm of, 95, 109

Monroe Doctrine, 135

Moscow State University, 74

Moscow summit meetings (1972, 1974), 59

Most Favored Nation (MFN) status, 68–9

movement, freedom of, 68, 93, 124–6

Mozambique, 61, 65, 136, 177

mutual assured destruction (MAD), 62, 64, 127, 186–8

mutual deterrence, *see* deterrence

mutual security, 127, 187–90

Napoleon Bonaparte, 29, 97

Nasser, Gamal Abdel, 56

nationalism, 11, 28; African and Asian former colonies, 4, 131–2; German, 159; Marxist/Leninist rejection of, 25, 27, 28; non-Russian, in USSR, 85, 118–20, 140, 169; Soviet, 27–8, 51–2, 85, 134, 139; Stalinist fusion with communism, 27–8, 169; U.S. 29, 30–1

national liberation movements, 79, 133, 176

NATO (North Atlantic Treaty Organization), 47, 88, 130, 150, 160, 163, 164, 178, 185, 188–90

Nazi regime, 56, 67, 140, 149

Nehru, Jawaharlal, 56

NEP (New Economic Policy), 83, 115, 180

"new thinking," 7, 87–91, 126–9, 163

Nicaragua, 135, 176, 182

Nigeria, 177

Nixon, Richard M., 61; détente policy of, 36, 59–60, 62, 66; and human rights issue, 69, 102, 103

Nkrumah, Kwame, 56, 131

"noncapitalist road of development," 131–2

North Atlantic Treaty Organization, *see* NATO

nuclear deterrence, *see* deterrence

nuclear equilibrium, 62–3, 99, 107, 126, 186, 187–8, 198

nuclear parity, 65, 126, 178, 189

nuclear peace, 43, 50

nuclear retaliation, 62, 186

nuclear sufficiency, 127

nuclear war, absurdity of, 4, 39, 43–4, 50, 62, 98

nuclear weapons, 3, 5, 39, 43–4, 45–6, 57, 62–3, 92–8, 99–108, 126, 161, 185, 197–8; abolition unlikely, 103, 128–9, 187; acquisition by USSR, 45; asymmetries between U.S. and USSR, 64, 188; countries in possession of, 99, 139, 188; intercontinental range, 99; intermediate range, 71, 72, 101, 180; MIRVs, 63; number of, 187; protests against, 100–1, 102; superiority question, 51–2, 57, 64, 126, 178–9, 187; *see also* arms control; military rivalry

order, Russian emphasis on, 94, 109, 118

Ostpolitik, 58

Pakistan, 143

Palestine Liberation Organization, 137

paradnost, 114

parliamentary government, 19, 20, 95

partiinost, 113–14

peaceful coexistence, 89

peasantry, Russian, 17, 19–20, 21, 24, 121

Peloponnesian War, The (Thucydides), 10

perestroika, 7, 81, 82–7, 88, 122, 169–70; in Eastern Europe, 156–8, 169; resistance to, 84; *see also* democratization; *glasnost;* liberalization

Perestroika (Gorbachev), 90

Pershing II missile, 71

Persian Gulf, 137

Philippines, 4, 33, 102, 146, 183

planned economy, 12, 15; Soviet, 23–4, 53, 55, 75–6, 83, 120

Poland, 28, 49, 150, 151, 153, 158, 160, 168–9, 184, 194; Bolshevik invasion of 1920, 26, 27; of 1980s, Army rule, 28, 71, 170; Solidarity movement, 60, 71, 104, 154, 158, 176; as Soviet client state, 26, 28, 45, 49, 149, 157–8, 175, 195–6; Soviet forces in, 164–5; uprisings in, 48, 55, 71, 79

Poles, in USSR, 119

Politburo, Soviet, 80–1, 155

political systems: liberal vs. communist, 11–12, 15, 20, 39–40, 69–70, 94; U.S. vs. other Western democracies, 31; USSR of 1980s, 76, 85–7, 95, 110, 113–18, 120–1

Potsdam Conference (1945), 45

Prague Spring, 154, 158, 168

Pravda, 74, 89

preemptive nuclear strike, 63–4

private enterprise, 32, 111–12

professionals, in USSR, 76, 85, 109–11, 113

property, private, 31; vs. collective, 12, 24

public welfare, 15; in USSR, 76

Radio Free Europe, 35

Radio Liberty, 35

Reagan, Ronald, 8–9, 61, 71–3; nuclear/arms control policies, 101, 102, 128, 161, 187–8; summit meetings, 41, 72, 200

Reagan Doctrine, 8–9, 133

realpolitik, 35–6

Red Army, 22, 27, 40; in Eastern Europe, 26, 45, 48, 149, 164–5, 176

religious freedom, lack of, 67, 92, 121

revisionism, Soviet, 115, 132

Romania, 49, 151, 153, 166, 168, 169; as Soviet client state, 45, 149, 156–7

Romanov dynasty, 19, 175

Roosevelt, Franklin D., 33–4, 45, 47

Russia, *see* Soviet Union; Tsarist Russia

Russian (October) Revolution, 19–21, 22, 25, 29, 115

Sakharov, Andrei, 85, 93, 94, 99, 107, 124

SALT (Strategic Arms Limitation Treaties), 96; SALT I (1972), 60; SALT II (1979), 59, 60, 61, 71

Sandinistas, 135

sciences, 90–1; in Soviet Union, 24–5

scientific agreements, U.S.-USSR, 60, 104

SDI (Strategic Defense Initiative), 9, 72, 161, 187

second-strike capability, 62, 186

security, "equal" vs. "common," 179

Shcharansky, Natan (Anatoly), 92–3, 94, 99, 124

Shevardnadze, Eduard, 87–8

Shultz, George, 138

social democratic parties, 15, 163

socialism, 14–15, 77, 85, 89, 111, 132, 150; "different roads to," 155; Marxist, 15–16, 17, 40; "in one country," 22, 27, 131; in Western Europe, 163; *see also* market socialism

socialist realism, 25, 74

social systems: liberal vs. communist, 12–13, 15, 69–70, 94–5; U.S. vs. other Western nations, 31; USSR of 1980s, 76, 95, 110–11, 114–15, 121

social welfare, 15; USSR, 76

Solidarity movement, 60, 71, 104, 154, 158, 176

Solzhenitsyn, Alexander, 18

Somalia, 136

South Africa, 36, 135–6

Southeast Asia, 100, 177, 184, 192; *see also* Indochina; Vietnam

South Vietnam, 36

South Yemen, 65

soviets (councils), 116

Soviet system (communist and collectivist), 11–13, 15–25, 39–40, 70, 173; authoritarian tradition of, 18, 19,

Soviet system (*continued*)
94–5, 109, 115–16; bureaucracy, 40, 74, 84–5; centralism vs. liberalization as Gorbachev's dilemma, 86–7, 156; dictatorship and terror, 18, 21–2, 24, 54–5; of dual authority, 22; failures of, 74; ideological underpinnings of, 24; roots and evolution of, 14–20; totalitarian nature, 116; Tsarist traces, 18

Soviet Union: Afghanistan as defeat for, 71–2, 133, 134, 192–5; aim of international equality, 51–3, 62, 64–7, 70, 78–9, 179, 192; Brezhnev "pre-crisis" era, 73–4; and China, 130–1, 133–4, 137, 141–4, 146–7, 166, 175, 177, 178, 185, 189, 191; civil liberties restrictions, 20, 21–2, 36, 67–9, 92–3, 103 (*see also* human rights issue); Eastern European domination, 28, 45, 46–50, 52–3, 55–6, 69, 88, 104, 140, 148–52, 155–60, 164–5, 175–6, 195–6; Eastern Europe as problem for, 150–60, 164–71, 177; economic autarky, 52–3, 90, 123, 180–1; economic planning, 23–4, 53, 55, 75–6, 120; economic reform, 83–4, 95, 111–12, 123, 126–7, 152, 154, 181–2, 184; economic stagnation and superpower decline, 75–9, 181, 183–4; emigration from, 68–9, 103, 107, 124–6; ethnic and religious minorities, 67–8, 85, 86, 118–20, 124–6; foreign investment in, 180, 181; foreign policy precept of territorial control, 175–7 (*see also* expansionism, Soviet); foreign policy changes and projected future, 175–82, 185; foreign policy under Brezhnev, 50, 53, 59–62, 64–70, 71, 89, 107–8, 132, 144, 179, 182, 186; foreign policy under Gorbachev, 73, 81–2, 87–91, 126–9, 132–4, 136, 143, 144–5, 146, 154–60, 164–71, 175–81 *passim*, 184–5, 190–1, 194–6; foreign policy under Khrushchev, 54–8, 64, 89, 131–2, 144; foreign policy under Stalin, 26–8, 45–53, 54, 55–6, 64, 89, 106–7, 130–1; Gorbachev's domestic reform goals, 7–8, 75–6, 79, 80, 82–7, 90, 95, 111–22, 172; Great Russian/Slav dominance in, 118–19, 121, 150; industrialization,

21, 23, 24, 75, 89, 181; and Japan, 144–6, 147, 167, 191; judicial and penal reform, 117; leadership turnover of mid-1980s, 79–80; as military power, 24, 57, 60, 71–2, 75, 98, 99, 126, 151, 164, 177–80, 189; nationalism of, 27–8, 51–2, 85, 134, 139, 169; "new thinking," 7, 87–91, 126–9, 163; non-Russian nationalities question, 68, 85, 118–20, 140, 169; nuclear capability, 45, 57, 63–4, 71, 178; nuclear inferiority abhorred by, 51–2, 57, 70, 178; nuclear policy, 63–4, 93–4, 126–9, 178–80, 186–8; police state, 22, 55, 124; political opposition as crime, 21–2 (*see also* dissent); rejection of Baruch Plan by, 45, 50–1; rejection of Marshall aid by, 46, 52–3; "second economy" in, 13; slow change in, 4–5, 7–8, 39–40, 76–9, 174; Stalinist terror regime, 21, 54, 67, 106–7; technological lag of, 77–9; ties to communist parties abroad, 27, 35; view of détente of 1970s, 65–7, 107–8; youth of, 74–5; *see also* Soviet system; U.S.-USSR relations; U.S.-USSR rivalry

space-based defense, 6, 72, 126, 187–8

space exploration, 55, 77

Spain, 163

Spanish-American War (1898), 33

Sputnik, 55

SS-20 missiles, 71

Stalin, Joseph, 3, 11, 17–18, 20–1, 22–3, 24–5, 37, 53–4, 55, 62, 76, 87, 95, 117, 119; death of, 41, 53–4, 109; denunciation of, 54, 115, 172; economic model of, 75–6, 83, 180–1; foreign policy of, 26, 27–8, 45–7, 49, 50, 52–3, 55–6, 64, 89, 106–7, 130; purges by, 20, 21, 54, 67, 106

Stalinism, rejection of, 115, 172

Star Wars, *see* SDI

Strategic Arms Limitation, *see* SALT

Strategic Arms Reduction Talks (START), 186

Strategic Defense Initiative, *see* SDI

"strategic quadrangle," 141–7, 191

Strauss, Franz-Josef, 160

Sukarno, 56

summit meetings, 59, 200; 1972 Moscow, 59; 1973 U.S., 59; 1974 Moscow,

59; 1974 Vladivostok, 59; 1975 Helsinki, 59, 69, 104; 1979 Vienna, 59; 1987 Washington, 115, 180; Reagan-Gorbachev, 41, 72, 200; tripartite agenda at, 104–5, 107
Syria, 60, 65, 134, 137, 138, 177

Taiwan, 142
Tatars, 119
technology, 46, 90, 99; Soviet lag, 77–9; U.S.-Soviet agreements, 104
Tehran Conference (1943), 45
territorial control, precept of, 175–7
terrorism, international, 139
Test Ban Treaty of 1963, 41, 57, 58
Third World: arms aid to, 56, 60, 72, 131–8, 141, 143, 147, 182; economic aid by USSR, 56, 133, 135, 177, 184; "noncapitalist road of development," 131–2; projection for future of, 138–47; Reagan Doctrine policy, 8–9, 133; Soviet influence declining, 79, 88, 134, 137–8, 176–7; Soviet policy reassessment, 132–4, 177; U.S.-USSR rivalry for influence in, 6, 8–9, 34, 37–8, 56, 58, 60–1, 64–7, 79, 88, 99, 130–47, 183, 190, 191–3, 194–5; *see also* Africa; Asia; Latin America; Middle East
Thucydides, 10
Time magazine, 88
totalitarianism, 116
Touré, Sékou, 131
trade, international, 34, 44, 46, 77, 90, 145, 180, 181; MNF status, 68–9; U.S.-USSR agreements on, 36, 53, 60
Treaty on Cooperation and Security in Europe, 59; *see also* Helsinki
Trotsky, Leon, 18, 22, 24
Truman, Harry, 8, 34, 45–6, 52
Truman Doctrine, 46
Tsarist Russia, 17, 18, 19–20, 23, 29, 49, 94–5, 175, 178, 180

Ukraine(ians), 119, 125, 150
United Nations, 34, 44, 45; Charter, 97
United States, 29–30; antinuclear protests in, 100–1, 102; Atlantic Alliance of, 130, 160–3; and China, 36, 142, 143, 146–7; civil liberties, 29–31, 94, 99; conservative views of USSR, 36, 61; Constitution, 30; federal deficit, 183; foreign policy before 1898, 32; foreign policy of 1898–1945, 33–4, 43, 45–7; foreign policy since 1945, 34–6, 45–7, 50–1, 54, 56–8, 65, 68–9, 166, 200; foreign policy of détente in 1970s, 9, 36, 58–62, 65–6, 69, 107–8; foreign policy of 1980s, 8–9, 41, 72–3, 182–3; foreign wars of, 30; human rights emphasis of, 100, 101, 105, 124–5; as ideological nation, 29–30, 32, 36, 69; internationalism of, 33–6, 42, 47, 65, 79, 139; isolationism in, 32–3; and Japan, 145–6; Jewish community, 68; as leader of Western coalition, 199; military strength, 60, 70, 71–2, 79, 98, 99, 178–9, 185–6; mode of change in, 4, 8; nationalism of, 29, 30–1; naval forces, 185–6; nuclear policy, 62–3, 93–4, 101, 102, 128, 160–1, 186–8; nuclear superiority, 51–2, 57, 178; nuclear superiority in question, 63–4, 71, 186; public disenchantment with 1970s détente, 61, 108; Reagan military buildup, 8, 102, 179, 182; relative superpower decline as victory for liberal principles, 183–4; Vietnam War as defeat for, 66, 192–3, 194; *see also* American system
U.S.-USSR relations: coexistence, 25, 38–9, 89–91; cultural and scientific exchanges, 60, 104; the Gorbachev difference in, 73, 82, 172–4, 182; "new thinking," 7, 87–91, 126–9, 163; trade, 36, 52–3, 60, 68–9; tripartite agenda of talks, 104–5, 107; Western Europeans' views of, 160–1; *see also* détente; summit meetings; U.S.-USSR rivalry
U.S.-USSR rivalry, 97, 172, 184–5; economic incompatibility, 46, 48, 52–3, 145; economic/technological, 77–9, 88; geopolitical, 99, 100, 175–7, 190–7 (*see also* East Asia; Europe; expansionism, Soviet; Middle East; Third World); human rights issue, 67–70, 92–8, 99–108, 122–6; as ideological conflict, 34–5, 36–40, 41, 48–9, 53, 64, 69, 90, 97, 173; military/nuclear, 3,

U.S.-USSR rivalry (*continued*)
5–6, 8, 39, 45–6, 50–2, 55, 56–7, 60,
62–4, 71–2, 92–8, 99–108, 126–9, 160,
164–5, 178–80, 182, 185–90, 197–9; *see
also* arms race

Vanik, Charles, 68
verification, arms control, 105–6, 115,
180
Vienna summit meeting (1979), 59
Vietnam, 28, 58, 137, 144, 146, 177, 183,
191; South, 36
Vietnam War, 42, 43, 59, 66, 137, 183,
192–3, 194; Soviet aid, 60, 65
Vladivostok summit (1974), 59

Warsaw, Poland, 26, 45
Warsaw Pact, 71, 168, 175, 188, 189
Washington, George, 32
Washington *Post*, 92
Washington summit (1987), 115, 180
Watergate scandal, 66
West Africa, 184
Western Europe: attitudes toward
USSR, 35, 149; defense of, 47, 71, 126,
145, 160–1, 162, 196; economies of,
161–2, 183, 184; NATO forces, 47,
130, 160, 164; postwar reconstruction of, 34, 46, 130; *realpolitik*-ori-
ented, 35–6; U.S. troops in, 47, 162;
views of U.S.-USSR relations in,
160–1, 163; *see also* Europe
West Germany (Federal Republic of
Germany), 5, 162–3, 171, 184; antinuclear protests, 100–1; *Ostpolitik*,
58, 60, 199; relations with East Germany, 156, 159–60, 163, 167, 170; Social Democrats, 15, 163; *see also*
Germany
Wilson, Woodrow, 33–4
"window of vulnerability," 64, 66
working class, 16, 25–6; in Russia,
17
World War I, 4, 11, 19, 33, 98, 178; Russian withdrawal from, 26, 27
World War II, 4, 11, 28, 33–4, 37, 41, 43,
44, 45, 47, 49, 50, 52, 53, 97, 149, 175,
178, 180

Yalta Conference (1945), 45
Yeltsin, Boris N., 85
Yugoslavia, 117, 137, 152–3

A NOTE ABOUT THE AUTHORS

SEWERYN BIALER is Ruggles Professor of Political Science and Director of the Research Institute on International Change at Columbia University, and a member of the Executive Committee of Columbia's W. Averell Harriman Institute for the Advanced Study of the Soviet Union. He was born in Berlin, Germany, in 1926, and was educated at the Institute of Social Sciences in Warsaw, Poland, where he received a doctorate in political economy in 1955, and at Columbia University, where he received a second doctorate, in political science, in 1966. In 1983, Professor Bialer became the first Sovietologist to receive a MacArthur Fellowship. He is the author of several books, including *The Soviet Paradox* (1986).

MICHAEL MANDELBAUM is Senior Fellow and Director of the Project on East-West Relations at the Council on Foreign Relations. He received a B.A. from Yale University, his M.A. from King's College, Cambridge, and a Ph.D. from Harvard University, where he taught in the department of government. He is the author or co-author of numerous articles and six books on international politics and foreign policy, most recently (with Strobe Talbott) *Reagan and Gorbachev* (1987), and *The Fate of Nations: The Search for National Security in the 19th and 20th Centuries* (1988).